THE
SUPERSTAR SHOW
OF GOVERNMENT

THE SUPERSTAR SHOW OF GOVERNMENT

BY
ROGER-GÉRARD SCHWARTZENBERG

TRANSLATED FROM THE FRENCH BY
JOSEPH A. HARRISS

FOREWORD BY
HARRISON SALISBURY

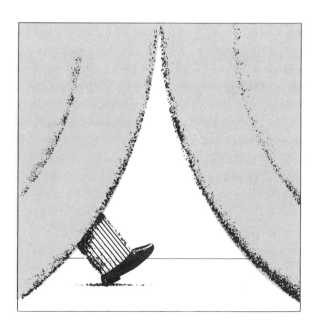

BARRON'S/WOODBURY, N.Y.

All inquiries should be addressed to:
Barron's Educational Series, Inc.
113 Crossways Park Drive
Woodbury, New York 11797

Library of Congress Catalog Card No. 78-835

Cloth International Standard Book No. 0-8120-5258-7
Paper International Standard Book No. 0-8120-2291-2

Library of Congress Cataloging in Publication Data
Schwartzenberg, Roger-Gérard.
  Superstar show of government.

  Bibliography: p.
  Includes index.
  1. Public relations and politics. I. Title.
JF2112.P8S3413   659.2'9'32   78-835
ISBN 0-8120-5258-7
ISBN 0-8120-2291-2 pbk.

PRINTED IN THE UNITED STATES OF AMERICA

85-4666

Contents

Foreword

There is very little about the apparatus, the methodology and the psychology of government which was not illuminated by Machiavelli in his medieval classic, *The Prince*. Indeed, the kinship of theater and politics, and of super-shows and super-politics was as clear to the Greeks and the Romans as it is to twentieth-century actors on the political stage.

If the Romans ruled by bread and circuses, if Greek democracy played to a Demosthean audience, if the Italian princes of the Renaissance triumphed through coups de theatre as well as carefully calculated doses of exotic poisons; then it should come as no surprise that today's political spotlight has played on such figures as "Super-K"—the embodiment of Henry Kissinger—as well as the photogenic Sadat and John F. Kennedy, that Mao Tse-tung has enchanted throngs of a million or more, and that television advisers have stood at the right hand of every American political candidate.

The virtue of *The Superstar Show of Government* is not that it adumbrates new principles of political theater, but that it shows how swiftly politics and the new technology of electronics have bonded their partnership, and how political figures have cut the pattern of their public images and stylized their campaigns to take full advantage of the new media.

And what may startle the American reader is Roger-Gérard Schwartzenberg's demonstration that the principles of political technology are universal. Television is employed as adeptly and massively in France as in the U.S. presidential primaries. The newly emerging rulers of black African states employ the same image-creating techniques as do the carefully coached candidates for the U.S. Senate. The Africans do not yet have access to depth opinion sampling, but opinion-studies and polling have swept like a hurricane across the western European democracies and are even being tested out in eastern Europe and the Soviet Union.

Roger-Gérard Schwartzenberg classifies and subclassifies various leadership images—the matinee idol, the father figure, the remote oracle, the friendly common man—and he demonstrates, with convincing evidence, that the public tends to alternate in its choice from one to another. One matinee idol seldom follows another. If a nation has long been led by an Eisenhower or a de Gaulle, it is likely to choose a "superstar" like Kennedy or a more conventional Pompidou as his successor. The swing of voters to the conventional Labour leader, Clement Attlee, in order to displace the dramatic Winston Churchill at the end of World War II was almost a classic example of this pendulum effect.

It may surprise some present-day Madison Avenue practitioners of political packaging to find that the real geniuses of practical politics, the charismatic leaders like Napoleon, Lenin or Mao Tse-tung, seemed to know instinctively those principles of leadership which would capture popular imagination and enable an individual to rise from the most lowly estate to a position of world significance. This genius is clearly innate although not a few charismatic leaders have studied the techniques of their predecessors.

The intimate relationship between politics and theater is extensively and searchingly explored by Mr. Schwartzenberg. Not only during recent years in American politics have men and women who made their first careers before the Hollywood cameras moved onto the political stage. Most successful mass political figures of the past have understood the importance of dramatic devices in capturing popular imagination. Hitler was not the first to harness techniques of mass psychology, to whip up mass emotion with Wagnerian spectacles staged in vast amphitheaters. Every successful Roman emperor employed the same device. Napoleon only trod the path well blazed by Caesar when he became France's First Consul.

The Superstar Show of Government deftly contrasts the countervailing principles of the "distant leader," the oracle who retires in silence and mystery to the mountaintop only to descend with a word to his followers in the moment of crisis; and the folksy common man who engages his fellow men by emphasis on his own commonality, the "Jes' plain Bill" characteristic.

What is educational in Mr. Schwartzenberg's analysis is the manner in which these basics transcend societies, race, and time. They work in Asia as well as they did in the late Boss Hague's

Jersey City. They have worked for ancient Chinese emperors as well as they do for contemporaries like Tito and Adenauer.

What is suggested here is that politics, being the science of human relations and government, does not really change. Its principles are imbedded in human characteristics, which have neither varied much over the millenia nor from civilization to civilization. In politics, all leaders employ the trappings of power. All invoke force when they feel it is necessary or to their advantage. All fall back upon theatrical devices. All draw upon the repertoire of human psychology to enhance their appeal. The leaders know they can win audiences by eloquence, and they achieve eloquence (if they do not possess it naturally, they achieve it by training and tricks). Few are able to eschew the advantages of dramatic surprise. Few fail to take every chance to elevate themselves over opponents or possible opponents. All are highly dependent upon the best possible intelligence which, in modern times, means accurate, frequent and effective polling. All understand the special mysteries of timing, and all understand (though they may not always admit it) the role which fortune plays in their careers.

One leaves *The Superstar Show of Government* with a profound sense of the continuity of human affairs; with a sense that, given necessary changes in time and circumstance, a political leader in one country probably could succeed in another— Khrushchev could have made a mark in U.S. politics, de Gaulle in post-World War I Germany, Churchill in post-World War II France. Nevertheless, in all likelihood, the Asian leaders could triumph only in Asia. It is difficult to imagine Mao Tse-tung triumphing anywhere but China, Gandhi anywhere but India, Ho Chi Minh anywhere but Vietnam. On the other hand, those who knew the late Chou En-lai could easily visualize him sitting at the head of an eighteenth-century French King's cabinet, taking Bismarck's role in Germany or, indeed being that very Prince to whom Machiavelli wrote his famous instructions.

HARRISON E. SALISBURY
Associate Editor, The New York Times
(Moscow Correspondent, 1949–54)

THE
SUPERSTAR SHOW
OF GOVERNMENT

PART ONE
The Cast

Politics used to be concerned with ideas. Today it is dominated by individuals; or, rather, by characters, for each ruler seems to deliberately choose a role and then play it as if he or she were on stage.*

The government itself is being transformed into a production company, with politics serving as the show's set and top officials as its stars. Thus personalization of power, true to its etymological roots, is carried to its logical conclusion. After all, doesn't the word *person* come from the Latin *persona*, meaning a stage mask?

AUTHORITY IN PERSON

Authority used to be an abstraction — a cold, impersonal legal concept for jurists. It was almost anonymous. That is how democracy began, after the struggle against the personal authority of monarchy and dictatorship.

Today the ruling power has a face — that of the official who wields that power. The art of politics has gone from the abstract to the figurative, with authority becoming humanized, personalized, in the dictionary sense of the term *to personalize* — "giving personal existence to an abstraction or an inanimate being."

A man — or a woman — personifies authority because he personifies the group over which he rules. He identifies with this group, and the group in turn acknowledges his leadership. He inspires respect through his prestige, his influence, his popularity. He is the authentic expression of the nation, the people, and the political party. He is their symbol.

Such a ruler is the very figure of authority, representing it in visible form. He *incarnates* it, giving a human shape to an abstraction.

Such words as *figure, represent,* and *incarnate* also belong to the vocabulary of the theater. Sarah Bernhardt incarnated l'Aiglon. De Gaulle incarnated France. What was it de Gaulle said on June 6, 1958,

---

*Show business seems to have taken over government. It has become the political superstructure of society, the state itself turning into show business, literally a Sate Spectacle. This is being done systematically to amuse and abuse the public, to divert the citizens in the most literal sense by making politics into a theater of illusion.

in Oran? "France is here. . . . It is here in the person of the man it has mandated to lead it."[1]

We must distinguish between the personalization of power and actual personal power, although the two often exist simultaneously. The term *personal power* designates an institutional reality: all power is concentrated in the hands of a single person, who controls all the apparatus of the state — what Bertrand de Jouvenel calls "the engine room." It is the assumption of all the powers granted by constitutional law. It is the tyranny of ancient times, absolute monarchy, or contemporary dictatorship.

The *personalization of power* is quite different. It derives not from institutions, but from collective psychology. An individual symbolizes the nation, the State, or the party. He represents the powers of the group that he incarnates, thus giving those powers a face — and sometimes a mask — visible to all.

Personalization can exist without personal power (as in the cases of Winston Churchill or Franklin Roosevelt). On the other hand, there can be personal power without personalization (as with Algeria's Houari Boumediène at the beginning). But the two often exist simultaneously (for example, with Joseph Stalin or Mao Tse-tung), one feeding on the other. Frequently, the "historic leader" comes to control all power (as with Tunisia's Habib Bourguiba). Also, the person who temporarily monopolizes state powers (after a coup d'etat, for example) ends up incarnating the nation in its own eyes (the later Boumediène).

Still, the face of power often conceals the fact that there is really no one behind it, as when the top official is merely a figurehead set up by the true powers who might be economic and financial groups, the technobureaucracy, etc., in order to deflect attention from themselves. If this is so, then the figurehead is nothing but a device where the spotlight can be focused while the real power is being exercised elsewhere — in the shadows, far from that shining image projected by officials.

THE IMAGE OF POWER

Increasingly, politicians attempt to create images of themselves to capture and hold public attention. These images are the more or less accurate reproduction of themselves. They are a collection of characteristics that each chooses to offer to public view. Each is a selection, carefully arranged. This scale model is, therefore, a figurative representation of reality — and a reconstitution of reality.

Such a reconstitution resembles the work of an artist. But this time the artist is working on himself, as in an autobiography or a self-portrait. This time the sculptor models his own statue, using himself as clay. He is both artist and model, creator and creation.

This work on oneself, this artistic production of oneself stems from the most blatant narcissism; the sort of narcissism that prompted Benito Mussolini to declare as his goal: "To make my own life my masterpiece."*[2] It is also the art of the happening, which consists entirely of its own staging.

But self-glorification is an art as old as the world. When Julius Caesar wrote *Commentarii de bello gallico,* what was he doing but striking a pose for his citizens? What was he doing if not making himself a star? The facts are there simply to enhance his portrait.[3] When Napoleon dictated his *Mémorial de Sainte-Hélène,* what was he doing but imposing his view of his character on future generations? He related reality here and there only to increase the credibility of his interpretation of events. Why has so much effort been spent through the ages on creating an image? For two reasons:

First, a powerful image strikes the public mind, creating or consolidating fame by serving as a visible, tangible symbol. Sufficiently characterized and individualized, the image captures the public's interest and holds its attention.

Second, the image is the outline — and the substitute — for a political program. A leader's profile today foretells his actions tomorrow. John Kennedy's dynamic image adumbrated the New Frontier. Just as in 1974 the modernist image of France's Valéry Giscard d'Estaing was an attempt to symbolize a leader eager to bring about change.[4]

The image thus serves as a label. It indicates the characteristics — real or supposed — and the performance of a "product" or of a political "brand." Indeed, it is legitimate to think in terms of "brand image" in this connection.

---

*In his preface to this book, the Duce wrote: "This is the greatest proof of abnegation that I can offer to the edification of my fellow men: to present myself."

A leader's image becomes the equivalent of a trademark, which identifies a manufacturer's products. It symbolizes the product's originality and value. Just as a detergent is advertised as getting the wash "whiter than white," a political candidate is advertised as "running a better government." Thus labeled, the candidate becomes a brand name product, easily identifiable and classifiable; at least this is so in theory.

Once the brand image is settled on, it is important to stick to it, avoiding any sudden changes in tone, style, or manner. This consistency gives the desired impression of dependable, solid character. It is sometimes known as "the golden rule of image coherence."[5]

France's Jacques Chaban-Delmas paid the price for not observing this rule in the French elections of 1974. From 1969 to 1974 he maintained the dynamic image of a man full of dash and elan. He was always buoyant and smiling, athletic and cordial. In short, he was the image of a brother. Then President Georges Pompidou died, and Chaban-Delmas attempted to change his role from prime minister to president. His posters showed him severe and preoccupied. He worked at speaking slowly and thoughtfully. He avoided smiling. Gravity — in the sense of weight — became his rule. In short, he assumed the image of a father.

This superposition of a new, different image within the relatively short campaign period contributed to his loss. The public was disconcerted, no longer recognizing the old Chaban-Delman "product," and it was unable to believe in his new image. As advertising people say, it is easier to create a new brand image than to change an old one. What would happen if Jaguar tried to assume the Cadillac image?

It is important to stay with the image once it has been shaped, but the result of this is that a number of leaders become captives of their own images. They are unable to change, constrained to remain in the roles they have given themselves.

Unable to modify his image of the aloof hero, de Gaulle was forced into a run-off ballot in 1965 and was finally defeated in 1969. President Giscard d'Estaing, reacting to the scare of the local elections of March 24, 1976, briefly tried a new style for his televised speech to the nation: his face was serious and his suit dark, his delivery was even and his eyes cold; there was a sober backdrop in a solumn office. Everything was changed from the youthful style and relaxed tone of his previous fireside chats. But this change was in vain. His new style was counter-productive; it confused the French, and Giscard immediately resumed his old image.

So a politician must be willing to stay with the role he has chosen for himself. He must consent to conform to the image spread by his propaganda. Thus he lives emprisoned in his own myth like the typecast actor.

The important thing for the politician is to create myths and symbols, even if they do not correspond to reality. The myth is sufficient unto itself. To be sure, it is better not to dissociate the real from the image too much. But more important than the reality itself is that the image be believed in. It should be believed in even if it is obviously a flattering pose, the way a painter poses his princely model.

What advice does Machiavelli give the Prince? He says to dissociate *being* from *seeming*. The Prince must be wily as a fox and strong as a lion. He must cheat and kill. But to reassure his subjects, he must "feign and disguise," composing a completely different persona for himself. Like Ferdinand the Catholic, that perjured warrior who made a great show of charity and religion, "Everyone sees what you appear to be, but few understand what there is within; and those few will not dare contradict the opinion of the majority, which is reinforced by the majesty of the State. . . . Common men believe only what they see. . . ."[6]

Since Machiavelli's day, the "art of lying" has refined its techniques, thanks to professionals in advertising, the media, and campaign management. Hannah Arendt denounces these practices, noting that politics amounts partly to create a certain image and partly to making people believe in the reality of that image.[7] The objective is to manipulate public opinion, to make it buy certain political brands. The goal is to sell an image on the electoral market, even if it means abusing and tricking the public and tampering with the truth. The truth no longer counts. It is an old-fashioned concept to many professionals, who confuse image and imagination. For them, the art of politics includes an increasing amount of set design and make-up, like the art of the theater.

THE STAR SYSTEM IN POLITICS

The politician could be authentic but he prefers artifice, simulating to the point of dissimulating. He creates for himself a persona that gets attention and strikes the imagination. He plays a role. Thus we often speak of politicians in a vocabulary borrowed from the theater, referring to "stars" on the "political stage" who captivate the "public" with their "act."

Each one wants the lead role, for politics has borrowed from show business Hollywood's star system, which started in the 1920s and which continues today, with Robert Redford, Dustin Hoffman, or Barbra Streisand. Today the world of political show business focuses its spotlights on a few superstars. No one wants to finance a high-budget film — or a political party — unless one or several well-known stars are in the cast.

We know what effect the star system had on the motion picture industry. At first it was the picture that dictated the role of the actor. Now it is the star that dominates the show. We no longer judge actors by their ability to interpret one of the roles in a film. We judge a film by how well it serves the actor.

The movie star is infinitely more important than the script or the director. Similarly, the star of a political party eclipses its program, reducing it to a simple "platform" for his personal ambition.

Politicians do this with the same rampant egocentrism and caprice as movie stars for whom nothing counts but their careers. What does a screen star care about cameramen and bit players? What does a star politician care about party members and organizational workers? Thus political life tends toward the singular — toward egopolitics. Thus public affairs as well are reduced to a solo performance played by a single instrumentalist.

Now the political spectacle focuses on one superstar. Alone on the stage, he monopolizes the public's attention with his one-man show. All the other acts are eliminated in order to center the show on him. The star is everything. Everyone else is either a bit player in the background or a spectator in the audience. This is how the political supershow works, the superproduction projected on the screen of government, with all eyes on one figure.

THE ROLES

The main problem for politicians who put personality before platform, is one of casting their own role. What image does one choose?

To be sure, political stars always project a composite image of various characteristics. But they soon find themselves typecast in one of several well-known roles of the political repertoire, often to the point of caricature:

There is the role of the hero. Aloof and above the battle, he is the rare exception; he is the savior, the providential leader, and often the idol. In theatrical terms, he is the *deus ex machina*.

There is the common man role, or Mr. Everyman. This is second-rate theater, where the understudy has been promoted to star.

There is the charmer who attempts to seduce more than to convince; this is the matinee idol.

There is the father of his country, the tutelary of authority. He plays the role of the noble, dignified father.

Then there are the female political stars, some mother figures, with all others in the supporting roles.

Depending on the historical moment and the mood of the nation, these roles follow one another in an almost logical order, as the chiefs of state rotate in and out of government. After a while, the hero tires, unable to maintain an epic pitch indefinitely. He is followed by the quiet, modest common man. But the nation eventually finds him boring and banal. So the people are ready for the charmer, who seduces, surprises, and makes some citizens nervous about what appears to be his instability. Tired of continual change and surprise, they are ready for the father figure. He lends an air of security with his experience and ponderous manner, especially in times of crisis.

There is nothing mechanical about this cycle, of course. But examples are not hard to find over the last 20 to 30 years of political life. In the United States, hero Roosevelt preceded common man Truman and everyman Eisenhower, who led the way for charmer Kennedy, who gave way to father Johnson.

In Fifth Republic France, de Gaulle preceded common man Pompidou, who led to charmer Giscard d'Estaing. "Every man is an exception," said Sören Kierkegaard. But today, every politician seems to be a stereotype.

Official portrait of Charles de Gaulle (1959).

The Hero

"A man bears glory within himself."
—VILLIERS DE L'ISLE-ADAM,
CITED BY CHARLES DE GAULLE

There's no doubt about it. The most important role, the one that the biggest political stars dream of, is that of the great man: the hero. The dream is to be the demigod of ancient mythology, suspended between heaven and earth.

The hero is that extraordinary man destined to go from one triumph to another until he reaches apotheosis. He is the man of great deeds and glory, idolized by mere mortals. He is the savior, almost the messiah. He is the providential leader, the brilliant chief, the best expression of the nation's soul, and the prophet of his race. His sytle is solemn, sublime, emphatic.

A whole generation of heroes left its mark on the 1930s and 1940s: Mussolini, Hitler, Franco, and Pétain. The role went unfilled for a brief period thereafter, but Franco lasted until 1975, enjoying 40 years of absolute power. And after the Second World War, de Gaulle reappeared in 1958 to give 11 years of heroic leadership to a different cause. When he resigned, and left the Elysée Palace, he visited the Caudillo and said, "You are General Franco. I was General de Gaulle."

At the age of 84, Marshal Tito *is* Yugoslavia. In the Soviet Union, Stalin died in 1953 and the 20th Party Congress began de-Stalinization in 1956. But a personality cult has begun there again with Leonid Brezhnev. In Romania, Nicolae Ceaucescu reigns as absolute master. On the Chinese island of Formosa, Chiang Kai-shek died in 1975, but Mao reigned until 1976 practically as emperor of the mainland Celestial Empire, and Hua Kuo-feng has succeeded him. In North Korea Kim Il-Sung continues his heavy-handed way toward glory.

The Third World has become the tricontinental land of charisma. In Argentina Juan Perón made a comeback in 1973, after losing power in 1955, only to die in 1974. In Cuba, Fidel Castro is, in his way, another *Lider Maximo*. In the Middle East, Gamal Nasser reigned, and died, like a pharaoh. In Tunisia, Habib Bourguiba is still the "Supreme Warrior." And in black Africa the heroes grandly preside over their faithful, whether it be the low-keyed Presidents Léopold Senghor (Senegal), Félix Houphouet-Boigny (Ivory Coast), Ahmadou Ahidjo (Cameroons), Daniel T. Arap-Moi (Kenya), and Julius Nyerere (Tanzania), or the bombastic General Mobutu Sese Seko (Zaire), Lule (Uganda), and Emperor Bokassa I (Central African Empire).

THE THEORY OF THE HERO

Heroes prosper and rule nearly everywhere, as if to confirm the notions of political thinkers dating back to antiquity. Xenophon was one of the first to praise the hero who commands the respect of all through his evident superiority. In his *Politics,* Aristotle acknowledges the authority of the exceptional leader who establishes himself as absolute master like "a god among men."

In his *Discourses on Livy,* Machiavelli also grants that exceptional men are carried to power by exceptional circumstances. This is the "legislator" or the "founder," the man who single-handedly establishes a regime, like Lycurgus or Solon. It is also the "dictator" vested, as at Rome, with temporary legal powers. These men come to power when the nation must "be defended against extraordinary events."[1]

Rousseau follows Machiavelli's thought closely. He also tolerates the "extraordinary man" in two exceptional cases: the "legislator" to found a State and give it its laws, and the "dictator" to insure its survival.[2]

These two hypotheses still apply to the leader as hero today. The ubiquitous "founder" in the Third World establishes a new state following decolonization and independence. The "savior" is in evidence even in some developed countries confronted with a serious crisis.

Next we have Carlyle's heroes.[3] They are clairvoyant prophets, inspired chiefs, infallible guides who hold their power not from men but from History, Destiny, God. This providential leader surrounds himself with mystery to underscore the supernatural character of his vocation. As a political artist, he rules through symbols to reach the senses of his people, rather than their reason.

Carlyle's hero is indeed a man of action, but his is a calm strength, not the brutal, savage violence of Nietzsche's "superman" which so influenced D'Annunzio, Mussolini, and Hitler.

Perhaps the best analyst of heroic leadership is Max Weber, who distinguishes among three sorts of authority and legitimacy. Traditional authority is founded on usages and customs, like that of the fuedal lord or the hereditary monarch. Legal-rational authority rests upon institutions and statutes like that of the modern State, in which citizens obey not the man, but the office he fills under the constitution. Finally there is the charismatic authority of the prophet, the hero, the wartime leader, the demagogue.

Charismatic is derived from the Greek word *charisma*, which means grace. In theology, charisma designates a special gift conferred by divine grace. Weber introduces this term in his political writing to designate "the special qualities of a person who is, as it were, endowed with supernatural or superhuman strengths or characteristics quite beyond those of mere mortals, or who is considered to have been sent by God, or who is otherwise exemplary and therefore considered to be a leader."

Thus certain leaders are so transcendently exceptional, thanks to this special grace, that men naturally follow them. The talent and influence they wield is worth any number of traditions or institutions.

As early as 1932, in *The Sword's Edge*, de Gaulle celebrated the gifts of "strong personalities: what Alexander called his hopes,' Caesar called his 'fortune,' Napoleon his 'star.' Others in their presence feel a natural force of command." One defers to them, for "certain men give off, as it were from birth, an aura of authority."[4]

It would be difficult to give a better definition of charismatic authority, or what Stanley Hoffmann calls heroic authority, as opposed to the routine authority of an ordinary leader.[5]

THE HERO AND HIS WORKS

Thus the Hercules-like hero has his work cut out for him or, rather, his functions, for this semisacred figure has three official duties: he must stage a show, he must develop the national dream, and he must provide the security of certitude.

More than any other beneficiary of personalized power, the hero is a showman for whom the "political scene" is truly stage scenery. To establish a theatrical rapport with the public and project himself above everyday routine authority, he must be a combination one-man band and miracle worker, giving a nonstop show. But this showman must also fulfill an oneiric function, for as the Bible says, "without a vision the people perish." As Chateaubriand advised, "lead the French with dreams," so the leader must rise above the prosaic and quotidian to outline a noble national vision composed of equal parts of myth, dream, wonder, and the irrational. Thus the hero becomes a prophet, if not a visionary.

In less-developed countries this prophetic-poetic function can be decisive, but it also retains its importance in advanced industrial societies. In a universe of statistics, in a mechanistic, materialistic world run by technicians, the people need new gurus to enlarge their horizons and sketch out a future that will be less drab, less abstract, more human.

Beyond furnishing glorious dreams, the hero must also provide certitude. Through his reassuring mastery he helps overcome the anxiety and uncertainty of changing, difficult times. The people feel secure following him, for the hero is farsighted and cannot make a mistake.

Fascism, for example, rests on this cult of the chief and the dogma of his infallibility. If they follow the Duce, the Italian people cannot fail. Article 8 of the Fascist militant's Decalogue declared, "Mussolini is always right." Nazism was also an act of faith in the Führer's person, who was idolized as absolute master. "I have no conscience," Goering said, "my conscience is named Adolf Hitler."

The question remains: how does the hero lend credibility to his image? Actually the "great man" uses two techniques: distance and pride.

The hero mythicizes and exalts authority, making of it something transcendent, fascinating, and mysterious. It becomes a strange and sacred activity to be exercised in secret and at a distance. The hero is obsessed with the need to avoid the ordinary, to place himself at the opposite pole from the simple, familiar, common man. He must remain distant, haughty, and proud, placing himself as far a possible from the people by withdrawing to a sort of empyrean or Olympus. There he is superior and sovereign, screened by legend. Such distance increases prestige by enhancing a mythical image, but it also has another advantage: it protects the hero from criticism. Far above the masses, appearing only in ritual ceremonies, the national idol eludes the critical faculty.

If only the czar knew, things would be different. But he is badly served by his counsellors and bureaucrats, while he remains all goodness and justice. Stalin knew well how to profit by the dividends of political distance, and the popular unrest, sparing him, concentrated on his underlings.

This haughty, majestic distance does not exclude, from time to time, a condescending visit from on high. On these rare occasions the prince manifests his interest in his loyal subjects, mixing with them while impressing them with how good he is to take the trouble. He allows them to approach him with their adulation, the way thaumaturgic kings of the past touched the scrofulous ill on the day of royal anointment.* So he plunges into crowds or invites himself to dinner with his fellow citizens, who are overcome with gratitude. Then he returns to his empyrean — or to his Elysée Palace or his White House.

DISTANCE

The best theory of distance is in *The Sword's Edge*. In 1932 de Gaulle celebrated in it the cult of the leader, of "the man of character."

---

*In his radio-TV address on December 31, 1974, Giscard d'Estaing on his return from the French Antilles declared: "They welcomed me with their eyes and with their hands. When I returned from the Antilles, my hands were covered with the scratches left by their fingernails when they shook hands with me." (*Le Figaro,* January 1, 1975)

"Nothing can be accomplished without great men."[6] "Both armies and peoples need excellent leaders; the rest follows naturally."[7] For men "can no more get along without leadership than they can without eating, drinking and sleeping."[8]

How then does the leader impose his authority? The third part of the book is entitled "On prestige," and its epigram is these words from Villiers de l''Isle-Adam: "A man bears glory within himself." It is a collection of ideas on how to fascinate public opinion. Of course, prestige is the result of a "natural gift," of "ineffable charm." But this innate "influence" can be cultivated. "The leader, like the artist, must perfect his gift by practice." How?

First, by keeping his distance from the masses. "A leader remains distant, for there is no authority without prestige and no prestige without remoteness. Beneath him, others complain in whispers of his haughtiness and his demands."[9] But thus does the master insure his superiority.

Next it is important to maintain the air of mystery and to transform authority into an enigma. "There is no prestige without mystery, for people do not respect what they know too well; no man is great to his valet."[10]

Neither must he underestimate the importance of looking the part. As a student of political aesthetics, the hero readily strikes a pose. He polishes his every gesture and calculates his appearances, like Amilcar in Flaubert's *Salammbô*. His public movements are as measured as Caesar's. Similarly, "it is well known that Napoleon took care always to show himself under conditions that struck men's imaginations."[11]

The oracle remains sibylline: "Soberness of speech accentuates the pose. Nothing so heightens authority as silence . . . Men instinctively dislike the verbose master. *Imperatoria brevitas,* said the Romans."[12] In sum, the leader's acts must always bear the mark of grandeur and an elevated character. "He must aim high, see far and think big, thereby distinguishing himself from common men with small minds."[13] The ransom for these leaders of men is solitude. "The leader deprives himself of the pleasures of letting go, of familiarity, even of friendship. He is fated to that feeling of solitude which is, according to Émile Faguet, "the misery of superior men."[14]

The first president of the France's Fifth Republic practiced what he preached, ruling "strong and solitary" like Alfred de Vigny's Moses. Distant, remote and haughty, he was above parliaments, parties, and contingencies. This attitude was appropriate from 1958 to 1962, during the Algerian crisis. But over the long term, it became tiresome. Proof of this came with the presidential election of 1965, when de Gaulle used two "heroic" techniques: mystery and silence. He kept his distance from everyone, including the voters.

The first round of voting was on December 5. Would the general be a candidate or not? No one knew. He played on mystery and suspense until November. To captivate and exacerbate public opinion, de-Gaulle delayed announcing his decision until the last moment.

As he had written in *The Sword's Edge*: "There is no prestige without mystery. . . . In planning projects, in expression and in general demeanor there must always be an element that others cannot quite grasp and that puzzles them, moves them and keeps them in bated breath." That is what counts: "Not revealing oneself, deliberately concealing a secret surprise that may be used at any moment."[15]

At the conclusion of the cabinet meeting on October 27, the minister of information announced that the general would make a speech on November 4. When journalists asked for guidance on what the president intended to discuss, the minister, Alain Peyrefitte, admitted: "The rest of us wonder just as much as you do."[16]

After the cabinet meeting on November 3, newsmen again asked Peyrefitte about de Gaulle's impending address. He answerd, "at the conclusion of today's meeting General de Gaulle repeated that he will speak to the nation tomorrow. The members of the cabinet will learn what he says along with the rest of the nation."[17] Even Prime Minister Georges Pompidou learned of de Gaulle's decision only on the afternoon of November 4.

That day, all France listened to that eight-minute TV address. In it, de Gaulle called for "frank and massive support from the citizens" to continue in office. Failing that, "France will have to undergo — this time without any possible recourse — governmental confusion even greater than it has known in the past."[18]

Having resolved the mystery, de Gaulle chose the tactic of silence. After his brief talk — which the press titled "Me or Chaos" — the general considered that he had said enough. To remain above the battle, to avoid lowering himself to the level of the other presidential candidates, he declined to use broadcast time available to him under normal campaign rules.

But this time his remoteness resembled a rejection of democratic debate of issues, and it rubbed the French the wrong way. De Gaulle noticed this *in extremis,* and agreed to make two TV speeches, on November 30 and December 3. During this first round of balloting he used only 23 minutes, in all, of the two hours available to each candidate. And this aloofness was one of the reasons for his falling short of a majority and having to participate in a runoff vote on December 5.

For this second round of voting, de Gaulle finally consented to act like a candidate, and to use all his TV time. On December 13, 14, and 15 French television broadcast three half-hour conversations between the general and a journalist, Michel Droit. The two were seated in armchairs in a salon of the Elysée Palace.

Suddenly the French discovered a different man, one who descended from his pedestal and spoke simply and spontaneously. His good-natured remarks, accompanied by shakes of the head and winks, bordered on familiarity. And at times the *deus ex machina* seemed to adopt the language of Sganarelle: "Anyone can jump on his chair like a young goat and bleat 'Europe! Europe! Europe!'[19] France is not the left! France is not the right![20] Let's not kid ourselves."[21]

It was new language by a new character: the hero had changed into an ordinary man, the leader had been transformed into a citizen-president. The exceptional man had become one of us, to insure his re-election.

But when the voting was over, the general returned to his Olympus. He adopted once again his old solemn, Zeus-like style. He re-established the distance between himself and the French people which he had briefly and regretfully narrowed. It was back to the *status quo ante.*

In a way, the revolt of May 1968 was against such haughty, remote authority. And de Gaulle again used the same technique: the relaxed tone of his chats with Michel Droit. For the second time — under pressure from the French people — the hero exchanged distance for closeness, aloofness for familiarity. Once again the great man assumed the role of the good guy.

PRIDE

The second device of heroic authority is arrogance. Full of pride, the hero does not doubt for an instant his talent, his lucky star — to the point of narcissism and self-adulation.

The very model of self-glorification is Stalin, lending his name to cities and raising monuments to himself. In 1948 his *Abridged Biography* was prepared, and Nikita Khrushchev explained how this was done in his address to the 20th Party Congress.

The text was submitted to Stalin before publication: "He was flattered and glorified like a god and presented as an infallible sage, the greatest of leaders, the greatest strategist of all time." Still, Stalin wanted more, and added other praise in his own hand, including the following: "Although he assumed his functions as head of the party and the people with consummate skill, and enjoyed the unreserved support of the entire Soviet people, Stalin exhibited no vanity, pretention, or personal aggrandizement."[22]

Other "socialist" leaders have been known to sing their own praises. Mao permitted a personality cult. North Korean President Kim Il Sung periodically buys pages in newspapers to advertise himself unabashedly, as in the following: "The great and immortal ideas of Djoutché constitute the quintessence of the revolutionary ideas of comrade Kim Il Sung, the respected and well-loved leader, eminent thinker and theoretician, and genius of humanity. Today, the ideas of Djoutché are at the center of all the progressive ideas of humanity, and the study and learning of them is the irresistable tendency of the age."[23]

As prophet of the "third way," Libya's Colonel Qaddafi has published *The Green Book* to provide the definitive theoretical solution to the problem of government organization."[24] After that, even the self-satisfied remarks of Habib Bourguiba seem modest, as when in 1969 the "Supreme Warrior" confided: "Two years ago I had that cardiac incident, and it was thought that I might die. People were weeping in the streets. They felt abandoned. I had only one thought: what will become of them? . . . I must get well. If I were to pass on, all would be jeopardized."[25]

How can one not accept the spontaneous praise of the Tunisian people? The following is a poem received by the newspaper *L'Action* from a reader who celebrated the proclamation of Bourguiba as president for life in 1975:

> Glory to the Supreme Warrior
> All honor to his superior soul
> Blessed be his fruitful labor
> Productive of joys extreme.[26]

THE HERO AND THE MONARCH

President for life: imperceptibly, the personalization of power turns into personal power. By monopolizing the state, the hero becomes a monarch in the etymological sense. In his desire to rule alone, to share no government powers, he acts like a king.

The title of president for life is his franchise, guaranteeing his position, and a number of heads of state have succombed to the temptation: Tito in Yugoslavia, Bourguiba in Tunisia, Francisco Masie Nguema Biyogo in Equatorial Guinea, H. Kamazu Banda in Malawi, Amin in Uganda, and Bokassa I in the Central African Empire.

Jean-Bédel Bokassa, an ex-captain in the French army, took over the Central African Republic after a coup d'état on December 31, 1965.[27] At first president of the Revolutionary Council, president for life of the only legal party, and holder of a dozen cabinet posts, he soon became a marshal and president for life. He awarded himself so many medals that he had to lengthen his uniform jacket — patterned on that of Napoleon's Marshal Ney — to wear them all. Still, that was not glory enough.

On December 4, 1976, the marshal proclaimed himself Emperor Bokassa I, and ordered a crown from a famous Paris jeweller. He decreed the transfer of the "imperial court" from Bangui to Beringo, "its ancestral home," and stipulated that the emperor would appear in public only for exceptional ceremonies.[28]

According to protocol, any person approaching Bokassa I must "salute him six steps away with a slight nod of the head." The correct answer to his questions during an audience is "Yes, Imperial Majesty." But "if the situation requires a negative answer," one must avoid an "abrupt no."[29]

Even in France the hero occasionally turns into a monarch without, of course, officially assuming the title and without going to ridiculous extremes. This is done by resuscitating the forms of olden times, a royal style inherited by the collective memory.

Thus Henri Pétain shaped a monarchial persona for himself. On July 10, 1940, the French State replaced the Republic. On the 11th of that month, the Marshal published three "constitutional acts" attributing to himself the powers of a French king. A reading of "Constitutional Act Number 2 describing the powers of the head of the French State" reveals this: "We, Marshal of France, Head of the French State, considering the constitutional law of July 10, 1940, decree: Article I, paragraph 1: The Head of the French State has all governmental powers. He appoints and dismisses cabinet members, who are responsible only to him. Paragraph 2: He exercises legislative power during cabinet meetings. . . ."

The royal style is obvious, from the majestic first person plural to all executive and legislative powers. And this, only four years after the victory of the Popular Front.

From then on, Pétain organized his pseudo-monarchy, including his portrait in private homes, letters to him from schoolchildren, and the stuffy ceremonies at the Hotel du Parc in Vichy. His visits to the provinces were full of pomp; the masses in the cathedrals are reminiscent of the ties between the throne and the church.

In the name of another cause, de Gaulle struck the same royal pose. Decades earlier he had graduated with honors from the War College — though the honors were not as high as he had wanted — with these official remarks in his record: "An intelligent, cultivated, and reliable officer; brilliant and easily competent; very solid. Unfortunately he spoils his unquestionable qualities with his excessive self-assurance, his low opinion of the ideas of others, and his attitude of an exiled king."[30]

Under the Fifth Republic, de Gaulle became truly the "republican monarch" dreamed of by Debré and Monick in 1943. He was an elected "monarch," to be sure, but for 12 years — the average reign before 1789.

The constitution of 1958, instituting the Fifth Republic, is in line with this. It puts the president in a monarchical position, giving him a supreme power of "arbitration," thereby placing him above petty quarrels and special interests. It makes him the guardian of national interests, or of the "common profit" as royal lawmakers would have put it. It places him above parties, factions, groups, central to the nation's institutions, like a *deus ex machina* ready to descend from his Olympus to set the collective destiny on the right path.

In any case, that is how the general interpreted "his" constitution. In truth, Charles de Gaulle was nearly Charles XI. The Fifth Republic was transformed into an elective monarchy founded on the plebiscitic referendum that periodically renews the subjects' homage to their sovereign.

Soon after his election to the Elysée Palace, the general made his attitude clear in a televised address on December 28, 1958: "Guide of France and head of the republican State, I shall exercise the supreme power in the large sense in which it is now conferred."

Five years later, his new decalogue was presented at his press conference of January 31, 1964: "It must of course be understood that the State's indivisible authority is conferred entirely on the president by the people who have elected him, that none other exists, neither ministerial, nor civil, nor military, nor judiciary, which is not conferred and maintained by him. . . ." Like a well-known predecessor of his, he had stated clearly, "I am the State."

De Gaulle derived his majestic self-assurance from a double feeling of legitimacy, i.e., his call for resistance of June 18, 1940, and by referendum of the French people. Similarly, Napoleon I reigned by the grace of God and by the grace of the people, which was signified by his anointment at Notre Dame, and by the grace of universal suffrage.

The historical investiture had greater value than the people's investiture. Beyond institutional legitimacy there was the feeling of his own personal legitimacy. Ranking above the referendums of 1958, 1961, and 1962 and the presidential election of 1965, to his mind, were his call of June 18, and his heroic vocation during the years 1940 to 1945. For those, like himself, who had been through the war, de Gaulle was not simply an ordinary leader, and he therefore had a greater right than others to govern France.

In the eyes of the general, this historical investiture had forged an unbreakable link between him and the nation, a mystical link in the sense France had known in ancient times. He had espoused France on June 18, 1940, the way the kings of France used to put on a wedding ring the day of their anointment. Marriage is an eternal sacrament that nothing can undo except death. President Pompidou alluded to this almost carnal relationship when his predecessor died: "General de Gaulle is dead. France is a widow."

For nearly 30 years, from 1940 to 1970, the general had felt himself to be the incarnation of national legitimacy, within or outside the framework of the nation's institutions. Thus, describing his departure from office in January 1946, he noted in his *Memoirs:*

> Although separated from their leader, the people continued to see in him a sort of designated bearer of sovereignty, a refuge decided upon in advance. They understood that this legitimacy remained latent as long as all went well. But they knew that it would be acknowledged, by general consent, as soon as the country once again ran the risk of being torn apart.
>
> My personal style during the following years was dictated by this mission that France continued to assign me. . . . All those who had dealings with me treated me as if, representing the supreme authority, I had received them in a national palace."[31]

This "exiled king" transported his legitimacy with him. This monarch without throne was reminiscent of kings whose place had been usurped. Charles de Gaulle, retired at Colombey and visited by his "legitimist" followers, is a bit like Charles X in Prague or Goritz.

Recalled to head the government and then the state in 1958, de Gaulle again joined historical legitimacy with electoral legitimacy, personal legitimacy and institutional legitimacy. Thus, politics ratifies history. Referring on December 28 to his election to the Elysée Palace, the general declared: "The national duty which has been mine for 18 years has been confirmed by this."

He was recalling the special ties between him and France, which existed above and beyond constitutional procedures and texts. During the tense moments of the Algerian War, the general proclaimed on January 20, 1960: "Well, my dear old country, here we are together again, facing a difficult trial. In virtue of the mandate that the people have given me, and of the legitimacy that I have incarnated for 20 years, I call on everyone to support me whatever happens."

He was very clearly affirming his double authority, that conferred on him by the people's investiture of the referendum and that, older and higher, of History and Destiny, if not of providence itself.

Thus did de Gaulle present himself as the depository of legitimacy "for 20 years," since the moment when in fact he occupied no constitutional office. He considered that his historical aura, his divine right placed him above the country's institutions, very much in the style and the tone of "the 40 kings who made France."

Until his last day, the "guide of France" was a king within the republic. Nothing could have been more royal that this republican president who restored the Trianon Palace at Versailles and who dreamed of the glories of ancient France. Charles de Gaulle was made for Rheims, Versailles, and Saint Denis, not for the National Assembly, the Elysée, and Colombey. Despite universal suffrage, he was the last of the Capetians, by the grace of History, if not God.

THE HERO AND DIVINITY

To all appearances, the hero has a special relationship with divinity. As in mythology, he is demigod, half-way between the gods and mortals, sent by the former to the latter.

November 20, 1975. General Francisco Franco has died after a month of death throes and 40 years of reign. He was like an awesome idol of Spain's ancestral religion.

Successor and predecessor of the *Reyes Catolicos,* Franco often staked his claim to Divine Providence, stating as early as 1937: "God has placed the life of our country in our hands to be cared for." The reference to divine right is explicit. Franco was proclaimed "Caudillo of Spain by the grace of God." The statutes of the Falange declare that he is "responsible before God and before history."[32]

Ensconsed in the Pardo Palace amid the etiquette and pomp of the Castilian monarchy and seated between Velázquez and Zurbarán, the Caudillo thus adds providential legitimacy to charismatic legitimacy.

This theocratic device is of course the underpinning of the last traditional monarchies. Hassan II belongs to a family that has reigned over Morocco since 1640 and which claims to descend from the Prophet. He has explained that "it is not Hassan II that is revered, it is the heir of a dynasty. . . . The people bow not before my person, but before the line of descendants from the Prophet." Like the caliph, he unites spiritual and temporal power. In virtue of the constitution of

March 10, 1972 (article 19), "the king, *Amir el Mouminine* (Commander of the Faithful) insures the respect of Islam."[33]

Similarly, King Khaled of Saudi Arabia is the guarantor of Law and Tradition. Imaum of the faithful, guardian of the Holy Places, he basis his power on divine right.

Marshal Amim, also a Moslem, told his people of his dreams, which put him in contact with God so that he could follow His command-ments. Dreams are the divine sanction for his actions. But the Ugandan president-for-life did not overdo the use of these voices and revelation — this rite of the prophet. "Do you often have dreams like this?" a journalist asked him.

"Only when necessary," came the answer.[34]

Still, heroic authority often strays from divine right and organizes its own cult. Using a backdrop of atheism or paganism, the hero replaces God. He becomes His functional substitute, providing the same services to the faithful: security, certitude, and peace of mind. Since authority cannot exist without some rite, authority becomes its own rite.

Nietzsche proclaimed the titanic hero who substitutes himself for God. "The superman," he explained, "destroys idols and assumes their attributes. The apotheosis of the human adventure is the glorification of the man-god."

Fascist and Nazi propaganda created a new religion of the state and of its providential chief. It transformed this savior into the idol of a new cult to be adored and adulated.

The substitute deity — Duce or Führer — is promoted with new sacrificial rites: appearances on the balcony of the Palazzo Veneto to receive the adoration of the masses or Wagnerian ceremonies at Nuremberg. The Third Reich and its high priests set up an ersatz Valhalla.

The Soviet Union also develops a pseudo-religious aura around its leaders, despite the letter Karl Marx wrote to Wilhelm Bloss: "When Engels and I became members of the secret service of Communists, it was on the condition that everything in its statutes having to do with the superstitious adoration of authority would be eliminated." And the *International* declares:

> There is no supreme savior
> Neither God, nor Caesar, nor Tribune.

But for half a century Lenin has been exposed in his glass coffin to the veneration of the people. And while he was still alive, Stalin was the object of a personality cult denounced by Khrushchev at the 20th Soviet Communist Party Congress in 1956.

THE PERSONALITY CULT

The personality cult began in December 1929, when Stalin's 50th birthday was celebrated with unheard-of-pomp. It became firmly established in the 1930s when Stalin, having vanquished his adversaries on the left and right, surrounded himself with lackeys.

Stalin personally encouraged this torrent of eulogy, which ended only with his death in 1953.* Roy Medvedev described him orchestrating this chorus of praise, stimulating his panegyrists, accepting the most excessive hommage.[35]

This propaganda provoked the collective delirium of an entire country, of the whole international Communist movement. Even those condemned to death sang to the glory of the secretary general. Before his execution, Lev Kamenev declared: "I adjure my sons to spend their lives defending great Stalin."[36] Shortly before being assassinated, Sergei Kirov, while opposing Stalin, called him "the greatest man of all time and of all the peoles."[37]

This veneration reached its apogee after the great purges of 1936 to 1938. "From 1938 on," observes Ilya Ehrenburg, "it is more accurate to use the word *cult* in its original religious sense. In the minds of millions of beings, Stalin was transformed into a mythical de-migod."[38]

He was changed into an idol, an earthly god who inspired adoration and reverent fear. The personality cult becomes a strange lay variety of religious conscience in a Socialist society. Describing this deification of Stalin, Medvedev notes: "Like all cults, this one tended to transform the Communist party into an ecclesiastic organization with a clear distinction between the flock and the high priests serving their infallible pope. . . . Just as believers attribute all qualities to God, so Stalin was found to possess all virtue."[39]

---

*The 23rd Congress decided to refer to the period 1933 to 1953 as "the period of the personality cult."

The Supreme Fetish exercised a veritable spell, with everyone devoted to him, everyone singing his praises. A "Song of Stalin" tells of his superhuman grandeur:

> Stalin you are higher
> Than celestial space
> And only your thoughts
> Are higher than you.
> The sun is brighter
> Than the stars and the moon
> But your mind, O Stalin,
> Is brighter than the sun.[40]

Another poem celebrates his incomparable genius:

> The stars of dawn obey your will,
> Your incomparable genius mounts to the skies,
> Your insight sounds the depths of the Ocean.[41]

He is the universal wise man, he is God:

> O Stalin, great leader of peoples,
> You who give birth to man,
> You who fertilize the earth,
> You who rejuvenate the centuries,
> You who braid the spring
> You who make the lyre sing . . .
> You who are the flower of my spring,
> A sun reflected by thousands
> Of human hearts. . . .[42]

Alexander Prokofiev affirms: "Stalin — I need say no more. Everything is included in this immense name. Everything: the party, the fatherland, life, love, immortality, all."[43]

Even Paul Éluard sings in this chorus:

> And Stalin to us is present for tomorrow
> And Stalin dispels unhappiness today
> Confidence is the fruit of his loving brain
> A reasonable fruit so perfect it is
> For life and men have elected Stalin
> To be their unlimited hope on earth[44]

GOD IS DEAD

The death of God is an unbearable idea for the faithful. Similarly, the death of the sanctified hero is a cataclysm for the faithful of this new cult; it causes them infinite anguish and distress.

Stalin's death was made public at dawn on March 6, 1953: "The heart of Lenin's companion, of him who continued the good cause, of the guide of the party and of the people, has ceased to beat." His body was exposed in the Hall of Columns beneath banked plants and red flowers. Then it joined Lenin's body in the mausoleum on Red Square. Women sobbed and held their infants up to see the holy relic. Symphonies and funeral marches added to the general desolation.

An entire people was in despair, moved by muted indignation. Since God is immortal, there must have been some terrible mistake. It is this feeling that explains the collective hysteria at Stalin's funeral, as at Nasser's, and even at de Gaulle's when the crowd filed sadly by the Arch of Triumph on that rainy night.

The stylish, charming leader does not provoke this delirium when he dies. Even when his death is inherently more dramatic, as was John Kennedy's, it is observed in silence. But the hero dies tragically, amid weeping and torment. His grandiose funeral — often dictated in advance by himself — is his last melodramatic number on stage.

Then consternation rules even the best minds. In 1953 Mao Tse-tung wrote:

> The greatest genius of our day, the great guide of the international Communist movement, the comrade of the immortal Lenin, comrade Joseph Vissarionovich Stalin, has said good-bye to the world forever. . . .
>
> All the writings of comrade Stalin are imperishable Marxist documents. We used to gather around him, ceaselessly asking his advice, and we never failed to receive intellectual strength from him. . . . Now we have lost our great guide and our most sincere friend, comrade Stalin. It is an immense tragedy! There are no words to express the sadness this tragedy causes us.[45]

Before long, Mao would organize — or allow others to organize — his own cult. At the time of the Little Red Book, that catechism of the new religion, he was considered the equal of a god, with portraits of him everywhere; his ideas were cited by millions of Chinese as if he were the Word Incarnate; he was even credited with miraculous powers. He was adulated and idolized as few emperors of the Celestial Empire have been before him.

His cult recalled a long tradition of devotion to emperors that the Chinese people do not forget easily.* It was just the way Stalin had used and accentuated the tradition of the czars.

In his *Memoirs*, Khrushchev compared the two idols:

> If you close your eyes, if you listen to what the Chinese say about Mao, and if you replace *Comrade Mao* with *Comrade Stalin*, you will have an idea of the state of things in those days. . . . Men like Stalin and Mao had one thing in common: to stay in power, they found it indispensable to claim that their authority came from heaven.[46]

For that matter, Mao himself described how to use this veneration:

> There are two sorts of personality cults. One is good, such as one whose object is the correct ideas of Marx, Engels, Lenin, and Stalin. We must venerate them eternally; if we did not venerate them, it would be very wrong. Since they represent Truth, why should we not venerate them? . . . A group should venerate its chief; if they did not, it would be very wrong. The second sort of personality cult is incorrect; it consists of following blindly, without reflecting, and that is not good. The problem is not whether to have a personality cult, but whether it conforms to the Truth.[47]

During the cultural revolution of 1966, the Red Guard served Mao's cult. He presided over their first demonstration on August 18. More than a million of them paraded on the Square of Celestial Peace, waving the Little Red Book and chanting "The Helmsman guides us over the seas." From dawn till noon, standing on the balcony overlooking the square and dressed in the uniform of the Liberation Army, Mao saluted his new revolutionary batallions. By the end of November he had done it seven times more, watching nine million Red Guards pass in review from all over China.

---

*In China, earthquakes are supposed to accompany the death of an emperor. China had several in 1976, including the one at Tang-Chan on July 28.

This was also when Lin Piao, the chief organizer of the cult, covered Mao with praise, calling him "the greatest supreme commander . . . the great helmsman," and even "Emperor Tsin." Busts, statues, and pictures multiplied everywhere, and Mao, the incarnation of his people, became a living god adored by 900 million faithful.

Thus China's anguish was infinite when Mao died at 82 on September 9, 1976. It was the same despair of the entire Russian people losing their tutelary divinity as in the death of Stalin.

Mourning lasted ten days. Thousands of Chinese filed by the foot of the Heroes of the People Monument on Tien An-men Square. A gigantic portrait of Mao hung from the 125-foot column that dominates the Square, and young and old alike bowed before it, often in tears. Inside the great People's Palace, the nation's leaders filed by Mao's body.

The whole country came to a standstill for the funeral on September 19. At precisely 3 P.M. 900 million Chinese stood rigidly to attention and observed three minutes of silence, while sirens screamed on factories, ships, and trains. In Peking's Tien An-men Square, a million people gathered, beginning at 7:30 A.M., to face Mao's immense picture in black and white and listen to the funeral oration by Hua Kuo-feng.

Silent and grieving, an entire nation wore mourning for the Chinese god. Shortly afterwards, on Tien An-men Square, Hua Kuo-feng laid the cornerstone of a mausoleum for Mao on November 24, much as the Soviet leaders had placed Stalin's body in Red Square.

FROM ONE CULT TO ANOTHER

But China soon had another idol: Hua Kuo-feng, who had become first vice-president of the party and prime minister in April 1976. Immediately following Mao's death, this leader of the "pragmatic" faction took the initiative against the "radicals" and ousted the "anti-party clique" or "the gang of four." They were Chiang Ch'ing, widow of Mao, and Wang Hung-wen, second vice-president of the party, Chang Chun-Chiao, first vice-prime minister, and the doctrinaire Yao Wen-yuan.

Henceforward, the New China News Agency declared, "these leaders have shown their true colors and have become as disgusting and despicable as dog droppings."[48]

As party president, Hua Kuo-feng directed his own cult. Four days of mass demonstrations all over China culminated in Peking on October 24, 1976, with a million people proclaiming him the heir of "the great Helmsman." Hua Kuo-feng, wearing a military uniform, appeared for the first time on the historic balcony of Tien An-men gate, where before only Mao had presided over mass demonstrations. He was receiving the vibrant hommage of the Chinese people — only six weeks after Mao's death.

On China's border, North Korea also practices the personality cult. It focuses on Marshal-President Kim Il Sung, "respected and beloved leader — "the nation's sun." Gilded bronze statues of him stand in every spot where he is supposed to have combated the Japanese during the war. His portrait — like that of Big Brother's — is everywhere. The village where he was born is a place of obligatory pilgrimage. The 2,896 places where he stopped to dispense his advice to the people are so many "holy places." The seat he occupied one day in the subway has been draped in satin and has never again been used. In P'yŏngyang, the Museum of the Korean Revolution devotes 95 rooms to his life.

There are countless books on Kim Il Sung, such as "Comrade Kim Il Sung is an Ingenius Thinker and Theoretician," or "President Kim Il Sung, the man who Guides Asia and the World." Also countless are songs like this one:

> Tell us, storm from the Manchurian plain
> Tell us, endless night of the dense forest
> Who is history's peerless partisan
> Who is the world's peerless patriot?[49]

Even in the U.S.S.R., despite its condemnation by the 20th Party Congress in 1956, the personality cult is returning — this time to the profit of Leonid Brezhnev, who has run the party since 1964.

At the 25th Congress in February-March 1976, all the Soviet orators praised his "personal merits." The first secretary from Georgia, Chevarnadzay, declared: "One of the greatest qualities of Leonid Ilich is that he never pretends to be a superman. . . . Great competence, breadth, a sharp mind, humanism, class, loyalty, firm principles, the art of penetrating to the bottom of souls, the ability to promote a climate of confidence, respect and scrupulousness among men, a climate that excludes blind fear, egoism, envy and suspicion — such are some of the qualities which we must learn and which we do learn from Leonid Ilich Brezhnev."[50]

Another delegate, Rachidov, was no less enthusiastic: Brezhnev is "not only the most eminent but also the most influential politician of our time. . . . He has immense modesty, brilliant talent, revolutionary optimism, a firm class position, good heartedness, and personal charm."[51]

Still another, Kounaiev, praised "his Titanic efforts." And Delegate Rassoulov described him as "a great statesman and party leader, gifted with immense organizational talent, with overflowing energy, knowledge of life and a great, sensitive soul." Delegate Voos saw in him "the unquenchable spirit of initiative, overflowing energy and immense capacity for work." Delegate Griskiavicius saw him as "a man with a great soul who incarnates the finest qualities of Man with a capital M."[52]

Each of the first secretaries from the federated republics added his encomium, all of which placed Brezhnev's earlier report to the Congress in a peculiar light: he had declared that there was no place in the Soviet Communist party for those "who surrounded themselves with flatterers."[53]

Nonetheless, the eulogies continued to flow. On May 8, 1976, the anniversary of victory in the Second World War, Brezhnev was promoted to the rank of field marshal and therefore to the summit of the military hierarchy, like Stalin. The same day, a bronze bust of Brezhnev was unveiled at Dnieprodzerinsk, his birthplace in the Ukraine. At the televised ceremony a member of the politburo and first secretary of the Ukraine, Chtcherbitski, declared: "Leonid Brezhnev's merits as a strategist and defense specialist have been recognized. . . . As a shining Communist representing the glorious galaxy of Leninist leaders, [he deserves] the respect and profound gratitude of communists, of the Soviet people, and of all the planet's inhabitants."[54]

At another ceremony at the Kremlin on October 14, 1976, Kirilenko asserted: "Leonid Ilich, you have deservedly received the profound love of millions of the earth's people. . . . Optimism and confidence in the world's progress flow from your words as from a spring. . . . The party and the people love you, Leonid Ilich!"[55]

The litany of praise increased as Brezhnev's 70th birthday approached. Thirty million copies of his full-color portrait were printed. Newspapers and television repeatedly ran his biography and gave details on the upcoming ceremonies. A photo album entitled *Leonid Ilich Brezhnev: Pages of a Life, Pages of an Era* was sold, making him out to be one of the key leaders in the Soviet victory in 1945 and responsible for Russia's achievements in space. A film on his career, *Story of a Communist,* was shown.

Leaders from the satellite countries — Erich Honecker (East Germany), Todor Zhivkov (Bulgaria), Edward Gierek (Poland), János Kádár (Hungary), Yumjaagiin Tsedenbal (Mongolia), and Raul Castro (Cuba) — visited Moscow, covering Brezhnev with decorations such as The Golden Stars, The Order of Liberty, etc. Like Communist Three Kings, they came bearing frankincense and myrrh.

The great day came on December 19. *Pravda* published six pages on Brezhnev and put his photo on page one. A Kremlin ceremony — live television — began at 11 A.M., with the chief dignitaries of the U.S.S.R. and its satellites participating.

Nikolai Podgorny presented the secretary general his fifth Order of Lenin, his second golden star as a Hero of the Soviet Union, and a ceremonial saber of the Red Army, all to celebrate his "eminent merits in reinforcing the defense capacity of the Soviet Armed Forces."[56]

That afternoon a great banquet was held lasting several hours, at which foreign guests and Soviet officials made over 30 speeches. Amid such ritual and devotion, the marshal-secretary general resembled a new Red Czar, a model of virtue ready for iconography. Twenty years after the Khrushchev Report, twenty years after Stalin had been removed from his pedestal, the U.S.S.R. has established a new personality cult complete with its simple-minded piety and thumping paeans.

TAKING GOD'S PLACE

Other leaders go even further, tending toward self-deification. They actually complete or replace established religion with their own cult. In such cases, references to fetishism and idolatry are not metaphorical but, rather, are real. Like Prometheus, the hero attempts to steal the secret from the gods to give his authority a religious dimension.

Thus Kwame Nkrumah, president of Ghana until 1966, created his own cult. He began his semideification in 1949, well before his country's independence in 1957. Describing the election campaign of 1951, which Nkrumah won, a journalist noted: "He has been virtually deified by the people, who attribute to him the virtue and universal imminence of an ancestral spirit. . . . His name has been substituted for that of Christ in religious hymns."[57]

The *Accra Evening News* called him "the greatest African of our generation," "Katamento" (He Who is Never False), "Oyea Dieyie" (Renewer of All Things), "Osagyefo" (Bringer of victories), "Kodokurni" (Brave Warrior), "Kasakrepo" (He Who Speaks For All), the "Redeemer" and the "Messiah."

In May 1961, the parliament in Accra discussed turning the house where Nkrumah was born into a museum. Its members compared Nkrumah to Confucius, Mohammed, Saint Francis of Assisi, Shakespeare, and Napoleon. Some drew parallels between his speeches and those of Buddha and Christ's Sermon on the Mount.

Jane Rouch noted during a visit to Young Pioneers, that they recited this litany:

> Leader: "Nkrumah is infallible"
> Chorus: "Nkrumah is our chief"
> Leader: "Nkrumah is our Messiah"
> Chorus: "Nkrumah is immortal."[58]

Today, President Mobutu of Zaire is also organizing his own cult. "I am the chief," he says with evident pleasure. "I like to be loved by my people. It feels good to know that one is loved. It would be worth killing for."[59]

Joseph Désiré Mobutu, son of the cook of Catholic missionaries, became Mobutu Sese Seko Kuku Ngwendu wa Zabanga (the cock that crows over victory, the unbeatable warrior who goes from one conquest to another). His titles include: Mobutu the Creator, Mobutu the Builder, Guide of the Zairian Revolution, Great Helmsman, Father of the Zairian Nation.

In the streets of Kinshasa and other towns, green signs proclaim "Mobutu Sese Seko, our salvation! Our only guide!" His portraits, bearing the words "Thank you, Citizen President!" are everywhere. Groups of "cheerleaders" roam the streets singing his praises.

From morning till evening the national radio station, The Voice of Zaire, pays its respects to him by broadcasting groups of singers who celebrate his life: "You are my father — Mobutu Sese Seki — You are my God — Kuku Ngwendu wa Zabanga." For one minute every evening before the 8 o'clock TV news, the screen is filled with clouds and the intermittent face of the celestial, clairvoyant Guide. God Mobutu.[60]

All public buildings have President Mobutu's portrait in their offices. The political bureau of the People's Revolutionary Movement (PRM), the country's only legal party, which Mobutu created in 1967, decided that places he honored with his presence would be sites of public veneration.

Nkrumah had developed his own philosophico-religious doctrine, "Nkrumanism," or "consciencism."[61] Likewise, General Mobutu laid down Mobutuism, which the permanent secretary of the PRM calls "a doctrine made up of the thought, the teachings, and the action of the president-founder of the PRM."[62] And the constitution's preamble proclaims: "We the Zairian people, united in the People's Revolutionary Movement, guided by Mobutuism. . . ."

The greater the influence of Mobutuism, the worse the state's relationship with the Catholic Church. In December 1974, Christmas ceased to be a holiday. The government ordered the crucifixes removed from the religious hospitals and from the nationalized parochial schools. They were replaced with Mobutu's portrait, just as the teaching of the Christian religion at school was replaced by instruction in Mobutuism. Radio announcers who previously called Mobutu "guide" and "father of the nation," now call him "Messiah" and refer to Christ as "that rebel Jewish prophet."[63] Thus is the hero deified.

THE HARDER THEY FALL

All the same, even the hero has to go eventually. Sometimes he is removed from the stage by death — like Stalin, Franco, or Mao — and the people are astonished to learn that he was mortal. Other times it is through the democratic process — like de Gaulle in 1969 — or a coup d'état — like Perón in 1955 and Nkrumah in 1966. The hero's fall is usually due to one of four causes.

First, he can be tripped up by failure. The hero reigns thanks to an unbroken string of successes. When the victorious general is defeated or when the prophet is wrong, his day is over.

The hero can also be upset by changed circumstances. Heroic authority, like that of the Roman dictator, works in times of crisis. When the crisis that created the need for it is safely past, the hero's charisma fades away. De Gaulle's prestige declined when the Algerian imbroglio was over, for paradoxically, heroes have the hardest time when things return to normal.

Then there is the fact that heroic authority does not wear well in a democracy. Aloof and distant, the charismatic chief inevitably looks down on his fellow citizens from the heights of his glory. After a while, this sort of condescension rubs democratic instincts the wrong way.

Finally, there is the problem of plain lassitude. After a while, grandeur is tiring. A people cannot live indefinitely in epic times any more than theatergoers want to see Shakespeare every night.

In the public mind, great leaders are associated with times of crisis and torment. After a period of that, a worn-out public wants to savor the calm after the storm, the quiet pleasures of the ordinary. Citizens turn from clashing cymbals to politics in a minor key; men on horseback become less attractive than those with a common touch. They want to be led by men like themselves.

So the hero is followed by the anti-hero. In this sense. Georges Pompidou in 1969 was an "anti-de Gaulle."[64] Similarly, Harry Truman replaced Franklin Roosevelt and Clement Attlee followed Winston Churchill. The old lion had promised nothing but "blood, sweat and tears," whereas Attlee held out the promise of simplicity and calm (too calm for some, judging by Churchill's well-known crack: "An empty taxi stopped in front of the House of Commons and Attlee got out"). And in 1953 Nikita Khrushchev, a man of the people, replaced Stalin, the Red Czar of the Kremlin. The common man succeeded the providential man, and demolished his cult. The demigod was followed by the solid Unkrainian, a man attached to the soil who knew about things like corn and who had a normal family life with a wife named Nina and a nephew named Adjubei; someone who spouted age-old proverbs and tapped a shoe on his desk at the United Nations to jeer a speaker.

This anti-hero of simple manners was the perfect example of the second major political role: the common man.

Just Folks

"I'm just a man like everyone else."
— JIMMY CARTER

The political leader sometimes appears as Mr. Everyman. He is the common man, the typical solid citizen who represents the average American, the average Englishman, or the average Frenchman.

He is above all banal, ordinary, and conventional, a virtual champion of normalcy. He is clearly one of us, reflecting back our self-image as faithfully as if voters had created him in their own likeness.

He incarnates middlebrow opinions, common sense, and the nation's idea of wisdom. Perfectly familiar and trite, he utters platitudes and commonplaces with the assurance of a veritable superstar of the pedestrian. His is routine authority par excellence.

How can we explain this triumph of the common, this B-movie of the political box office? It is largely through the function of its stars.

As the ordinary man, the star represents what the philosopher Roland Barthes calls "the happiness of identification." Since the public can easily identify with this self-made man up from the ranks, it feels a natural attachment to him.

He also offers the simple pleasure of conformity, his reassuring platitudes increasing the public's feeling of security. As a virtuoso of the conventional, zealously promoting notions popular with the masses, he tends to unify the nation by reinforcing its cherished beliefs. His stage trick is to tranquilize with routine.

The advent of the common-man politico means everyone is finally equal, even if this equality is only apparent. He has populist reflexes and incarnates the little man in his struggle against the big shots. Enough of triumphant heroes! It's time for the underdog to have his day!

President Gerald Ford, Mr. Everyman, making his own toast at the White House.

Thus the common-man role satisfies the public's yearning for egalitarianism, especially when that common man succeeds the hero with the hero's superior ways. Happy nations have no troubles, and they don't need heroes.

Thus it was with some severity that Cyrus Sulzberger entitled his book on the years 1963–1972 *The Age of Mediocrity,* it being a time which followed "the last of the giants." It was under the sign of leaders with a human dimension like Johnson, Nixon, Wilson, Heath, Pompidou, and the like.[1]

To be sure, this list of common men is not exhaustive. To be complete it would have to be drawn up for each country and each culture, for the average Frenchman is not the average American, who is not the average German, and so on. Each politician who plays the common man reflects the typical citizen, but that typical citizen is not the same everywhere. Each one bears the mark of the national character.

Still, it is possible to sketch the traits in a way that holds good for every country. The common man comes from a modest family that was neither poor nor rich. He went through secondary school, but rarely university. He is the opposite of a patrician or an intellectual, just as he is unsophisticated. He leads a calm, simple family life, and indeed simplicity is one of his cardinal virtues, along with common sense and hard work.

FROM SAINT-CHAMOND TO MONTBOUDIF

1952. The French National Assembly, including several Gaullist members, installed Antoine Pinay as prime minister and minister of finance. De Gaulle is said to have remarked bitterly, "I did not save France in order to turn it over to this Monsieur Pinay."

This Monsieur Pinay is indisputably Mr. Everyman. A small businessman running a family leather concern, he learned his economics from his tannery's balance sheets, without benefit of university training. He was the mayor of the small town of Saint-Chamond. Wearing his customary little porkpie hat, he had made a nice modest career for himself: mayor, general counsel for his region, member of the National Assembly, cabinet member at 57 years old, and finally prime minister at 61.

How did the French see him? Jacques Fauvet, a political journalist, wrote: "Monsieur Pinay is a singular man because he is a simple man. His name, his face — which leaves political cartoonists nonplussed — his way of speaking, his little hat, his politics, everything about him is simple."[2] Another journalist, Françoise Giroud, did this sketch of him:

> He is 61 but looks 50, has gray hair, the prominent forehead of the irascible, lively, direct brown eyes, medium height, a sense of irony, a delicate liver, a feel for the soil, the ability to always spend one franc less than he possesses, a tin ear for foreign languages, giving the general impression of being cut from thin but good quality cloth — Monsieur Pinay, pure, fast-dyed wool, closely resembles a great many Frenchmen of his age who habitually gripe about the government.[3]

In fact, Antoine Pinay played the role of the average Frenchman quite deliberately. He knew full well that his character made it easy for the public to identify with the government. He knew it would put the masses — the man in the street and the average housewife — on his side, whatever other politicans thought of him. So he carefully cultivated his exemplary banality with every media interview and every trip through the country. He made it clear that he sought to be nothing special. He did not pretend to possess bravura and grace (like the charm leader) or superior intelligence (like the hero). No, he was strictly a common man with common qualities.

The first of those qualities was the common sense of a moderate, careful, practical man. Then there was his lengthy experience as a provincial sage, as well as his obvious goodwill and taste for hard work. There was also his toughness of character. Finally, and above all, there were his almost ostentatious honesty and simplicity.

In April 1952, Pinay invited a sampling of wholesale butchers to lunch — a simple *pot-au-feu*, naturally — and paid the bill himself to emphasize the government's anti-inflation campaign. In September 1959, he left his official car in the garage as a sign of government austerity and took a taxi to the Elysée Palace for a cabinet meeting. Even Gaullism had adopted Pinay, who was de Gaulle's finance minister from June 1958 to January 1960.[4]

In 1969, as in 1965, Pinay would have gladly run for president, but by then Georges Pompidou had upstaged him in the role of Average

Frenchman. As mentioned earlier, Pompidou was the perfect "anti-de Gaulle," the anti-hero. Louis-Philippe succeeding Charles X. Once again a low profile was the order of the day.

A native of Montboudif, grandson of peasants, son of a school teacher, professor himself before becoming a state counsellor, then a banker and then prime minister, Georges Pompidou had made it. But this cultivated, successful man carefully retained the style of the average Frenchman, accessible and easy with others. His style was marked by direct, concrete language, a cigarette hanging waggishly on his lower lip, the crafty look of a peasant, a comfortable bourgeois paunch, rough simplicity, and a feeling of nostalgia for the soil.

But, like Pinay, Pompidou's character was essentially petit bourgeois, complete with the prejudices that go with it. The average Frenchman he represented did not live in a housing development for the poor; neither did he work on an assembly line. Rather, he resembled a peasant from central France, proud of his few acres of land, or a provincial shopkeeper who liked to be his own boss and who detested students, longhairs, and abortion: someone who was a bit chauvinistic.

Pompidou identified so much with this role that he actually knew little of the real Frenchmen of his day. For a brief moment he saw them — to his astonishment — in May 1968. But afterward he returned to his prudent, ponderous, and circumspect ways, resembling a Frenchman of the 1930s more than one of the 1970s, and one who had read neither Giraudoux nor Jules Romains.[5]

MIDDLE CLASS

With Harold Wilson, simplicity is not only deliberate, it becomes downright ostentatious. This, despite the fact that his career was marked by many successes: he was a graduate and later a professor at Oxford, a member of parliament at 29, a cabinet member at 31 (the youngest since Pitt), leader of the Labour party at 47, and prime minister at 48 (the youngest in a century). Wilson won four elections: 1964, 1966, February 1974, and October 1974. He was prime minister for a total of seven and a half years, from 1964 to 1970 and from 1974 to March 1976, before voluntarily leaving office and retiring at 60.

What success! But also what modesty! The nonhero par excellence, Wilson loved to cultivate a low profile in contrast with his eminent ability. This son of a Yorkshire druggist resolutely clung to a middle-class manner.

In practice, that meant bluntness, a generally good-natured style, a pipe between his teeth, total indifference to clothes, a quiet family life with his wife Mary, peaceful vacations reading whodunits in a little cottage in the Scilly Isles, and a definite distaste for decorum. When he returned to power in 1974, Wilson eschewed 10 Downing Street in favor of his own house a few blocks away.

In sum, he was the very opposite of Tory England — the sort that goes in for clubs and grouse hunting — and specifically the opposite of that of Lord Home, whom he beat in 1964, and of Edward Heath, who, although the son of a carpenter, had adopted upper-class habits like yachting and conducting an orchestra along with his Tory politics. Heath had lost so much contact with his origins that he ended up in continual confrontation with the unions, leading to his defeat by Wilson in 1974.

Wilson, on the other hand, adopted the opposite brand image, going so far as to exaggerate typical British traits. He underlined his simple tastes, such as tea and beer rather than champagne or red wine. He steered clear of cosmopolitan political friendships, unlike Aneurin Bevan or Hugh Gaitskell. He even kept his distance — he, the product of the university meritocracy — from intellectuals, especially Marxists. He admitted — he, the head of the Labour party — that he had never been able to get past page two of Marx's *Capital*.

Wilson did everything to pass as the ordinary Englishman, down to and including designating a successor with the same style: James Callaghan, who took over the Labour party on April 5, 1976, thus becoming prime minister.

Callaghan is a middle-of-the-roader, a man who works at striking a happy medium between his party's two extremes. But beneath this moderate exterior lies the great political skill that has enabled him to avoid taking clear-cut positions on the large questions which have divided the Labour party since the war. His positions are all the more difficult to grasp in view of his low-key performances in the Commons. But Callaghan prefers to spend his time and talents on keeping in touch with his constituents. In 30 years he has missed only four meetings of his local Cardiff party group.

At 64, with his John Bull profile and ultra-British style, this political pro is extremely popular. For *The Observer,* his success stems from "his feel for what simple people are thinking. He is a one-man public opinion poll. Ask him what he thinks of Picasso or the death penalty or hoodlums, and you will get the majority view."[6]

For Sunny Jim — or Big James or Uncle Jim — possesses the people's common sense, thanks to his roots. The son of a Royal Navy first mate, he left school at 15 for a modest job in a tax office to help his widowed mother. Of all Wilson's possible successors, Callaghan is the only one who did not attend a university. Soon he took up union work and joined Labour, where he rose steadily.

Like Wilson — but this time as an authentic Mr. Everyman — Callaghan is proud of his simple life: his peaceful family life with his wife Audrey, their small apartment in Kensington Oval in a modest London neighborhood, the farm in Sussex where he likes to be photographed feeding his pigs and sloshing around in the mud. And like his constituents in Cardiff, he dearly loves James Bond thrillers and rugby matches.

Proud to be of the working class, proud of his union contracts, proud of his simple life and common sense, Big James definitely provides the majority of his compatriots "the happiness of identification;" even more than Harold Wilson, which is saying a lot.

ORDINARY PEOPLE

The year 1976 saw two other politicians successfully play the common-man role, upstaging charm leaders who are a bit too sure of themselves.

In Sweden, the Social Democrats lost power in the September 19 elections after 44 years in office. The new prime minister was Thorbjörn Fälldin, 50, the essence of anti-sophistication, a true anti-Palme.

A gnarled, massive, phlegmatic man, Fälldin makes the most of his peasant-like gaucherie and uncouthness compared with the high-flown intellectualism of Olof Palme, the former prime minister. To show what an average Swede he is, he often allows himself to be photographed at his farm in Aangermanland wearing jeans and an old shirt as he tends to his sheep and hoes his potato patch.

His square shoulders, rough hands, and perennial pipe are good props as he supports the ecologists and champions the return-to-the-land movement. This common man readily assures his fellow citizens that "we politicians are ordinary people, after all. We shouldn't fool the public by pretending that we can do everything."[7]

Two weeks after the Swedish elections, on October 3, West Germany too, held legislative elections. On the left, the SPD party was led by the outgoing chancellor, Helmut Schmidt, renowned for his economic expertise, his intellectual arrogance, and the outspokenness that has earned him the nickname, "Schmidt the Lip."[8] Cold and distant, the chancellor alternated biting sarcasm and complicated analysis of problems, refused to shake hands in the street or sign autographs. Still, he managed to intrigue the public with his habitual Hamburg sailor's cap and his ability to play the great organ in Passau Cathedral with its 17,000 pipes and 208 keys.

On the right, the CDU party was led by Helmut Kohl, head of the Rhineland Palatinate state since 1969. Tall, hefty, and 46, the "black giant" exuded the easy nonchalance of an experienced manager of public affairs. With his unspectacular moderation on issues, he resembled a provincial notary.

But while Kohl possessed neither panache nor superlative mental powers, his frank simplicity reassured millions of Germans who saw themselves in him, a candidate who dared come out foursquare for "those fine virtues of work, morality, punctuality, fidelity."[9]

As it happened, the CDU did not beat the Socialist-Liberal ticket on October 3. But it garnered a respectable 48.6 percent of the vote behind the quiet Kohl, who so skillfully played the role of a man "like you and me."[10]

1974. America, weary of Watergate and the shady dealings of Richard Nixon, that Machiavelli on the Potomac, seemed to have a dream — nostalgic, retro-dream about the past, in general, and about Harry Truman, in particular.

Truman, the small-time haberdasher from Missouri, succeeded the patrician Roosevelt in 1945, after being his vice-president. Truman, the average American from the Midwest, had carried the presidential election in 1948 despite polls and every other indication to the contrary, by campaigning on the theme of the common man.

In 1975 he became almost a folklore figure as the object of a cult called Trumania. There were tee-shirts bearing his face and the words,

"America needs you, Harry Truman." Two bestsellers* were published and one play *Give 'Em Hell, Harry!*, were done about him. This one-man show featured James Whitmore and showed Truman relieving General Douglas MacArthur of his command, taking on Senator Joseph McCarthy and the Ku Klux Klan, using his own stamps on personal mail, and cooly assessing Stalin. All this was seasoned with his reflections on his wife, Bess, his daughter, Margaret, and his mother-in-law. In short, he was shown as a citizen-president, a good husband, and a father, honest and self-effacing.

THE QUIET MAN OF THE WHITE HOUSE

To be a Truman or nothing was perhaps Vice-President Gerald Ford's ambition when he replaced Richard Nixon on August 9, 1974. *Time* called him "A man for this season." This simple man was indeed the right one to heal America after Watergate, this ordinary man who seven months earlier had said: "What our nation needs is ordinary people, upright people, loyal people. These are qualities we should be proud of. But they are qualities that have been neglected."[11]

In his seven-minute televised inaugural address — "just a little chat among friends" — the new president asserted, "our nation's long nightmare is over. Our constitution works. Our great republic is based on a government of laws and not of men. Here, the people are sovereign."[12]

In his dealings with the sovereign people he represented, he strove for an exemplary banality. As one of his friends observed, "Gerald Ford is just Jerry. He is no different from your next-door neighbor."[13] Ford *is* the average American, and the typical congressman from Grand Rapids, Michigan. But in 1974 he came to represent not just Michigan's Fifth District, but the entire nation. "I plan to follow my instinct for frankness and good faith," he said. And this alone was enough to delight Americans, who were convinced that "Mr. Clean" would sweep the Augean stables. His frank, cordial, and relaxed style was refreshing after the Byzantine intrigues before him.

---

*The memoirs of his daughter, Margaret Truman Daniel, titled *Harry S. Truman,* and *Plain Speaking* by Merle Miller, an account of conversations with the 33rd president, sold 2.5 million copies.

It amounted to a honeymoon, and in July 1975 the quiet man declared his candidacy in the presidential election of November 1976. "People know what I have done," he said. "They know that I am honest."[14] "Mr. Right" had thrown his hat in the ring, campaigning as "a decent human being." He was going to show that anyone, even an ordinary congressman who had become president by accident, could be elected to the nation's highest office; even "plain old Jerry," who called on the common sense of his fellow citizens.[15]

He confessed in an interview, "I am the first to admit that I am not a great orator, but I'm not so sure that the American people want that. I think they are more interested in honesty, loyalty, and a feeling of security."[16] Ford was simple, perhaps too simple, for after a while his mediocrity bored more than it reassured. And then there was his evident awkwardness.

Lyndon Johnson, who disliked him, once said, "Ford has played too much football without a helmet." And he also claimed that Ford was the only man he knew who could not "chew gum and walk at the same time." Soon the president had made so many *faux pas* that "the ridicule problem," as *Time* called it, became unavoidable.[17] Ford banged his head, fell in front of Austrian Chancellor Bruno Kreisky (on an airport gangway in June 1975 in Salzburg), stumbled in front of Egyptian President Anwar Sadat, took two memorable falls for photographers on the slopes of Vail at Christmas 1975. "He has a trick knee as the result of an old football injury," his friends explained.

The president tripped over long words (it took him eight tries during a speech in Atlanta to pronounce *geothermal*), toasted "the great people of Israel" with Sadat, introduced his new secretary of commerce, Elliot Richardson, as "Elliot Roosevelt."*

Would he be "the first president to be chased from office by laughter?" wondered Nicholas von Hoffman in the *Washington Post*. In any case, Ford's position declined, with his own party seeming at one point to prefer Ronald Reagan as its candidate.

Ford won the nomination after all, only to go down to defeat before Jimmy Carter. The problem was that he had not just *played* the role of the common man. Ford *is* the common man, with all the shortcomings that that implies.

---

*During the campaign on October 16, 1976, Ford declared, "I'm happy to be in Pontiac," when he arrived in Lincoln. The day before he had surprised students at the University of Iowa by saying he was "happy to be in Ohio." *Le Monde* October 19, 1976.

The spectacle of a truly ordinary man is monumentally boring; that is the cruel lesson of Ford's presidency. Banality is only bearable when simulated with genuine acting talent to heighten the colors, like naive painting as done by a consummate artist. The image has to be worked on, polished, and projected by an intelligent and cultivated political artist, the way Harold Wilson did it. And in this role Jimmy Carter is the flamboyant superstar — the wide-screen, Technicolor common man.

A SIMPLE HEART

June 1976. America was celebrating its Bicentennial. It commemorated the American dream of a just and free society. It referred to the Founding Fathers with their purity and Biblical simplicity. And it compared them to its leaders of the last 15 years: the sophisticated intellectuals from the East led by Kennedy, who stayed on under Johnson; the shyster lawyers and image makers from the West under Nixon. It dreamed of old-fashioned leaders from small towns, full of common sense and uprightness. There was, of course, the good Jerry Ford, but he was disappointing.

And then came James Earl Carter asking everyone to call him Jimmy. He was unctuous, had blue eyes beneath silvery hair, and was eternally smiling. In his voice there was a drawl of the Deep South, in his walk was the easy swing of a farmer. He came out of Plains, Georgia (pop. 450), to talk about love to America. "My strength comes from people like you," he said. "Together we can make a government as good, honest, and full of love as the American people."[18]

Carter played the new man: the outsider of humble origins, the heartlander against the Establishment and the professionals of Washington. A stout-hearted crusader for traditional values, Carter represented integrity, hard work, honesty, civic responsibility, patriotism, free enterprise, economizing, and respect for parents and God.

James Reston noted that Carter was mainly "a reflection of our past, the symbol of a simpler world that has disappeared;"[19] he was a man of the people able to understand the needs of ordinary folks. At the

Democratic Convention in July 1976, Carter gave a populist address attacking "the political and economic elite," "the big-time swindlers who never went to prison," and "the perpetual links between money and power." Instead of this, he promised to protect the humble, the weak, the disinherited.

The address was very like an old-time sermon:

> "I say to you that our nation still has its best times ahead of it. Our country has come through a bitter trial, but the time of healing is at hand. We want to be able to believe again, to be proud again. We want to be able to believe in truth again. I have often spoken of love. . . . We can have again an American government that rejects scandal, corruption, and bureaucratic cynicism, that will again be as honest and competent as our people."[20]

Like all of Carter's campaign, the convention, which concluded with a speech by Reverend Martin Luther King, Sr., carried a note of religious fervor, with the constant repetition of the words *God* and *love*. As a pillar of the Baptist Church, Carter taught Sunday school as his father had before him. He has also served as a deacon in Plains, and preached in nearby churches.

The preacher now has America for a parish. He is constantly invoking God and Biblical values, in the way Baptists speak directly to God in everyday words. "Is it true," he has been asked, "that you pray 25 times a day?" Answer: "I've never counted. But I would say that in the course of a busy day that would be about right."* And he added: "Whether I win or lose, I believe I will be able to accept the outcome calmly, without regret or animosity and even without profound disappointment, thanks to my relations with Christ and God."[21]

Carter campaigned with the Bible for a platform and with God as his campaign manager, eager to restore "the old principles of religion and morality that insure the world's stability." On July 18, three days after being nominated by the Democratic Convention, Deacon Carter taught Sunday school in Plains, explaining — for 37 minutes — the meaning of the Biblical expression, "God is love."[22]

---

*This was the famous interview in which he said, "I have looked on many women with lust in my heart." *Playboy*, French edition (November 1976).

Whether deacon, plantation owner, naval officer, or governor, Jimmy had the perfect biography of the self-made man. In 1924, Jimmy was born in Archery, three miles from Plains. He describes life there in his autobiography *Why Not the Best?*: "We lived in a wooden house beside the road. For years we pumped our water by hand. The yard was full of dogs, chickens, ducks, and turkeys. From early April to the end of October we never wore shoes and rarely wore a shirt, except to go to school or church."

But his father, Earl, diversified his crops, became a peanut wholesaler, and opened a general store. His mother, Lillian, a registered nurse, worked 12 hours a day for $6, then went home and worked 8 hours more. In 1966, at 68, she enrolled in the Peace Corps and stayed two years in India. Young Jimmy soon followed in their footsteps and showed good business sense, a key quality of the American Protestant ethic:

> At the age of five, I sold peanuts in the streets of Plains. I managed to make a dollar per day, sometimes five on a Saturday. When I was nine, I had saved enough money to buy five bales of cotton at the low price of five cents a pound. I kept those bales in a barn belonging to my father until I could sell them a few years later for 18 cents a pound. Then I had enough money to buy five houses, and until I left home to enter the Naval Academy I received a total of $16.50 rent per month.

Carter served in the navy 11 years, assigned to submarines during the Second World War. In 1948 he passed exams to become an officer and engineer. In 1949 he asked to join the first training program for nuclear sub crews. That was when he studied nuclear reactor technology and atomic physics, and met Admiral Hyman Rickover.

"What was your position in your graduating class at the Academy?" Rickover asked him.

" 'Fifty-ninth in a class of 820, sir,' Carter answered. "I sat waiting for a compliment that didn't come," Carter relates. Instead, he asked, 'Did you do your best?' I was about to say yes when I remembered who he was, and that there were times when I could have worked harder. I swallowed hard and answered, 'No Sir, I did not always do my best.' He looked at me for a long moment and asked me a question I have never been able to forget: 'Why not?' "

When his father died, Carter resigned from the navy to take over and develop the family business. In 1964 he became a senator in the Georgia legislature, and then governor of the state in 1970. In 1976 he started campaigning for the Democratic nomination for president against a dozen better-known and wealthier rivals. "Jimmy Who? Running for what?" were the reactions in those days.

But on November 2 he beat Gerald Ford in the race for the presidency. Carter was the good old boy with the big smile and an edifying background as a boy scout. He was the dutiful man who feared God; he was the honest man who had made it by dint of hard work. He was the respectful son, faithful husband, model father. He was the average American — Jimmy Carter, "one of us" — who told audiences during his campaign, "I don't pretend to know everything . . . I'm not any more capable or intelligent than you . . . but I have a feeling that you are talking to the next president of the United States."[23]

But behind this innocent facade lies a wily professional, an angelic Machiavelli. For this peasant was a naval officer and nuclear physicist; this Bible-citing deacon is good at being vague about his options. "Trust me," he says, as if that were enough of a program.

"Am I not one of you?" Carter asks, with his uncommon intelligence, peerless will, and credentials in atomic engineering. What a dream candidate! What "happiness in identification!" Never before has the average voter been encouraged to feel so intelligent, so charming. Never has the common man put on such a show, such a scintillating color super-production. Never has the ordinary shone with such appeal. With Jimmy, every average American feels like a president and political superstar.

It takes all an actor's talent to carry off this role without becoming a bore like James Callaghan, Georges Pompidou, or Gerald Ford. The public quickly tires of such authentic banality, however much it may have welcomed a respite from the previous hero (de Gaulle) or villain (Nixon). The problem with the boring common man is that citizens are unable to rise above their own ordinary status by identifying with him and his prosaic low profile. So they eventually turn toward another kind of show, the more amusing one put on by the charm leader.

President Carter at a televised news conference (1977).

West German Chancellor Helmut Schmidt (left) with French President Giscard d'Estaing (right) at the economic summit in London (1977).

The Charm Leader

*"I believe that political action always
involves a certain amount of provocation."*
—VALÉRY GISCARD D'EESTAING

These are good times for charm leaders. A quick survey of them would include the Kennedy brothers, Henry Kissinger and Jerry Brown in the United States, Pierre Trudeau in Canada, Olof Palme in Sweden (until 1976), Jeremy Thorpe briefly in Great Britain, Helmut Schmidt in West Germany, and Jean-Jacques Servan-Schreiber and Valéry Giscard d'Estaing in France. There are many others.

Each in his own style attempts the same thing: to surprise, captivate, and please his audience of citizens. Each conceives of politics as the art of seduction, if not as a branch of show business.

BROTHER, JUNIOR EXECUTIVE, DANDY

The charm leader often projects a brotherly image, implicitly promising moral support in the conflict with a society made by parents. Whereas the paternal or maternal image is usually associated with repressive authority,[1] the fraternal image brings to mind democracy as a process of opposition to personal power and the status quo.[2]

Like Kennedy, Giscard d'Estaing is a "brother" who succeeded a "father." The New Frontier mobilized the latent feeling of hostility toward "father" Eisenhower. Giscard's Advanced Liberal Society claims to increase liberty (the vote for 18-year-olds, legalized abortion) and oppose "the solitary exercise of power."

In order to be effective, this brotherly image has to coincide with a youth wave. The 1960s, for example, were hit by the first wave of the

1945 post-war baby boom, and during that decade France was increasingly influenced by the youth culture.

The brotherly image also needs world peace and prosperity to flourish, just as the charm leader, whether JFK in 1960 or VGE in 1974, is the fruit of peace and the affluent society. But as soon as there is a crisis on the horizon, the atmosphere of anxiety makes the paternal image more appreciated. The public is willing to turn over the government to a brother when everything is going well, but let a storm blow up and it prefers an old hand to see it through.

In any case, the charm leader has to have a young image — even if only relatively so. In November 1960, Kennedy was elected president at 43. In 1974, Jerry Brown was governor of California at 36. In 1969, Palme became Sweden's prime minister at 42. In 1974, Giscard d'Estaing entered the Elysée Palace at 48, the same age as Trudeau when he became Canadian prime minister in 1968.

Often in his forties or fifties, the charm leader usually is about ten years older than that other "modern" fixture of industrial societies, the young executive; but they have several points in common.

First of all, they are covered with degrees from famous universities, whether Harvard, the London School of Economics, the Institute for Political Studies, and so on. Impressed by their own learning, the "new mandarins," as Norm Chomsky would say, have a shared smugness.

Next, they all typify the myths of their age — speed, action, success — promoted by advertising and the media. They are above all mobile, dynamic, on the move. Indeed they incarnate the politics of movement and action.

Henry Kissinger, for instance, was always jumping into an airplane, going from Jidda to Moscow, from Washington to Islamabad. Jeremy Thorpe traveled by hovercraft, while Giscard d'Estaing (not content to hold his cabinet meetings in Paris), moved them occasionally to the provinces. They all play man-in-a-hurry, jumping here and there, attaché case in hand.

Up at dawn, the young executive goes all out to climb his company's success ladder, proving by his constant travel that he is aggressive, persistent, and dynamic. The charm leader also makes a point of appearing dynamic, starting his day with breakfast meetings, jumping from airplane to helicopter, from one time zone to the next.

The young executive and the charm leader also share the same conviction: you can sell just about anything to the public. Selling a product or a candidate all comes to the same thing for these young Turks of the techno-structure. The trick is to ignore what the consumer really wants, either in terms of goods or politics. Effectiveness is proven by manipulating the public's desires through advertising or propaganda.

It began with politicians imitating business managers to appear modern and up to date. But today the shoe is on the other foot, with many a company president reigning over his board meeting like a nation's president running a cabinet meeting.

The charm leader is particularly concerned about his style, recalling dandies like Beau Brummell, the Earl of Shaftesbury, Count d'Orsay, and Benjamin Disraeli.[3] "I attach great importance to style," says Giscard d'Estaing. "Style is the esthetic of action." He also likes to spring surprises, confirming Baudelaire's dictum: "Dandyism is the pleasure of surprising others."

Giscard confesses, "I believe that political action always involves a certain amount of provocation because you must get a reaction."[4] Like the dandy, the charm leader can't resist when someone dares him, "Surprise me!"

Dandies can be provocative, but they go only so far, knowing that society tolerates a certain liberty of mores, a certain insolence. As one observer noted, "they may despise society, but dandies refrain from criticizing it with violent diatribes. . . . Dandyism defies a society's manners, not the political system."[5]

Sartre is right about the dandy: "He makes gratuitous gestures, but he is perfectly inoffensive, violating none of the established laws. . . . And the ruling class always prefers a dandy to a revolutionary."

A dandy's defiance of convention remains minor, like the real influence of a charm leader. "I am certain," Giscard d'Estaing has said, "that posterity will retain no image at all of me."[6]

Still, one trait does distinguish clearly the charm leader from the dandy. Whereas the dandy scorns egalitarian sentiment in the name of a new aristocracy, the charm leader pays lip service to democracy while striking his eccentric, superior pose.

For millions of Americans, observed M.B. Levin, the Kennedy brothers have class and exciting lives. They are seen associating with poets, scientists, religious leaders, pretty women, and statesmen. But that does not prevent them from campaigning night and day. They are elegant, but not afraid to get their hands dirty. They are rich but they work hard. They can drink vintage wine or Coca-Cola. They are sophisticated, but they can rub elbows with the man in the street.

In short, they are a combination Proust and Zola, Fitzgerald and Steinbeck, the Great Gatsby and the Katzenjammer Kids.

From the best families and the best schools, married to high society debutants, living in the best neighborhoods, and often millionaires, they combine simplicity — even if feigned — with distinction to satisfy democratic egalitarianism.

Levin concludes that without quite being like us, they are not too different. In other words, they symbolize the impossible but fundamental American double ideal: aristocracy and equality.[7]

Familiarity, simplicity, or modesty can be a weapon in politics. In everyday life, they are inherent and natural to many people. The hero shuns them, preferring the aloofness that is becoming to a providential chief. But for a charm leader they are humanizing, preventing too much superiority, which could put the public off. Needless to say, such simplicity is often simulated.

Whereas the hero cultivates superiority and distance, and the common man tends to familiarity, the charm leader works it both ways. He is alternately distant and close, different and similar, superior and equal. In the final analysis, his brand image is created by the retinal superposition of two contrasting images. Not only can he live with his contradictions, he is proud of them, fascinated to be so complex, as if Narcissus had a double. He is the prince of ambiguity and ambivalence: two-faced.

LEADER AND STAR

This same duality can be found in a certain phase of the motion picture star system. The political hero is the movie star of the 1920s and 1930s — legendary, distant, and remote. Living a life of white Rolls Royces, blue swimming pools, and pink champagne, they are poles apart from the average spectator. Living isolated in his Olympus and well above us mere mortals, the political hero cultivates the same legend. Clearly, Garbo and de Gaulle have much in common.

The charm leader, on the other hand, is more like the stars of the 1940s, 1950s, and 1960s. To be sure, the star still has uncommon beauty and presence, and he lives like no one else. But his private life is an open book; he allows photographers to shoot him strolling with his children or cooking dinner.

The star today is at least half-way down to earth, admitting to a daily life like the rest of us and expressing ordinary sentiments. He has become close and distant, similar and different. All of today's "Olympians" practice this duality: movie stars, sports champions, political leaders, and crowned heads. Who is not familiar with the latest sentimental problems of Soraya? But who also has not heard of the doings of the Persian monarchy?

The Olympian is a man or woman like the rest of us, yet continues to lead the life we can only dream of. He excites both sympathy and admiration, but more admiration, for the citizen (or spectator) transfers to the leader (or star) all his unrealized longing. By identifying with the charm leader, the citizen vicariously exercises power, even imagining that he is participating in summit conferences and "living" other adventures.

Thus, we have the need for a certain glamor by the electorate and the failure of politicians playing Mr. Everyman who are really only that. This explains, for example, Hubert Humphrey's failure when he ran for the Democratic nomination against Kennedy in 1960. The worst thing about his campaign was its very simplicity and clarity, Theodore White reported. Humphrey was just like his audiences. And a president, unfortunately for Humphrey, had to be different from everyone else.[8]

Against John Kennedy, the patrician charmer, Richard Nixon made the same mistake. Nixon wanted to identify with others. He was obsessed by the desire to seem to be just an ordinary guy.[9]

Unlike the charm leader, the common-man politician does not make the public dream. It is pleasant to identify with Robert Redford, rather than with Bob Hope; with John Kennedy, rather than with Hubert Humphrey or Gerald Ford.

So the charm leader keeps up his double game of Prince Charming and Tom Sawyer. This worldly patrician-mandarin, wealthy and well educated as he is, is also cool and relaxed, spontaneous and blatantly simple. He loves sports, ordinary pleasures, and family life.

PATRICIAN AND PLAYBOY

The charm leader is almost never a self-made man. On the contrary, he is usually the heir of a wealthy family, known for its power and conservatism.

Kennedy's father was a former ambassador to London, and apologist for Nazism. Jeremy Thorpe, former leader of the Liberal party in Great Britain, was the son and grandson of Conservative members of Parliament. Trudeau's father was a rich landowner, and Palme's was a well-known businessman. Giscard d'Estaing, who bears a noble name, is an honorary member of the Society of the Cincinnati and claims to be a descendant of Louis XV on his mother's side.

These patricians naturally attend the best schools. The Kennedy brothers went to Harvard, although Edward had his difficulties over cheating on exams. Thorpe attended Eton and Oxford's Trinity College, where he was president of that training ground for future statesmen, the Students Union. Trudeau attended at one time or another the University of Montréal, Harvard, the Institute of Political Studies in Paris, and the London School of Economics. Palme studied at the "school of princes," Beskow, then at the exclusive Sigtuna Humanistika, and finally at Law School after taking a bachelor of arts degree at Kenyon College in Ohio. Giscard d'Estaing graduated from France's elite Polytechnique and then went on to the prestigious École Nationale d'Administration.

These patricians naturally marry young ladies of the best families, like Jacqueline Bouvier for John Kennedy. Thorpe's second marriage was with the divorced wife of Count Harewood, a relative of the Queen. Giscard d'Estaing married Anne-Aymone de Brantes, one of France's titled families.

Often, the charm leader adds a touch of sophistication to his image by assuming the role of playboy. He lets it be known that his qualities of seduction are widely appreciated. Trudeau was credited with a number of affairs, for instance, with Barbra Streisand. Although there were the usual denials, the opposition was visibly displeased when the singer sat in the House of Commons in Ottawa and received winks from the prime minister.

With his flowered shirts and boutonniere, Trudeau the man about town, created enthusiasm, especially among the ladies, akin to Beatlemania, which was dubbed Trudeaumania in Canada. Finally in 1971 the golden boy got married — to Margaret, a 21-year-old student

29 years his junior. At a campaign rally in Vancouver in 1974, she introduced him to 1,500 cheering supporters as "a beautiful guy, a very loving human being who has taught me a lot about loving." The vexed supporters of Trudeau's rival, Stanfield, the sixtyish leader of the Conservatives, waved a new banner at their next rally: "Stanfield is a lover too."[10]

But Lucky Pierre is not the only one to cultivate the image of a companionable dilletant. Before marrying Nancy Maginnes, whom he shows off proudly, Henry Kissinger was very much the playboy, dating starlets like Jill St. John. Both parties profited by the publicity, getting the attention of voters and producers alike. Kissinger cultivated the image of the swinger, one of his biographers wrote, but many suspect that he plays Don Juan above all for the photographers. He sidles up to a beauty at a party just in time to be caught by the photographer.[11]

A poll done by the German magazine *Jasmin* found Helmut Schmidt to be "exceptionally attractive." As early as 1970, 40 percent of German women considered him the politician with the most charm.[12]

On the verge of snobbism, Jeremy Thorpe struck a pose of elegant eccentricity. Often dressed in an Edwardian double-breasted vest, flowery tie, and heavy watch chain, the Liberal leader aimed his last campaign in October 1974 at women voters. His posters showed him raising an admonitory finger with the caption, "Women will decide." Unfortunately, a male model named Norman Scott claimed in court in May 1976 that he had had homosexual relations with Thorpe, who had to relinquish leadership of the party he had run since 1967, despite his denials.

John Kennedy, on the other hand, has left a record as an authentic lover. In 1976 a Senate committee investigating the CIA and its alleged assasination plots against foreign heads of state took the testimony of Judith Campbell Exner, a 41-year-old, blue-eyed brunette. According to the committee's report, she had been "a close friend" of President Kennedy, having had "frequent contacts" with him from the end of 1960 to mid-1962, a period during which she knew Mafia chieftains Giancana and Roselli, who were alleged to have had a contract from the CIA to kill Fidel Castro.*

---

*The truth about the "contract" may never be known. Giancana, who was to be heard by the committee, was riddled with bullets in his fortified house in Chicago on June 20, 1975. Roselli's body was found in a floating barrel off Miami on August 7, 1976. None of the three men Mrs. Exner "knew" between 1960 and 1962 is alive today, all having died violent deaths.

The investigation led first by the Senate and then by the press established that Mrs. Exner had not served as intermediary between the president and the two mafiosi. But she had indeed been Kennedy's mistress, having been introduced to him at a Las Vegas party by Frank Sinatra.[13] In fact, the deceased president appears to have had more than one affair. In the book *Winter Kills,* Robert Condon goes so far as to tally up 1,600 mistresses. An artist friend of Kennedy's commented, "If all the women who claim to have slept with Jack had really done it, he wouldn't have had enough strength to lift a teacup."[14] The published list of women linked romantically with JFK include Kim Novak, Janet Leigh, Angie Dickinson, Jayne Mansfield, Rhonda Fleming, and especially Marilyn Monroe, who sang at his birthday party in 1962.*

Two young women reportedly were on the White House staff, not for secretarial duties, but to render sexual services to the president. These two "assistants," who often accompanied him on official trips, were known to the Secret Service by the code names "Fiddle" and "Faddle."

At the Nassau Conference in 1962, Kennedy reportedly told Harold Macmillan, the honorable British prime minister, that Kennedy had violent headaches if he went too long without a woman.[15] And hadn't he written in *Profiles in Courage* that "a statesman has to think with his heart?"

Compared to Kennedy's record, the rumors about the Elysée Palace in 1974 look mild indeed. Thomas Ferenczi wrote about the French president:

> The presidency is a profession, not the priesthood. It is not supposed to take up a man's entire life. As is well known, Giscard d'Estaing chose not to live in the Elysée with his family. He has been known, for example, to spend the night at the Grand-Trianon at Versailles. During weekends he often disappears without anyone's knowing whether he is at Chanonat in his parents' house, at Authon in the house of his wife's family, or elsewhere . . .
>
> The private life of the chief of state, who likes to live the normal life of any citizen, worries his security services, who

---

*See Earl Wilson, *Show Business Laid Bare* (1975). Hubert Bryant's *Dog Days at the White House* (1975) gives an account of the comings and goings at the White House and around its swimming pool.

fear he may have an automobile accident or be the target of an assassination attempt. There have been rumors of several near-misses, including an early hours accident with a milk truck. True or false, the rumor, which was officially denied by the Elysée, has itself become a political fact.[16]

Kennedy, Trudeau, Giscard, and other charm leaders appear to have a lively private life. Does this offend the public? No, it observes such things with amusement, just as it follows with interest his official trips and summit meetings. The citizen-spectator lives vicariously through such leaders, the way he projects his dreams through movie stars to escape the hum-drum of the daily grind. The charm leader, a peerless showman, helps him escape boredom and frustration. He participates in his own way in the leader's election wins and his feminine conquests. He feels gratified to be represented by this high-liver, delighted to watch this melodramatic show.

All the same, the leader cannot appear too exceptional, so he does more ordinary things to promote the public's identification with him. He practices a sport or two, for instance, but only those that augment his prestige, because of their risk or costliness.

Trudeau is an ardent swimmer and diver, goes underwater fishing on the French Riviera or the shores of Honduras, has a black belt in judo, and goes skiing at Courcheval, standing in the tow line like everyone else. In September 1974, at a party picnic in Vancouver, the prime minister spotted a trampoline and performed a series of impressive jumps on it.[17] His style is both sporty and risqué. During the 1968 campaign Trudeau, who liked to drive sports cars in a fur hat and coat, was asked whether he intended to give up his Mercedes. "Which one," he asked, "The car or the girl?"[18]

Giscard d'Estaing follows suit. He skis, hunts bear in the U.S.S.R. or big game in Africa, plays tennis, or — more democratically — soccer, with his hometown team of Chamalières, after which he answers journalists' questions in the locker room, stripped to the waist.

SLUMMING

From time to time, the charm leader affects a low-brow style, again to promote the public's identification with him. It may be pure snobbism to add this incongruous touch to the patrician's portrait, but democracy and the mass media must be satisfied.* After all, one of the best ways a high official can captivate the public is by being unconventional.

The charm leader is by instinct unpompous, knowing, with Montesquieu, that "solemnity is the shield of the stupid." He prefers to be spontaneous, relaxed and cool, at opposite poles from the solemn, heavy hero.

One day Trudeau left an elegant official reception by sliding down the banister. Another day, he showed up at the House of Commons wearing a Lacoste sportshirt, sport jacket, and sandals. In Sweden, Palme campaigned in jeans and took the bus to his office. Giscard d'Estaing also adopts this relaxed style in defiance of protocol. De Gaulle would have said of this haughty patrician, this cold technocrat, that "his problem is people."[19] So he tries a bit of everything to maintain contact with the people.

Even before his election to the Elysée, Giscard made a conscious effort to create an image of simplicity. On February 5, 1964, he appeared on television wearing a V-neck sweater and no jacket. The next day, after a party meeting in Vincennes, he took the subway to return to his office in the Finance ministry. On July 28, 1969, wearing a checked shirt, he played the accordion during the taping of a TV show. He played it again on June 25, 1973, at the world accordion festival in Montmorency. On December 20, after a cabinet meeting at the Elysée, he walked back to the Finance ministry, saving about a pint of gasoline.

Giscard multiplied his contacts with the public and fractured protocol after his election to the presidency, seeming to want to give an American style to his administration. In May 1976, he laid a bouquet of violets on the tomb of John Kennedy and said, "his attempt to bring spontaneity and gaiety to public life was and still is what the public wants."[20]

Questioned in Marseille on February 27, 1974 about "the Giscard style," he replied: "this new style of French government interests the whole world. Many people in other countries feel that this more natural

---

*This affected familiarity is often the lot of princes and kings when the winds of democracy are blowing. Thus Louis-Phillipe played at being a "citizen-king." He did away with regal ceremonies and walked through Paris wearing a gray hat and carrying his "large sentimental umbrella" as Heine called it, under one arm. Occasionally he stopped to chat with construction workers.

and direct way of conducting public affairs is the way of tomorrow.''[21] To promote greater ''simplicity in human relations'' that he says he favors, the new president made a number of surprising gestures.

At his inauguration on May 27, 1974, Giscard went up the Champs-Elysées, not in top hat and tails riding in a limousine, but wearing a business suit and on foot. On June 12, he invited a young schoolgirl named Blandine to visit the Elysée, with the president as guide. On Bastille Day, he chose a new itinerary for the traditional parade, routing it through the working-class neighborhoods from Place de la Républic to Place de la Bastille. On August 10, he made a surprise visit to two prisons in Lyon and shook hands with the inmates. A few hours later he had arrived on the Riviera for a vacation and was photographed water skiing near a mansion loaned to him by a French noble.

He posed for his official photo on August 26, wearing neither formal attire nor the usual tricolor sash. The next day, while a taped speech by him was being telecast, he was having dinner with his son Henri in a restaurant near Les Halles. On September 4, he took his daughter Valerie-Anne to the movies on the Champs-Elysées to see Ken Russell's *Malher*. On the 11th, he presided over the first cabinet meeting of the Fifth Republic to be held outside Paris, in Lyon. And on Christmas Eve he invited the garbage men of his neighborhood to share breakfast with him in an Elysée salon.

The year 1975 also began with the unexpected, when Giscard and his wife had lunch with residents of an old people's home. On the 22nd they dined in the home of a certain Mr. Cucchiarini, a Parisian picture framer. Indeed, on New Year's Eve the president had expressed the desire to ''have dinner periodically in the homes of French families of all classes.'' On January 3 he added: ''I plan to begin with the Paris area and then to the provinces, at least once a month. I believe we must rethink relations between the chief of state and the nation's citizens. We have to show that chiefs of state are like other citizens, and my objective with these meals is to stay in contact with public opinion.''[22]

There were, in fact, several such dinners. On February 28, the president was in the home of a truckdriver in Voisin-le-Bretonneau; on March 30, it was with a sales manager in Tours, and so on. Asked about the results, he commented, ''these dinners in the homes of Frenchmen have helped me make a discovery: as far as the people are concerned, there is no insurmountable problem in communicating with a president. I believe that I have had the same sort of contact with these persons that any two Frenchmen with different activities can have.''[23]

On January 27, he did away with the wearing of official decorations at Elysée receptions. He celebrated his 49th birthday on February 1 by taking his family to see a popular play — and sat, not in a reserved box, but in ordinary orchestra seats. After an imposing dinner for cabinet members on February 19, everyone democratically played cards, checkers, chess, and scrabble. When West German President Walter Scheel was invited to dinner at the Elysée Palace on April 23, Giscard's former German nanny, Frau Zervas, was invited too. And the same day he moved up the time of a televised speech by 15 minutes so as not to interfere with the telecast of an important soccer match between Saint-Etienne and Munich.

Some last but not the least important examples of this charmer's style includes the Christmas tree celebrations at the Elysée for the children of the official mansion's staff. On December 18, 1974, Teddy Bear, a TV favorite of French children, was escorted to the tree by the president. "He's too busy and he has lots of work and responsibilities, but he likes to talk. Who is it?" teased Teddy Bear. "Giscard!" chorused the children. On cue, the president parted red curtains and appeared to chat with Teddy: "I remember you. We met at the television station where we both were on programs, but not at the same time." He concluded, almost wistfully, "I'm not Santa Claus; if I were, I would have a pretty costume and I would be famous all over the world.''[24]

For Christmas 1975, 500 children were assembled in the Elysée's ballroom. The cabinet meeting had considerately been transferred to the Paris suburb of Marly so the children would not interfere with it, and vice versa. When he arrived, the president sang a popular children's song, "la Peche aux Moulse," with his young guests and tried to get his dog, Jugurtha, to do tricks. Then he sat at the electric piano to accompany a popular singer, Claude François, in "Silent Night, Holy Night."*

On December 15, 1976, the guest of honor was another star of children's television, Casimir, The Nice Monster. He was joined by a

---

*This (media) event was good for the cover and eight inside pages in the weekly magazine *Jours de France* (December 29, 1975).

longtime French favorite singer, Annie Cordy, who led the president and his guests in the politically appropriate song, "Things Will Be Better Tomorrow."[25]

Many observers praise this new style. It is not, after all, more democratic to lift the veil of myth surrounding authority, to remove its aura of mystery? Moreover, this style might influence society for the better by encouraging other elected officials to be more democratic. Like stars in other fields, the charm leader could become a model of comportment on which to pattern the fashions and mores of the day.

Finally, these observers point out that if the chief of state is to "sell" his policies, the best way is to establish empathy between himself and the public. This increases confidence in him and enhances comprehension. Without his charm, would Roosevelt have been able to implement the New Deal?

Other observers, however, are more critical. They fear that such gimmicks make politics dependent on advertising and public relations — another form of show business and comic strips. Doesn't this make the presidency a sort of round-the-clock spectacle, with elegant small talk only skimming the surface of the country's real problems? Indeed, all these gadgets amount to a smoke screen, the skillful artifice of change concealing the lack of real change.

The president may have read too much of Marshall McLuhan and decided that the medium *is* the message, that form can replace substance, that "style" can replace solid government policies. And there is always the possibility that all this is designed to divert the people from their real problems and needs, that this close-to-the-people style hides policies that are fundamentally against the people's interest.

So some critics call this demagoguery, and say that it is no more than the art of appearing to be simple in order to increase a popularity rating. Who can tell? It can be fun to watch the show, but is this what the public really expects? Long ago that perceptive observer La Bruyère wrote: "The French character requires gravity in the sovereign." *Sovereign* is an apt word here, for Giscard d'Estaing deliberately practices ambiguity in his style, which is at times familiar and at times distant, partly relaxed and partly ceremonious.

As an admirer of Louix XV, from whom he claims to descend, Giscard d'Estaing has given his presidency several traits of monarchy, especially since 1976. The Elysées' etiquette has been modified in small ways that reveal a taste for old-fashioned protocol.

Unlike his predecessors who, like all heads of household, were served after their dinner guests — or simultaneously if those guests were themselves heads of state — Giscard now is served first. Above the Elysée flies his personal flag. In its salons, Louis XV furniture has slowly been replacing the modern pieces brought in by Georges Pompidou. When a head of state now visits the Elysée, he crosses its courtyard on foot as cavalry trumpets sound and an honor guard salutes.[26]

On May 20, 1975, Giscard celebrated his first anniversary as president by having the cabinet members gather solemnly in the elegant "Gilded Salon." Having arrived to strains of the Résistance hymn that has become Giscard's theme music, "Le Chant du départ," the cabinet members exited from the Elysée courtyard on foot to the sound of an ancient military march.[27]

At the chateau of Chambord, hunting luncheons have lost the rustic character Pompidou liked and become solemn receptions. And every time the president returns to Orly airport from an official trip, he expects to be greeted by music played by several different regiments. Thus the charm leader is sometimes Gavroche, sometimes a monarch.

But the job does not last forever, for it depends on youth and dynamism. No one can play the charm leader indefinitely, any more than an actor can play the matinee idol forever. At 58, Trudeau was not able to last against Joe Clark, the 37-year-old Conservative.

Sometimes the charm leader is able to make the change into the role of noble elder of his nation. In 1961, West Germany's SPD party chose the younger, more telegenic Willy Brandt as its candidate for chancellor, preferring him to the older Ollenhauer. But as the years passed, Brandt changed gradually to become more paternal during the 1972 campaign, if not quite a new Konrad Adenauer.

But in the end, the public tires of the charm leader, with his seductive qualities eventually looking more like instability. His rakish nonchalance, his carefree manner become unbearable over the long term, especially if an economic or international crisis strikes. Then the public turns away from the relatively untried "brother" and toward the paternal authority figure who promises greater security. In times of crisis, the charm leader yields to the sexagenarian.

Former Canadian Prime Minister Pierre Trudeau leaving his Parliament Hill office after the 1972 elections.

Marshall Henri Pétain, leader of the Vichy Government of France during World War II.

Our Father

*"I was very touched by a placard that said
'Barbarre, we're fed up!' If the people
are starting to call me Barbarre, there's
really something between us."*

—RAYMOND BARRE[1]

Authority is traditionally legitimized by the father image. Monarchs are supposed to exercise paternal authority over their family of subjects, from whom filial obedience is expected; Louis XII was called "Father of the People." The czars of Russia also had that image, being called familiarly *batiouchka,* or "little father of the peoples."

More recently there was Georges Clemenceau, "Father of Victory," and from 1940 to 1944, Henri Pétain, who might have been called "Father of Defeat." His Vichy government affected a paternalist character, even if Pétain alternated between roles of hero and father. In his radio address of October 31, 1940, after Montoire, he declared: "Until now I have spoken to you as a father. Today I speak to you as chief." The paternal image was also the one chosen mainly by de Gaulle from 1958 to 1969.

In Germany, the father figure was old Marshal Hindenburg, president of the Reich from 1925 to 1934. Then Adenauer, *Der Alte,* assumed the role of chancellor and rigid *paterfamilias* from 1949 to 1963.

Stalin also had a paternal image, taking up the "little father of the peoples" role and sometimes being known, even outside the U.S.S.R., as "Papa Stalin."[2] In a funeral eulogy in March 1953, Rakosi mourned "Our Father Stalin."[2] Cholokhov cried "Goodbye Father! What an awful feeling it is to become an orphan! The Party, the Soviet people and the workers of the world have become orphans."[3]

November 20, 1975. Franco dies at 82, and in a message broadcast to the country the prime minister, Carlos Arias Navarro, announces the death in a voice shaking with emotion: "Spain is not a widow. She is an orphan."[4]

In the Third World the paternal theme is also frequent. All Haiti knew President François Duvalier as "Papa Doc." And it is especially in countries that have recently acceded to independence that the leaders use the father image. Nasser, among many others, was known as "The Father of the Revolution." Before being assassinated in August 1975, Sheik Mujibur Rahman of Bangladesh was "The Bengal Tiger" and "The Father of the Nation." General Mobutu is "The Father of the Zaire Nation." And Marshal Amin reveled in the nickname "Big Daddy."

On the other hand, Marshal Bokassa promulgated an ordinance in February 1976 — before he made himself emperor — forbidding his fellow citizens from calling him "Papa," "Dear Papa," or even "Father of the Nation." Henceforth he was to be called simply "The President for Life" or "Marshall of the Central African Republic." Only members of his family and the party politburo were allowed to continue to call him "Papa."[5]

The father image remains current, nonetheless. Throughout the world leaders are known as noble father, father of the country, or of the nation, founding father and even eternal father. In fact, two sorts of father can be discerned: heroic-paternal authority (the revolutionary chief or founder of national independence, usually called "father of the revolution" or "father of the country," but who is close to being a hero figure) and routine paternal authority (the sage full of experience and wisdom, the "quiet father" who is more of an ordinary man).

If advanced age is useful to the former, it is indispensable to the latter, for greater age naturally enhances the father image. To be the nation's paterfamilias it is useful to be seen bent beneath the weight of years. Indeed, to be a septuagenarian or even an octogenarian is no handicap.

In 1940, Marshal Pétain was 84 years old. To some Frenchmen this was an advantage. "His age gives him added greatness," wrote one. "The old soldier's image reaches the purity of an archetype. . . . He is the ghost of Merovaeus, the 'wise old man' of medieval times."[6] More than a father, he was a grandfather, almost an ancestor. He was the survivor of another age, the nostalgic symbol of former, better times.

In French history, disasters, wars, or national crises have often provoked this turn toward a peaceful or victorious past to palliate the anxiety of the present. At the moment when the people feel lost, the old protector brings reassurance. They have included 73-year-old Louis Adolphe Thiers in 1870, Georges Clemenceau at 76 in 1917, 71-year-old Gaston Doumergue in 1934, 84-year-old Petain in 1940, and de Gaulle at 67 in 1958.[7]

Even during the period of reconstruction, the father image remains attractive. Adenauer owed a good part of the admiration he inspired to his advanced age and his governmental longevity of 14 years as chancellor. The new "Iron Chancellor" turned out to be "The Wise Old Man." Mao finally died at 82, but Marshal Tito at 87 is still the patriarch of his people. And Brezhnev at 73 is, perhaps, following in his footsteps.

THE MODEL OF PATERNAL AUTHORITY

What sort of man is behind the paternal image? Or the avuncular one for that matter, there having been "Uncle Ho" in North Vietnam and today, England's "Uncle Jim" Callaghan. What character traits go into the makeup of this model of paternal authority?

The first is wisdom. The "father" is the man of experience, the one who knows everything, thanks to his years. He is the man who can handle any situation with acumen and moderation. He is in the image, for instance, of the Ivory Coast's Houphouet-Boigny, the wise septuagenarian of Yamoussoukro. Born in that village and the descendent of a long line of tribal chiefs including Queen Pokou, he had been a doctor, head of a plantation, member of the French National Assembly from 1945, and cabinet member five times from 1956 to 1958 before becoming the president of the Ivory Coast republic in 1960. He was reelected in 1965, 1970, and 1975.

The second paternal trait is knowledge and competence, the ability to master complex problems beyond the grasp of "ordinary citizens." In modern industrial societies with their subtle political and economic techniques, this theme of technocratic competence is essential. It's the "Papa knows best" syndrome, with citizens playing the role of the child dazzled by the father.

This man of wisdom and knowledge is above all a man of authority. He incarnates firmness, forcefulness, the ability to make decisions and impose his will. This *macho* leader often uses a strong-sounding vocabulary and the first person singular. He will say "I have decided" rather than "the government has decided."

The father character plays to his best audience when he makes a show of authority during a crisis. General de Gaulle's popularity was at its zenith from 1958 to 1962, while the Algerian war lasted. During the May-June 1968 crisis, however, it went through two phases. First his popularity waned when it appeared that he could not cope with the situation. Then, after his imperious speech of May 30, it became clear that he had things in hand, and his popularity rose again.[8]

Clearly, the father figure must, above all, make the people feel secure. President Georges Pompidou also filled this protective role, even though his authority was more routine and heroic. Even if, as some said, "a man of breadth succeeded a man of stature."[9] The second president of the Fifth Republic did not exactly galvanize crowds, but he knew very well how to make them feel secure.

When Giscard d'Estaing inaugurated the monument of his predecessor in Saint-Flour on November 13, 1975, he said of Pompidou: "France felt his full authority during those troubled days of 1968, let us not forget it. By his ability to negotiate day and night, he carried a worried and self-doubting France through that long, difficult passage."[10]

When Raymond Barre took over France's prime minister's office at Matignon in August 1976, he filled a role that had remained vacant since the death of Pompidou. Three characteristics particularly fitted him for the father role.

First, he had a reputation for wisdom, a thoughtful image, and a paternal tone. This coincided with a solid-looking physique that gave him the reassuring appearance of the typical *paterfamilias*. Also, this former professor always seemed to address his audience as if they were children, or at least his disciples.

He was clearly a man of knowledge. As a university professor and expert on European problems, he was said to be the best economist in France, at least as far as Giscard d'Estaing is concerned, who introduced him as such to the television audience.[11]

Finally, Barre's massive, resolute appearance gives him an air of authority. This "General Joffre of economics"[12] has energy and stage presence. He does not hesitate to raise his voice if need be. Speaking to a group of business leaders, he defined his policy as one of "truth, continuity, and firmness."[13]

As far as firmness is concerned, Barre is rivaled by his predecessor, Jacques Chirac, who became president of the Gaullist party, the Rally for the Republic, on December 5, 1976. One observer called him "this superman, this super guy, this super Chirac,"[14] for this "Cadet of the Republic"[15] has become a chief in his own right.

His official portrait has many touches of the "heroic." He has had a brilliant career: member of the National Assembly with deputy cabinet rank at 33, full cabinet minister at 38, prime minister at 41. He has military bearing, as befits the valedictorian of the Saumur military academy. He has an almost carnal love of political conquest, as in his native Corréze region which is "head over heels in love with him." His natural dynamism led Georges Pompidou to call him "my bulldozer." And his handling and love of authority, if not Caesarean or Bonapartist, is at least Gaullist.

Like de Gaulle, Chirac made "an appeal to the people of France,"[16] similarly posing as a providential man sent to wake up the country. Ready to confront the economic and political crisis (which always favors the charismatic leader), he offered to save the Gaullist majority, the Fifth Republic, and indeed France itself.

Chirac pulled off a surprise on January 19, 1977, when he announced on television that he would be a candidate for mayor of Paris. He indicated this, despite the fact that Giscard had already backed a different candidate.

As of early 1977, the Gaullists had a triumvirate to propose to voters: Chirac in the hero's role, Giscard d'Estaing as the charm leader, and Barre as the father figure. In other words, the hussar, the marquis, and the bourgeois.

FROM SUBMISSION TO REVOLT AGAINST THE FATHER

As has been seen, the paternal image is based on the public's desire for authority. It is the very model of authority imposed from above, as described by Harold Lasswell, the idealization of political authority as a substitute for strong paternal authority in our still patriarchal society.[17]

The father symbolizes the rigor of order, the state that dominates and dictates. He quells discontent, not by giving satisfaction, but by repressing it. "By his authority, he blocks the expression of aggression, rejects criticism and substitutes his will for that of the muzzled individual citizen. He also calls on the country to transcend its petty quarrels and pull together, thereby sublimating any feelings of discontent."[18] In short, paternal authority represents the political superego. It asks for abnegation, sacrifice owed to the country or to the party. But this essentially repressive authority could not succeed if it did not appeal to certain individuals ready to yield to it either through personal inclination or social conditioning.

Certain psychic or characterological factors favor yielding to the paternal image. They tend to correspond to the receptive personality described by Erich Fromm or the complaisant type of Karen Horney. They need to admire and obey, to be dominated and even mistreated by others, provided they receive a minimum of security and help in exchange.

This passivity especially favors the "heroic father" who asks for a blank check and who receives it from those only too happy to give themselves up to a master who will take care of everything. As Freud said of the "great man":

> Most human beings feel the imperious need to admire some authority by which they may be dominated and sometimes even mistreated. Individual psychology teaches us where this collective need for authority comes from: it is born of the attraction to the father. . . . All the character traits we attribute to the great man are those of a paternal figure. . . . Firmness in his ideas, strength of will, resolution in action — these are all part of the paternal image.[19]

But the strength of the paternal image becomes, in the long run, its weakness. This "protective political father"[20] ends up by unwittingly provoking the classical "revolt against the father."[21]

As a psychoanalyst, Gérard Mendel, also notes: "This political father, by his very existence, castrates adult citizens, who are transformed into children. It is as if they had lost some of their virility. This ideal Father is therefore necessarily a castrating Father in political and social reality, a superego and not an ego ideal."[22]

One either submits — which is the most frequent case — or rebels — the minority attitude — against this abusive father. De Gaulle experienced this rebellion. He posed as the indispensable father, keeping his people in a state of symbolic childhood. So the people forced him into a runoff vote in 1965, and then revolted completely in 1968. This was helped along by the demographic changes due to the baby boom, young adults wanting to affirm their adulthood. So an entire people, led by youth, liquidated its Oedipus complex.

Even Jacques Chaban-Delmas admitted it: "I revered General de Gaulle as a national symbol and I loved him like a father. Many Frenchmen did the same, for better or worse. May 1968 was also a revolt against the father."[23]

As time went on, the general's successor, Georges Pompidou, also came to play more and more the same father role and ended by inspiring lassitude rather than awe in a people that does not like to feel minor.

Indeed, the paternal image is on the decline today. Knowledge and techniques are advancing at such speed that the experience of age is a handicap more than an advantage in understanding the world.[24] Only those fresh from their training possess the information necessary to deal with "future shock."[25] In short, in a universe of planned obsolescence, the father no longer has the competence to impose his authority. Whereas before the son tried to imitate the father, today the father often tries to ape the younger generation, usually without much success.

So the political father yields sometimes to the brother. Eisenhower, Brandt, and Pompidou withdraw and are replaced by Kennedy, Schmidt, and Giscard d'Estaing. The scales come back toward the charm leader, who appears to be better adapted to run an economy based on expansion and innovation.

Let economic growth stop or other crisis develop and the public will turn from the father figure to the hero, that superfather who has the virtue of paternal authority plus an aura of grandeur and mystery. Since the hero is not only knowledgeable, like the father, but also infallible, he is better suited to providing the certitude and vision the people need in such times.

Former Prime Minister Indira Gandhi (1978).

The Political Nonwoman

*"I do not consider myself as a woman,
but as a person practicing a profession."*
—INDIRA GANDHI

I say the political *non*woman for two reasons. First, there are very few women heads of state or even cabinet ministers or party leaders, owing to the sexism and male chauvinism that has kept them in subordinate positions in government.

Second, the rare women who reach the top do everything they can to dispense with their femininity. As Mrs. Gandhi put it, "As prime minister, I am not a woman. I am a human being."

To be sure, it would be sexist to claim that there is such a thing as a specifically feminine political identity deriving from "feminine nature." That would be confusing nature and conditioning, and it would be hazardous to expect special sensitivity, compassion, or tolerance from women political leaders.*

Still, it is disappointing to see some of them uncritically accepting male values instead of inventing a political counterculture composed of other ways of thinking and acting. But how could they, after all? As long as the participation of women in public life does not reach a certain threshold, a certain critical mass, they cannot really affirm their true identity. They cannot do it with only a few token political

---

*Still, in Northern Ireland, the Women's Peace Movement of Mairead Corrigan and Betty Williams gave this example in 1976, when they attempted to stop Catholic-Protestant confrontation. See *Newsweek* (December 13, 1976) for an interview with Mrs. Williams entitled "We are Capable of Kindness."

positions as a base.* So it is natural that the few who have made it to prominence start, by imitating their masters, rather as a decolonized people start by copying their former colonizers.

So in order to minimize their intrusion into the men's club that is public life, women copy masculine styles of wielding authority, often to the point of parody, by heavily adopting male attitudes. As the press often puts it in such cases, they are "the only man in the government." But is that a compliment or a sad commentary on their betrayal of their sex?

In any case, there are masculine stereotypes they cannot imitate; the "ordinary woman" counterpart of the "ordinary man" does not exist. Our patriarchal societies require such exceptional qualities of the women it allows into politics that it is safe to say that sexism will have disappeared when mediocre women — like so many male cabinet ministers — will be members of government. We are a long way from that, at least to any significant degree. Neither does the female charm leader exist, for if women played on their femininity the way men exhibit their virile seductiveness they would be accused of frivolity and coquetry. Thus there remain the roles of heroine and mother, respectively, the counterparts of the male heroes and father figures.

THE MATERNAL MODEL OF AUTHORITY

The maternal image is in fact double, and this ambiguity works in favor of a certain return to matriarchy.

First there is the maternal image as antithesis of the paternal image. Whereas the father image represents the virile virtues of authority, dynamism, decisiveness, and self-assertiveness, the maternal image calls up other qualities. "The libidinal elan toward the mother — considered as source of life, love, warmth, nourishment, sensory satisfaction, and gratifying response — is interiorized, personified, and unified in the unconscious in the image of the Good Mother."[1]

---

*In West Germany, there are only 38 women among the 518 members of the Bundestag. In Italy, there are 54 women out of 630 members of Parliament, and 9 out of 490 in France. The present French administration of Raymond Barre includes four women out of 36 cabinet members. On the other hand, the Swedish cabinet formed by Fälldin in November 1976 included five women out of 20 members, counting Mrs. Karen Söder, 48, who was minister of foreign affairs.

It is the image of the Virgin Mary, "Mother of all misericord." It is the image of the motherland, of "France, mother of arts, arms and laws . . ." It is the stereotype of the giving mother.

It is, for example, the image of Queen Juliana, matron queen of the Netherlands. It is also that of Golda Meir, the Russian *babouchka,* or eternal mother of the Bible. The day she became Israeli prime minister in 1969, she said, "I only knew that now I would have to make decisions every day that would affect the lives of millions of human beings. I believe that is why I cried."[2]

But while this double image of maternal authority includes motherly care, it also implies punishment. There is the giving mother, but also the one who is the source of frustration, for the child inevitably learns that mother can refuse as well as give; she can even castrate. This is the image of the archaic mother: "The archaic mother is the source of all good things (the "consumer society"), but also of all the ills that afflict us (the cruel mother, the Medea who devours her children). This mother is therefore a castrater. And we know that the archaic maternal superego causes more anxiety (annihilation complex) than the paternal superego (castration complex)."[3]

This bipolar image corresponds to a duality of attitude toward authority. On the one hand there is the image of an authority that rules and forbids, maintains order, and deprives of pleasure. On the other there is the image of an authority that offers the services and benefits of the welfare state.

Indeed, certain male leaders have incarnated this hard and vengeful image of the archaic mother. That is how some explain Hitler's success in Germany: "The Germans voted for the Fürher because they were subjected during their childhood to authoritarian mothers, castraters who suppressed every sign of a budding personality. A compulsion to repeat made them repeat their childhood in a manifestation of collective neurosis."

The autocratic absolutism of the czars also corresponded in the Russian collective unconscious to an archaic maternal image, and this explains the rise of Stalin. "Beneath his appearance as a father, Stalin, like the czars, was unconsciously felt by the Russians as the archaic mother. The idea of losing him provoked in them an anxiety similar to that of the hungry infant left alone as punishment, who has fantasies of the destruction of his mother." This leads to "fear of being abandoned and the need of an appearance of security through total submission."[4]

As it happens, women political leaders often deliberately choose the image of the cruel mother who imposes her will rather than that of benign, generous authority. Even so, the one image is usually mixed with the other, as when she veers toward the heroic-maternal authority, with its emphasis on domination and constraint. Many of these women come to power in countries at war, like Israel and India, or in a state of semi-civil war, like Sri Lanka (formerly Ceylon).

MOTHER INDIA

July 21, 1960. Mrs. Sirimavo Bandaranaike becomes the head of the Sri Lanka government, succeeding her husband, who was prime minister from 1956 until his assassination in September 1959.

Mrs. Bandaranaike was, at first, the grieving but activist widow at the head of the Liberty party that she led to victory in the elections of 1960. Then she was head of government, and the alchemy of power transformed this timid and self-effacing widow into a political boss who was often authoritarian and sometimes brutal. In March 1971 she crushed the insurrection by the "Guevarist" youths and allowed a repression that reportedly cost 15,000 lives. Mrs. Bandaranaike's crowning success came on August 16, 1976, when she opened the Fifth Conference of Nonaligned Countries in Colombo.

Indira Gandhi, another Asian, also inherited power, but through family ties. Born in 1917 of an aristocratic Brahman family, she was the daughter of Jawaharlal Nehru, first prime minister of India from 1947 to 1964. In 1942 she married Feroze Gandhi, by whom she had two children before his death in 1960.

At first, Mrs. Gandhi was her father's confidante, hostess, and companion during his official trips. At his death in 1964 she became minister of information for his successor Shri Lal Shastri, who died in 1966. Then the chiefs of the Congress party agreed to elect Mrs. Gandhi to leadership because of her father and because her name reminded the public of the Mahatma. Being a woman, she should be easy to manipulate, they thought.

But they were wrong. The new prime minister turned out to be strong-willed. The Congress party split in 1969, the left wing supporting her, the right wing hostile to her. Mrs. Gandhi decreed the dissolution of the parliament and organized early elections for March 1971. Criss-crossing India by plane and helicopter, she won a landslide for her party, the New Congress. From then on she imposed her will ruthlessly, firing high officials in several Indian states. In late 1971 India beat Pakistan in the short war to support Bangladesh. In 1976, India became a nuclear power.

But on June 12, 1975, the Supreme Court in Allahabad annulled her election to the parliament, charging her with fraud. With her post as prime minister in danger of being revoked, Mrs. Gandhi proclaimed a state of emergency on June 26, giving herself almost dictatorial powers.

Political liberties were suspended, the press censored, and thousands of political opponents arrested.* Moreover, Mrs. Gandhi's party controlled all the states as of March 1975, when Gujarat, the last one still hostile to her, was placed under federal control. In autumn 1976 the parliament considered 59 amendments to the constitution that conferred quasi-unlimited powers on the prime minister.[5]

On January 20, 1977, Mrs. Gandhi relaxed the state of emergency somewhat, lifting censorship, although the press had to conform to a code of good conduct. Opposition leaders were released from prison, but many militants remained locked up.[6]

Despite such obstacles to democracy, the legislative elections in March 1977 brought about Mrs. Gandhi's defeat. But before her defeat, this daughter of Nehru prepared her son Sanjay to succeed her, as if she were invested with some historic mission or bore some dynastic legitimacy surpassing democratic rule. She ceased to be the benign mother and became the archaic mother, authoritarian and vengeful. Draped in her sari, Mrs. Gandhi incarnated Mother India, *Bharat Mata,* and published an essay entitled "On Being a Mother." "My public task has often separated me from my children," she wrote. "Still, they realize it is important, for I am attempting to play my role in constructing a better future for all the children of India."[7]

This mother figure also poses as a national heroine, identifying herself with her country and instituting a personality cult. Her

---

*How many? The figure 80,000 was cited by Thierry de Scitivaux on television station TF1 in January 1976. "Figures mentioned abroad are greatly exaggerated," the prime ministrer replied. (*Le Monde,* January 23, 1976). On December 31, 1975 and September 3, 1976, *Le Monde* mentioned several tens of thousands arrested since June 1975, and *Newsweek* (February 16, 1976) estimated their number at between 50,000 and 100,000.

supporters claimed "Indira is India and India is Indira." A new book was published in 1975 containing Mrs. Gandhi's speeches and writings and bearing the simple title, *India*. Her picture was on billboard everywhere with the caption, "The people thank the prime minister for saving the nation."

That same year, the new empress of India wrote a magazine article entitled "The Secret of My Success." In it she confided that "when I was a little girl, the teacher asked me what I wanted to be and expected me to answer 'teacher, doctor, or lawyer.' But I answered, 'I want to be like Joan of Arc!' "[8] She often mentioned that "I have always been fascinated by Joan of Arc," she told French television.[9] Again, evoking her childhood: "My favorite pastime was making speeches, standing on a table in front of the servants. All my games were political games. I was like Joan of Arc perpetually burned at the stake."[10] Joan of Arc, the French national heroine, freed that country from the English yoke. But Joan of Arc was the anti-woman, the woman who became a soldier, the woman who became a man.

This woman who, like Mrs. Bandaranaike and Mrs. Isabel Perón, was prematurely widowed, often said, "I do not consider myself as a woman, but as a person practicing a profession."[11] Despite her sari, her fragile appearance, her soft voice, Mrs. Gandhi personified perhaps better than anyone else the refusal of a feminine political identity. In her case, *heroine* is of feminine gender only in the purely grammatical sense. Her style of authority remains masculine, her system of values virile, as if the deliberately repressed instincts that exist no longer have any use, as if the exercise of power was everything to her — just as it is to so many male leaders.

THE SEÑORA AND THE IRON LADY

"Do men really think they are the only ones who can wear pants?" asked Isabel Perón in the land of *machismo*.[12] Born in 1931, having lost her father at the age of six, Maria Estela Martinez became a dancer in a folk dance group. It was then that she took the pseudonym of Isabel, shortly afterward meeting the ex-President Juan Perón in 1956 in the Happyland cabaret in Colón, Panama.

Isabel became his private secretary and then his wife in 1961, succeeding Eva who had died in 1952 and who had been known as "the Madonna of the shirtless," and "Mother of the Innocent." Isabel never replaced Eva in popularity, but the elections of September 23, 1973, made Juan Perón the president and Isabel the vice-president. When he died on July 1, 1974, she became president of Argentina.

Isabelita — Little Isabel — seemed too tiny and fragile at 43 to handle the job. But through hard work she became "La Señora," and even "L'Excelentisima Señora," ruling the country from the Casa Rosada with stern authority. She reshuffled the government to give it an extreme right bias, purged the labor unions, muzzled the press, established order in the universities, and proclaimed a state of emergency on November 6, 1974, which gave her the right to arrest hundreds of "leftists."

At her side was Lopez Rega, her private secretary and minister of social welfare, whom Argentinians called "the sorcerer" because of his open belief in spiritualism. But this former police corporal abused his power and so exasperated military and union leaders that he was forced to resign on July 17, 1975.

Stoic and resolute, Isabelita remained in power. Her last speeches were as vehement as ever and were accompanied by the fascist salute. But the results were too negative: galloping inflation, her party divided, an alarming number of political assassinations, and the country on the edge of civil war. On March 23, 1976, the army ousted her.

London, February 4 and 11, 1975. The 276 Conservative members of the House of Commons were voting for a new party leader. Would it again be Edward Heath, its leader since 1965, who had been prime minister from June 1970 to February 1974, but who had led the party to two defeats in 1974? Would it be Whitelaw, the former "proconsul" in Northern Ireland? Or would it be Mrs. Margaret Thatcher? It was Mrs. Thatcher.

At 49, this woman thus became the chief of the Conservative party, that misogynic gentlemen's club, and leader of the Opposition. What was more, this woman who was going to lead the Conservatives came from a modest background. Born of a lower middle-class family (her father was a grocer, her mother a seamstress), Margaret won a scholarship to Oxford, where she studied chemistry before taking a law degree and specializing in fiscal questions.

This self-made woman was elected to the House of Commons in 1959, and two years later she was undersecretary of social affairs. When the Conservatives returned to power in 1970, Heath named her minister of education. Mrs. Thatcher proved to be a combative, ultra-conservative cabinet officer, raising the prices in school cafeterias and eliminating free milk in schools. It was the latter measure that earned her the schoolboy chant, "Thatcher, Thatcher, milk snatcher."

Although she pretended to defend the middle class, Mrs. Thatcher — married to an oil industry manager — kept her distance from her humble origins. This "Pasionaria of privilege," as Labour leader Denis Healy called her, warred against the Welfare State.

Blonde and pink-skinned, always sporting a fresh hairdo beneath a green or fuchsia hat, dowdily dressed and affecting an upper-class accent, Mrs. Thatcher was no more faithful to her sex than she was to her class. She hard-headedly practiced all the virile qualities of dynamism, strict order, and organization. Some go so far as to allege that she had twins because it was more efficient to have all her children at once.[13]

Time called her a "tough lady," while a Tory colleague said "she's a tigress." Another asserted "she's a new Joan of Arc."[14] Thus Mrs. Thatcher became a female parody of the strongman, sedulously avoiding any semblance of a specifically feminine political identity.

FEMININE POLITICS

Britain's Labour party has also had several women cabinet minsters. There was Mrs. Barbara Castle, 66, at Social Affairs, Mrs. Shirley Williams, 46, at Consumer Affairs under Harold Wilson, and Education under James Callaghan. Like Mrs. Thatcher, who had the education portfolio before her, she may one day become her party's leader. If that happens, Britain's prime minister will necessarily be a woman, whether Labour or Conservative.*

---

*Other women politicians include Mrs. Ella Grasso, elected governor of Connecticut at 55 in 1974, the first American woman to become governor without succeeding her husband (as did, for example, Mrs. Lurleen Wallace). Mrs. Grasso declared, "Women in power can be as tough as anyone." (*Time,* January 5, 1976). In 1976 another woman, Mrs. Dixie Lee Ray, became governor of Washington. There is also Mrs. Anne Armstrong, U.S. ambassador to London since 1976, a Texas Republican called "Sugar and Steel" by *Time* (January 19, 1976).

In December 1974, Mrs. Shirley Williams candidly informed the public of her dilemma: she was a practicing Catholic divorced from a husband who loved another woman and in love with a remarried widower who was ready to divorce to marry her. "If my confessor says that I don't have the right to remarry, I am ready to live with the man I love without being married. But living in sin is just as bad. So what can I do?"[15]

All the gossip columns worried about this in print, along with their readers. Plenty of advice was offered, and it was obvious that the public liked such charming spontaneity in a cabinet officer.

In France, another woman, Simone Veil, minister of health[16] enjoys great popularity after her dignified support of more liberal abortion laws. Public opinion polls periodically put her at the top of the list of most-liked government officials, even ahead of the prime minister.

Occasionally Mrs. Veil shows signs of a feminine political style not lacking in charm. Revealing not weakness, but real simplicity, she once said, "it would worry me if I became another sort of human being just because I was a cabinet minister."[17]

Here and there, bit by bit, perhaps, a new political style is developing that will be less pompous and wordy, that will deal with concrete problems of daily life without being theatrical, without staging and stars. One day public office may be conceived of not as a narcissistic power game but as a service.

Priority might be given to listening to others and paying attention to their needs, not to gradiose honors and the derisory ceremonies of masculine style politics. Perhaps it is not illusory after all to hope that women might make a contribution to a new kind of politics, not necessarily feminine, but more human and dedicated to the commonweal.

President and Mrs. John F. Kennedy sailing off Hyannis Port, Mass.

The Private Life of a Public Man

*"I want to be more than a rose
in my husband's lapel."*
—MARGARET TRUDEAU

Privacy. What meaning can that term have for a political leader? Everything about him — age, state of health, athletic prowess, morals, conjugal relations, family life, house pets — is on exhibit. His life is literally an open book.

BIRTH CERTIFICATE

An older candidate for public office will boast of this superior experience. A younger one will emphasize his youth to underline his dynamism and fresh approach to things.

Age can "sell" as a synonym for maturity and wisdom. It promotes the father figure image so valued in times of crisis or war, as noted previously. De Gaulle even used it to dispel any doubts about his democratic sentiments: "Does anyone think that at 67 I am going to become a dictator?" Adenauer, Gaspari, and Mao all reached their zenith at advanced ages.

But age can also become a handicap easily exploited by the opposition. De Gaulle's age of 75 was harped on during the presidential campaign of 1965, when younger voters were incited to murder — politically speaking — the father figure. One adversary,

Jean Lecaneut, then 45, said, "General de Gaulle is still worrying about problems our fathers had, whereas I am trying to address the problems that will confront our sons."[1]

Youth is associated with imagination, innovation, and modernism. Lecaneut's advertising presented him as "a young man looking toward the future." It added: "In the age of space exploration, we need a young leader."[2] De Gaulle's only rebuttal was in the form of a confession: "I am what I am. I don't pretend to be perfect, and I don't deny my age."[3]

Nine years later, during the presidential campaign of 1974, Giscard d'Estaing, then 48, attempted to use this argument against François Mitterrand, who was in fact only ten years older. In their TV debate on May 10, 1974, he suddenly stated: "The thing that surprises me about this debate, Mr. Mitterrand, I will tell you simply, is that you are a man of the past."

And Giscard emphasized to the voting public: "If you elect me, it will be France among all the great countries of the world that will have the youngest president."[4] Indeed, had he not been a member of the National Assembly at 30, an under secretary at 33, and minister of finance at 36?*

Youth, of course, is one of the distinctive traits of the charm leader. Jerry Brown became governor of California at 36. Palme was prime minister of Sweden at 42. Trudeau took over the same post in Canada at 48.

Kennedy was 43 when elected president, and the physical difference between him and Eisenhower was striking at the inauguration on January 20, 1961. As Kennedy put it then, "Let the word go out that the torch has passed to a new generation of Americans."[5]

The truth is that the much-desired youth image is the product of cinema and television, thanks to close-ups. Age mattered little in theater or opera, even in adolescent roles. How old, after all, was Sarah Bernhardt when she played l'Aiglon? But today, with movie and TV news coverage showing up every crow's foot on a leader's face, youth is the symbol of vitality.

---

*Mitterand could have turned this to his advantage by noting that at 30 he was the youngest minister of the last two republics.

HEALTH REPORTS

Health is as important as youth to today's leaders, confirming their youthful image of vigor and dynamism. Woodrow Wilson noted that "we must always choose our nation's leader from among athletes who know how to pace themselves — a very limited category." Because the job of president or prime minister is physically taxing, the smart candidate will prove he has a robust constitution by vigorously criss-crossing the country.

That makes the campaign a sort of endurance test. In the United States it lasts from at least the first primaries in February and March to the election in November. That gives ample time to verify whether candidates to the White House have the physical stamina it takes.

In 1960, British Labour leader Hugh Gaitskell admitted his astonisment at the punishing pace of an American campaign. "I don't see how you do it," he told the press. "Frankly, three weeks of campaigning are enough to exhaust me. I suppose that after that, being president of the United States must seem like a vacation."[6]

In fact, John Kennedy's health became an issue during the 1960 campaign. During the Democratic Convention, Texas Governor John Connally, who supported Lyndon Johnson, asserted during a press conference that Kennedy had Addison's disease and could not stand the rigors of the presidency. Kennedy's doctor immediately published a health bulletin denying this. The irony, of course, was that Connally would later be in the car in which Kennedy was assassinated in Dallas.

Kennedy did have problems with his back, due to a wound incurred during the Second World War, and he had to wear a special brace. The campaign was therefore particularly trying for him. When the candidate with the ready smile got back to his hotel room, he took off the brace, relaxed in a hot bath and sighed with relief: that was the only sign he gave of the suffering he was going through.[7]

Another difficulty Kennedy had came during the Oregon and Indiana primaries, when he lost his voice. That did not keep him from giving his scheduled press conferences, however. Instead of answering questions orally, he wrote them out on large sheets of yellow paper which Pierre Salinger, his press secretary, then read to the newsmen.[8] Thus was born the mute press conference.

On the Republican side, Richard Nixon also had difficulty maintaining the hectic pace. His press agents gave the following figures on the candidate on November 7, 1960: he had flown 65,500 miles, appeared at least once in 188 cities and towns, made over 150 speeches and been seen in the flesh by ten million persons.[9]

But even a good athlete can trip up in such an exhausting marathon, and at the end of August, Nixon knocked his kneecap against a car door and the injury became infected. He had to lie in Walter Reed Hospital from August 29 to September 9 with his leg in traction, losing two full weeks of campaigning.

The presidential knee also figured in the 1976 campaign between Ford and Carter. The White House released a complete report on its tenant's health: "Mr. Ford has trouble with both knees, which have been operated on in the past, but he compensates for this with vigorous physical exercise when he rises at 5:30 A.M. and with daily swims of 400 yards in the open-air pool he had built at the White House. He sleeps well, having to get up only once to relieve himself, and has experienced no nervous disorders following the two assassination attempts against him. His teeth are stained by nicotine. His testicles are normal and symmetrical. The president has no depressive tendencies. His stool is brown and well-shaped."[10]

Steady nerves are as important as good physical strength for a president. The Democratic Convention nominated Senator Thomas Eagleton, 42, for vice-president on July 13, 1972, as George McGovern's running mate. But it was soon learned that Eagleton had been hospitalized three times for nervous problems between 1960 and 1966, and that he had received electrotherapy twice. McGovern had to find another running mate.

SPORTS

To prove his strength and project a dynamic, virile image, the leader has to be — or appear to be — athletic.* It's best if he plays team sports, showing he knows how to work with others.

Jacques Chaban-Delmas, the former French prime minister, outclassed everyone on the golf course. Moreover, this former rugby

---

*At 72, Mao himself proved his endurance by swimming 10 miles in the Yangtze River on July 16, 1966.

player — he was on the French national team against England in 1945 — played practically all sports and had photos to prove it. While president of the National Assembly he continued to play excellent tennis, making the semifinals in the French National Open. He also jogged with France's track star, Michel Jazy.

Giscard d'Estaing also has tried to appear to be an all-around athlete. Although he does not play tennis, he accompanied his two sons to Roland-Garros for the finals of the French Open. He let himself be photographed water skiing during the summer of 1974 and swimming in December of that year in the same pool as Gerald Ford and Henry Kissinger during their summit meeting in Martinique. He skied at Courchevel in 1975, 1976, and 1977. He even gets in a bit of flying, having taken the controls of his helicopter during a surprise visit to a low-income housing development on June 13, 1975.

Helicopters and airplanes generally are an important symbol for today's leaders, establishing beyond doubt that they are modern and use the fastest means of transport available. When Franklin D. Roosevelt wanted to underscore his image as a daring, innovative candidate in 1932, he took a plane to the Democratic Convention in Chicago to accept the nomination. Forty years later, Henry Kissinger played a sort of flying Metternich, jumping from one jet to another for his trips to the four corners of the world — omnipresent, omniscient, and the fastest superstar in diplomacy.

Jean-Jacques Servan-Schreiber, French political leader and former publisher of the news magazine *L'Express,* also uses aeronautical symbolism. He learned to fly fighter planes in the United States in 1944, and he still flies his own plane, decorated with the Cross of Lorraine, the region he represents in the National Assembly. In April 1970, he flew the Greek composer Mikis Theodorakis out of Greece to escape the colonel's oppressive regime. Even at home he often wears a Mae West vest over his shirt and tie, creating the image of a flying political superman.

CAESAR'S WIFE

Besides these physical qualities, the leader must also demonstrate certain social ones, particularly concerning his family. It is as if he had to illustrate Article 4 of the Declaration that preceded France's revolutionary constitution of the Year III: "No one is a good citizen unless he is also a good son, good father, good brother, good friend, and good husband."

Good husband: to correspond to the traditional stereotype of proper morals, the leader must be married. The public tends to worry about bachelors, as could be seen in the case of Edward Heath. Just before the British elections of October 10, 1974, the former prime minister was questioned by TV newsmen about the absence of women in his life. Heath, his face tense, admitted that this was perhaps lacking in his life, but added firmly that those who asked questions about such subjects could "go to hell."[11]

Divorced men are just as worrysome, as Adlai Stevenson's case showed during his unlucky attempts to win the White House against Mamie Eisenhower's husband in 1952 and 1956. Ever since, some politicians have refused to divorce so as not to compromise their chances, both in the United States and in France. In 1974, Mr. and Mrs. Jacques Chaban-Delmas were both systematically smeared for being divorced before marrying each other.

But morals evolve, especially in America with its high divorce rate, and divorce is no longer the cause of reprobation it used to be. Thus Gerald Ford was able to choose Nelson Rockefeller as vice-president in 1974 and Robert Dole as running mate in 1976, despite the fact that both had been divorced.

Candidates' wives participate actively in their husbands' campaigns and, if they are elected, in their activities at the White House. During the last 25 years this role was played by Mamie Eisenhower, Jackie Kennedy, Lady Bird Johnson, Pat Nixon, Betty Ford, and Rosalynn Carter.

In 1960, Jackie Kennedy assisted her husband very effectively. "That campaign," Pierre Salinger has noted, "was hers as much as the senator's. . . . Dave Powers liked to tease Kennedy by saying, 'It's not you so much as Jackie that half the people turn out to see.' " And everyone remembers Kennedy's crack during his official trip to France: "I am the man who accompanied Jacqueline Kennedy to Paris, and I have enjoyed it."

Ironically, Jackie wrote a note to her press secretary about the upcoming 1964 campaign the very week of her husband's assassination: "If Pierre [Salinger] can get me and the children in a bubble bath on the cover of *Look,* I guess I'll have to do it."[12]

As of July 1976, *Time* noted that in 14 months of campaigning, Mrs. Carter had been in 34 states and made nearly as many speeches as her husband. When Betty Ford and Nancy Reagan made their entrances at the Republican Convention in Kansas City in August 1976, they were measured on the applause meter. To make sure she won, Mrs. Ford danced the Bump with singer Tony Orlando.[13]

In France, candidates' wives remain more discreet. Georges Pompidou explained why: "I don't think it is proper for a woman to wear herself out in a presidential campaign. . . . My wife is terribly important to me, and I hope this is true of all husbands."[14]

But in 1974, wives played a more important role in the French presidential campaign. After her husband's election, Mrs. Giscard d'Estaing continued to help out, not only by playing Lady Bountiful and being a good hostess at the Elysée Palace, but also as the president's special envoy on several occasions and by sharing the TV screen with him during the traditional New Year's speech on December 31, 1975.

THE SECOND SEX

In France and elsewhere the candidate's (or president's) wife is shown off to humanize his image and promote the notion that he lives a normal family life like any citizen. Women voters are supposed to be particularly susceptible to this.

But the First Lady remains, nevertheless, an auxiliary to her husband, typecast in a supporting role, always in the wake — or the shadow — of her husband. Faithful, patient, and submissive, she serves the interests of his career in the classic situation described by Simone de Beauvoir in *The Second Sex*.

The leader's wife is also typical of *The Feminine Mystique* outlined by Betty Friedan, alienated in a society that denies her any identity of her own, that obliges her to "stifle her own personality," and condemns her to "existency by proxy." She lives only as a reflection of her husband, her children, her home, the victim of masculine supremacy. As Kate Millett analyzed it, "everything that is creative and self-fulfilling is for the man. The woman's lot is limited to domestic and sexual services, subaltern tasks, and the education of the children."

Thus the president's wife can have only one objective: to support her husband as his devoted and attentive servant, full of admiration for everything he does. She plays Penelope to his Ulysses.

Giscard d'Estaing's mother has confided: "One day when I was taking tea with Valy, he asked me, 'Mama, do you think I have a great future ahead of me?' I replied, 'I will tell you when you introduce me to your wife.' Well, I believe that Anne-Aymone is a woman who can help a man have a great future. . . . She has always freed him of inner worries, and knows how to stay discreet."[15]

This role of help-mate extends to the point of identification, with the wife usually having been chosen in his own image by the leader.

The charm leader, for example, marries a woman who is good at alternating between equality and superiority, closeness and aloofness, familiarity and distinction. Jackie Kennedy was incomparable in this role. She was spouse and mother, but also a brilliant, sophisticated woman dressed by the likes of Oleg Cassini and Hubert de Givenchy. She cut a figure in the Jet Set while being cultivated and intelligent, making them a truly star couple to be admired by the American public.

Jackie redecorated the White House with antiques and gave it a style worthy of the prestigious official receptions given there, where guests were served on gold-plated dishes, and wine was poured in crystal glasses.

There was the Pablo Casals concert in honor of the governor of Puerto Rico on November 13, 1961, attended by composers like Leonard Bernstein, Aaron Copeland, Norman Della Joio, Ray Green, and Roy Harris. In 1962 there was the reception in honor of André Malraux, where Isaac Stern, the cellist, Leonard Rose, and the pianist Eugene Istomin played a trio. And it was in cooperation with Malraux that Jackie arranged to have the "Mona Lisa" visit the United States.

The White House was thus the country's semi official meeting place for artists and intellectuals. During a dinner party for Nobel Prize winners, Kennedy observed that the White House has never known such a talented gathering, except perhaps when Thomas Jefferson dined here alone.[16]

Mrs. Imelda Romualdez Marcos, 47, the wife of President Ferdinand Marcos, "the Philippine Kennedy," also projects the image of patron of the arts, thanks in part to construction of a luxurious cultural center in Manila, and member in good standing of the Jet Set. Against a backdrop of fast planes, yachts, and games of polo she cultivates friends like Dr. Christian Barnard and Gina Lollobrigida.

Newsweek asked Mrs. Marcos once, "as the First Lady of a country that is still relatively poor, aren't you embarrassed to have your name listed among the world's richest women?" Answer: "Of course it is embarrassing. It looks so materialist. In reality I'm the least materialistic person in the world. And all those reports about my being in the Jet Set. How else could I travel around the world to do all these things for my people? By paddling a canoe? And how else could my Jet Set friends come to see me? By paddling a canoe?"[17]

But when it comes to playing the unpretentious role, the charm leader's wife is also good at adopting a less sophisticated image. Thus Margaret Trudeau, 27, accompanied her husband on an official trip to Latin America in February 1976. In Cuba she showed up wearing blue jeans and a tee-shirt (with *Margaret* printed on the back) dating from her husband's latest election campaign. Before long she was calling the Cuban prime minister "Fidel." At an official dinner in Caracas, she insisted on singing a song she had composed in honor of the wife of Venezuelan President Carlos Andrés Pérez, that went, "I want to sing for you, sing a song of love." In any case, Margaret said clearly that she did not intend to be "a lady of good works who goes around opening day-care centers."[18]

But that is precisely what the wives of the father figure and common man leaders do. The political Mr. Everyman needs a Mrs. Everywoman at his side who is a good housekeeper, who is economical and prudent, and who dresses in year-before-last fashions. She must possess simplicity and a moral tone far removed from the women's movement. She is Mamie Eisenhower in the United States, Germaine Coty in France, tending her kitchen. She is the archetypal Mrs. Smith or Madame Dupont, shuttling between making jam and caring for her grandchildren. Even the very active Mrs. Jimmy Carter projects this image, returning home every weekend to wash and iron her husband's shirts after a hard week of political campaigning.[19]

Occasionally, when the common man appears really too common, his wife becomes more popular than he is. That seems to have been the case with Betty Ford, who inspired badges proclaiming "Betty's husband for president in '76" during his campaign. Known for her frankness, Mrs. Ford gave a much-noted interview on the CBS *60 Minutes* show in August 1975.

To underline how much she favored equal rights for women, Mrs. Ford called the Supreme Court decision legalizing abortion "a great, great decision." Asked about marijuana, she replied that she supposed that her four children had tried it, and that she probably would have done so herself when she was young: "It's the sort of thing that young people have to experiment with, like their first beer or their first cigarette." As to her husband, Mrs. Ford observed calmly, "he still enjoys a pretty girl, but he really doesn't have time for outside entertainment because I keep him busy."

The conversation then turned to premarital sexual relationships. What would her attitude be if her daughter, Susan, who v as 18, told her that she had had an affair? "Well, I wouldn't be surprised. I think she is a perfectly normal human being like all girls. If she wanted to continue it, I would give her advice on the subject."[20]

Such liberal views shocked certain circles, but they won Mrs. Ford other friends. Her popularity only increased when she underwent an operation in September 1974 for breast cancer. When the First Lady attended a premier of Alvin Ailey's dance company — she was a former student of Martha Graham's — it was not long before she jumped up on the stage to improvise a number with a member of the company, Judith Jamison.

But not all leaders' wives project this image of happiness. Indeed, in her book *The Power Lovers: An Intimate Look at Politicians and Their Marriages*, Myra MacPherson, a journalist for the *Washington Post*, decided after interviewing 30 famous couples that successful conjugal and family life is nearly impossible in politics. For one thing, candidates have to campaign day and night, weekdays and weekends, instead of being with their family. And their wives, who quickly learn to suppress any expression of personal opinion, have to run a gauntlet of political assistants, groupies, and fans to be with their husbands. The demands of the candidate's electoral district are not the only she must compete with. As Myra MacPherson notes, "the sort of person who chooses politics as a career is not at ease in personal relationships. He often prefers above all the roar of the crowd.''

Mrs. Joy Baker, daughter of Senator Everet Dirksen and wife of Senator Howard Baker, declared that politics had destroyed her personality. Lady Bird Johnson has remarked that a politician should be born an orphan and stay a bachelor. And Joan Kennedy defined herself with a single word: *Vulnerable*.[21]

Vulnerable: how can a woman stand this life of self-effacement and devotion to her husband's career? The candidate's wife must participate actively in his campaign and make speeches. She must be a model of virtue and propriety. Recalling her husband's election as governor of Georgia, Rosalynn Carter confided: "I woke up one morning in a panic. I suddenly realized that I must be perfect every minute."[22]

She is permanently exposed to the eyes of the public and to her critics, to photographers' lenses and television cameras. She lives in fear of a word or a gesture that might be detrimental to her husband. In short, she becomes public property, an extension of the public man she married. "What will be Rosalynn's role in your administration?" President Carter was asked. Answer: "I will use her as an extension of myself."[23]

The politician's wife must bear many constraints on her personal freedom and must handle many tasks. Mrs. Ellen Proxmire, ex-wife of the senator from Wisconsin, said of the leader's wife, she is first and always a mother, cook, chauffeur, seamstress, and housewife, but she is also a counsellor, social worker, campaign agent, and even TV personality.[24] Such husbands are usually utterly egocentric, thinking only of their careers. In 1960 Hubert Humphrey decided to run for the Democratic presidential nomination without even informing his wife, Muriel, who sent him a bitter telegram: "Let me know if I can be of any help." What is more, charm leaders are tempted by groupies and amorous fans who follow them around, provoking occasional affairs and making them victims of their much-touted sexual powers.

Some wives finally cannot stand it. Some, like Abigail MacCarthy, Mieke Tunney or Phyllis Dole, decide to divorce. Some take refuge in alcohol or drugs; others simply have nervous breakdowns.

There was the case of Joan Kennedy, who reacted to the double shock of the Chappaquidick affair (in which Mary Jo Kopechne, one of her husband's secretaries, was killed in odd circumstances in 1969) and the cancer of one of her sons by sinking into alcoholism (she was arrested for drunken driving) and having a breakdown. Edward Kennedy's wife had to be hospitalized in a psychiatric clinic for a long stay in 1974.

It was also in 1974 that the Canadian prime minister's office let it be known that Mrs. Trudeau would spend ten days in September in the Royal Victoria Hospital in Montréal for a rest and a checkup. But she called a press conference at the hospital to rectify this official version of events. "I am under psychiatric treatment for emotional stress," she confided, "but I hope to be well soon." Her husband was angry, fulminating that "the press has no right to be here." Margaret nevertheless maintained her version, confirming that being the wife of a politician can create enough nervous tension to send a woman to the hospital for psychiatric care.

Later, in February 1976, Mrs. Trudeau was criticized for her behavior during that official trip to Cuba and Venezuela. She called a radio station in Ottawa and, almost sobbing, said: "I don't think I have done anything wrong. If you follow protocol to the letter, you become a robot."[25] During this half-hour talk she also said, "I want to be more than a rose in my husband's lapel. I refuse to be shunted aside the way I have been in the past."[26]

Even Betty Ford admitted to a certain amount of difficulty when her husband became minority leader in the House of Representatives in 1965. Even this well-balanced woman had to ask help from a psychiatrist. "I had completely lost any sense of my own usefulness," she said.[27]

Thus there is often a very large gap between reality and the image of self-fulfilled happiness that politicians' wives attempt to project. Their children, sometimes transformed into no more than performing animals in a side show, often are no happier.

THE FAMILY CIRCLE

The leader's children, and even grandchildren, play an important part in humanizing his character. In this sense, the governor of New York, Hugh Carey, has established a sort of record as the father of 12 children. In January 1975, the 51st governor of New York rented a bus to transport his family from New York to his new official residence in Albany.[28]

The presence of children and grandchildren is important to accredit the image of father (or grandfather) of the nation. They also serve to certify the Mr. Everyman as an ordinary loving father like everyone else. In the case of the charm leader, they attenuate his brilliant intelligence and style by giving him homely dimension. Only the hero figure forbids everything that — like women and children — might show him as less than superhuman. General de Gaulle's wife and children, for instance, were carefully kept out of the news.

The younger the child, the better he "sells" the product, as is well known in TV advertising circles. The sight of an infant makes the potential buyer — or voter — melt with sentiment. Moreoever, young children symbolize the still-active sexual potency of the charm leader, even one in his forties or fifties.

In 1960 Caroline Kennedy was three years old and Jackie gave birth to John-John in November, a few days after the presidential election. The previous September the candidate alluded to the coming baby when he was in Oregon, excusing Jackie's absence by saying she had "other appointments." The public loved it, and the next morning, in North Carolina, the line became, "my wife has other duties." Everyone chuckled. That afternoon, the wording was more explicit, "my wife is expecting a baby." The next day, in the San Joaquin Valley, it was, "my wife will have a boy in November." That afternoon in Los Angeles, the subject was hot enough to make the press conference. "How do you know it will be a boy?" a newsman wanted to know. Answer: "My wife told me." And the press conference ended in general laughter.[29]

After their father's election, Caroline and John-John gamboled all over the White House, showing up in the most unexpected places. One day, Caroline ventured into the briefing room where newsmen were waiting for the president. One of them asked her what her father was doing. "Oh, he's upstairs with his shoes off, taking it easy," came the reply. Another time, when Kennedy was holding a press conference in Palm Beach, Caroline suddenly appeared in her nightgown, wearing her mother's bedroom slippers.[30]

1974. Trudeau was campaigning and exhibited Justin, two and a half, and Sacha, six months, both born on Christmas Day. "Lucky

Pierre!'' the saying went. "Even God had only one son on Christmas.''[31] In December 1974, Justin, who would soon be three, appeared in pajamas and shook hands with Mr. Hoveyda, the prime minister of Iran who was the guest of honor at an official dinner.[32] Shortly afterward the Trudeaus had a third child: a boy, Michel, who accompanied his parents on an official trip to Cuba at the age of four months, in February 1976.

Jimmy Carter played the same game. His eight-year-old daughter, Amy, impish and uninhibited, was at the center of his campaign. Like the spiritual sister of Huckleberry Finn, plus the Carter smile, she ran a lemonade stand in Plains, Georgia, with the profits going to the Democratic party.

Besides Amy, with her blonde bangs and freckles, there were her three brothers: John, 29, James Earl III, 26, and Jeff, 23. Children this age naturally can play less on the public's heart strings, but they had the advantage of being able to participate actively in their father's campaign.

There was also, of course, the faithful spouse, Rosalynn, 49, and it had even been said that "Rosalynn (was) a better campaigner than Jimmy.''[33] Mrs. Carter often talked politics with her husband, but played down that part of her character, saying modestly, "he needs to know what people think who are less intelligent than he is.''[34]

How admirably this political wife conformed to the stereotype! Carter was fortunate in also having an admirable mother, Lillian, 77, who says, "I finish everything I start. Jimmy takes after me in that." There was also Jimmy's brother, Billy, who stayed in Plains like a good redneck, but who also granted 300 interviews in July 1976. And there were the two sisters, Gloria and Ruth.

Before Jimmy Carter reached the White House, Gerald Ford had put his family on stage as part of his show, including his wife, Betty, and his children, Susan, 19, Steve, 20, Jack, 24, and Mike, 26, as well as Mike's wife, Gayle, also 26.

Earlier presidents had done likewise. Johnson had Lady Bird and their two daughters, Lynda and Luci. Richard Nixon had Pat — also known as "Plastic Pat" — and their two daughters, Tricia — a very active propagandist that the press situated "slightly to the right of Ivan the Terrible" — and Julie, who just happened to be married to Dwight Eisenhower's grandson.

In France, presidential campaigns are beginning to imitate this model. It was a timid imitation in the 1965 and 1969 campaigns, but it became blatant in 1974, when the candidate's family was put squarely on stage. This was especially the case with Giscard d'Estaing, with his wife Anne-Aymon, their two sons, Henri and Louis, and their two daughters, Valerie-Anne and Jacinte. Jacinte even figured at her father's side on one of his official campaign posters.

And once their father was at the Elysée, the president's two daughters got even more press coverage, with both on the cover of the popular weekly magazine *Jours de France* within a few weeks of each other. The issue of May 19, 1975, headlined "The fairy tale of Valerie-Anne, Queen of the Azalias," a story about her attending festivities in Norfolk, Virginia. On September 1, 1975, the cover showed her younger sister on horseback, with the headline, "Jacinte's equestrian exploits."*

BESTIARY

Sometimes the family circle even includes domestic animals, those faithful companions of that friend and defender of all, the leader. This proves his goodness and sensitivity, despite disagreement by Jonathan Swift, who held that "A man who hates children and animals can't be all bad."

Roosevelt's dog Fala was famous, but in 1952 Nixon's cocker spaniel, Checkers, earned even greater fame, on which more will be said later. Under Kennedy, horses, ponies, dogs, and hamsters coexisted in the White House, where there were never less than about 15 domestic animals, according to Pierre Salinger.[35] This menagerie included Sadar, the horse given to Jackie by Pakistani PresidentAyub Khan; Macaroni, Caroline's pony; Charlie, a fox terrier; Shannon, an Irish Cocker given by de Valera; Pouchinka, offspring of Laika, the first space dog, which was the gift from Khrushchev to Mrs. Kennedy. And then there were Caroline's hamsters whose antics were reported by the women's press.

---

*Valerie-Anne got seven pages inside; Jacinte six.

Today the Elysée is full of canines. There are two labradors, Reale and Candy, a Weimaraner, Jugurtha, and another dog, Justine. One journalist wrote that Giscard d'Estaing arrived at a meeting at the chateau of Rambouillet flanked by a labrador and "another dog of indeterminate race." But the president called him shortly afterward to specify that "There are no dogs of indeterminate race here. That dog was from the Auvergne." And during a TV talk on April 22, 1975, that was filmed near a window looking on to the Elysée's grounds, the president inquired of the film crew, "did you get the two dogs going by?"

As can be seen, every detail has its place in the meticulous staging of the leader's show.

PART TWO
The Show

Once the role has been chosen, the show has to be staged, using theatrical or cinematographic techniques to better mix political art and artifice. These techniques involve "mediapolitics": politics degraded by the mass media of the press, radio and television, and by the show business people called campaign managers.

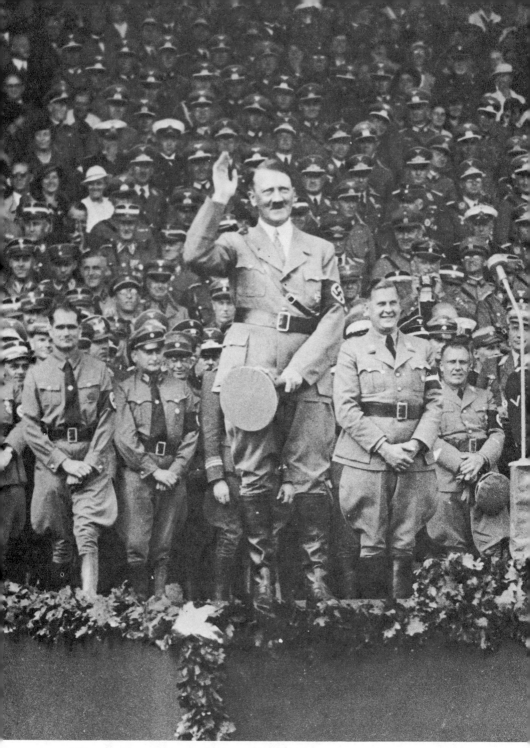

Hitler addressing a Nazi party convention in Nurenberg (1935).

The Art of Politics

*"The leader, like the artist, must have his
natural gifts polished by professionalism."*
— CHARLES DE GAULLE

Robert Redford admits that "I was naive when I produced *The Candidate*. I believed that it would have an impact on the elections of 1972 because it showed the public how it is manipulated and tricked, and how much politics resembles show business."[1]

In the United States and elsewhere, leaders become actors, veritable political performers in a show made up of artifice and illusion, tricks and slight-of-hand. They in fact form a subspecies of dramatic art.

THE GOVERNMENT AS THEATER

"All the world's a stage, and all the men and women merely players; They have their exits and their entrances; and one man in his time plays many parts."

On July 30, 1975, General Gowon, smiling and relaxed, quoted Shakespeare's *As You Like It* and accepted with good grace the new coup d'état that had overturned his government. Soon afterward, the former president of Nigeria enrolled at Warwick University in Britain to study political science.

Not all leaders have such a sense of humor, but many behave like stage actors. Some, like Augustus, declaim at the end; "Acta est fabula."* Others recall Nero, who murmured as he committed suicide, "Qualis artifex pereo!"**

The French kings were fond of theatricals. Louis XIV danced in some of the ballets put on at his court and occasionally participated in the "royal entertainments" at Versailles. In 1664, the king, wearing a gilded breastplate and riding a horse livried with diamonds, had a role in *La Princesse d'Elide*.

Like his remote predecessor, Napoleon was very good at creating his own role. Like Louis XIV, Napoleon enjoyed the company and advice of actors and actresses. Queen Hortense noted in her memoirs, "the most famous actors were successively invited to dinner at Malmaison. One after the other I saw Talma, Mlle. Raucourt, Mlle. Contat, and Mlle. Fleury."

In 1931, Pétain prepared his acceptance speech on his entry to the French Academy by taking diction courses from an actress at the Comédie Française. At about the same time, de Gaulle wrote in *The Sword's Edge*, "the leader, like the artist, must have his natural gifts polished by professionalism." Later it was reported that the general took lessons from several actors at the Comédie Française.

The generation of leaders of the Second World War was the last to be heavily influenced by the theater, which was soon to be replaced by the cinema and television. But whether Hitler, Mussolini, Churchill, Roosevelt, de Gaulle, or Stalin, they all admired and imitated stage stars.

There were evenings in the Kremlin when the great actor Mikhoels gave a recital of scenes from *King Lear* with Stalin as the only spectator. In Germany, Bertolt Brecht, who was to caricature Hitler in *The Resistable Ascension of Arturo Ui*, noted that "it is said that Hitler took declamation and poise lessons from a small-time actor named Basil." In Brecht's play, Arturo Ui learns to strike a pose and to move with the "imposing presence" of a Shakespearean actor.[2]

Today, Habib Bourguiba appears to be the last survivor of that generation of leaders. His brother, who is the director of a theater

---

*"The play is over," the words with which Roman plays traditionally ended.
**"What an artist I am putting an end to!"

group, has taught much about dramatic art to "the supreme fighter," who in fact is known by some of his student rebels as "the supreme comedian." Speaking of his youth in Paris, the Tunisian president has confided: "My great love was the theater, the Comédie Française and especially the Odéon, which was then run by Firmin Gemier. What a great artist Gemier was! And when René Alexandre played Salluste in *Ruy Blas*, he gave you goose pimples! It was enough to make your head spin!"[3]

Wherefore this passion for the theater among political leaders? In a word, what is it that links the theater so closely to authority?

THE THEATER OF THE HERO

First, the political hierarchy resembles the hierarchy of show business. At the top are the first-ranking actors, who get the best roles. We often speak of politicians as if they were "stars" on the "political stage"; and the layout of a parliament or house of congress resembles nothing so much as a theater.

Second, and above all, the dramatic repertoire offers a wide range of stereotypes for political actors to pattern themselves on: the matinee idol (equivalent of the charm leader), the wise old father, the understudy suddenly thrust into the star's role (as is the "common man" leader), the mother, and the hero. Especially the hero, who is often cast as a great warlord or even a demigod.

And since the theater is often a theater of illusion with a repertoire based on hero stories, it is hardly surprising if the last generation of leaders formed by the theater tends to be men playing heroic characters inspired by the theater of their youth.

The theater is of religious origin, and it has retained certain liturgical aspects. Many authors and directors compare a play to a ceremonial or even to the mass. The Grotowski school of thought holds that the theater has no value except as a rite, a sacred ceremony of communion with the player.

Speaking of this "sorcerer's art," Jean-Louis Barrault writes: "It is like a lover's rendezvous, including the excitement, the giving of self, the appetite, exchange, mutual comprehension, communion, and final orgasm. Hallelujah! What a religious service, and also what an orgy!"

And he writes further: "The stage is a sacred object. . . . At the theater you don't listen, you receive."[4]

What a model for the political hero! He who dreams of apotheosis and of being a demigod, venerated by his public in an atmosphere of secular religiosity which does away with any rational analysis as a sacrilege. The charismatic leader likes nothing so much as to be considered a prophet and waited-for Messiah, a *deus ex machina* descending from his empyrean to help mere mortals with their problems.

Thus it was that the Third Reich staged gigantic spectacles, often in the evening, at Nuremberg, complete with spotlights and torch-lit processions. There were flags, standards and banners, emblems and cabalistic signs, uniforms and chants. With its romantic sumptuosity and Wagnerian overtones, the Hitlerian stage setting was reminiscent of a long-forgotten mass liturgy.

These ponderous affairs stage-managed by Goebbels culminated with the arrival of the *deus ex machina*, which had been preceded by a slow-paced ceremony. The apparition of the Magus was delayed as long as possible to use to the maximum the device of "waiting" that Marcel Mauss has studied.

A great ceremony in Nuremberg Stadium began in the morning with the arrival of "assistant directors." Delegations began arriving at 12:30 P.M. and took up their places behind their bands, each arrival being the occasion for salutes and cheers. At around 7 P.M. the party dignitaries arrived, followed by a period of recollection and solemn anticipation. Then Goebbels and Goering arrived, and finally Hitler himself, to be greeted by an enormous ovation. At the microphone, the Führer seemed to be trying out his voice for the first few minutes as he worked to establish an emotional contact with a crowd that was exhausted from waiting hours for its idol. The "hero," who mounted the rostrum to a roll of drums, also had a keyboard on the speaker's stand that enabled him to modulate the lighting at will.

The Nazi Opera included everything imaginable to create an effect of awe and illusion, including machinery to produce surprises of appearance and disappearance — as when Roehm and his group disappeared through a trap door. With all its stagecraft, this sort of theater did not only lend a sacred character to authority. It also magnified it through an opulent decor symbolizing wealth and, therefore, power.

As Roland Barthes writes in "The Ills of Theatrical Costuming," the third ill of theatrical costuming is money, a hypertrophy of sumptuosity, or at least its appearance.[5]

There are feathers, velvets, spangles, furs, silks, plumes, diadems, necklaces, and jewels. All these theatrical props have their equivalent on the political stage. There are heavily bedecked uniforms, marshal's batons, medals, bunches of decorations including cordons, crosses, stars, and palms. Dictator's outfits in the 1920s, 1930s, and 1940s would astonish even a theater costumes expert, as would that, today, of Marshal Idi Amin or Emperor Bokassa I. All such dress uniforms reveal a certain taste for theatrical costuming and play-acting.

The luxury of their decor is in harmony with their uniforms. Their quarters are decorated with marble, mirrors, gilt, chandeliers, and heavy curtains connoting prestige and ostenation. With their inevitable two basic colors, red and gold, the whole is designed to symbolize power and wealth.

Red evokes blood, sacrifice, ritual. In short, the supreme power of thanatocracies: death. Gold symbolizes both abundance and the solar myth.[6] The typical colors of the theater are thus those of heroic politics. For that matter, aren't heads of state always invited to the theater or opera during official visits?

When they get to the theater, they find a decor appropriate to supreme power: red carpets, luxurious draperies, trumpet fanfares, palatial marble, crystal chandeliers, and velvet plush. The decor of power is exactly the same as that of the theater.

GRAND PANJANDRUMS

With the support of all this luxurious gimmickry, the heroic actor creates a fabulous character poles apart from the average spectator. The model for such a character is "The Sublime," Sarah Bernhardt fascinating her public with her extravagance.

The Grand Sarah connoted remote mystery, even in her townhouse on Boulevard Péreire with its atmosphere of an oriental basaar full of carpets, copper trays, and divans. She also used stuffed wild animals and bear skins, and even a coffin lined with white satin — in which she liked to welcome her visitors — to promote the aura of myth around her.

Paris rendered a monumental tribute to her on December 9, 1896, at the Théatre de la Renaissance. Sitting on a throne in the middle of the stage, "The Sublime" received the rhymed offerings of poets while an orchestra played a hymn to her glory composed by the famous Gabriel Pierné. She was indeed, as Edmond Rostand had called her, "the Queen of poses and the Princess of gesture." With the mysterious character and deliberately hazy biographical details she created for herself, Bernhardt was truly the model to be followed by many leaders aspiring to the role of heroic authority figure.*

As de Gaulle put it in *The Sword's Edge*: "The great of this world prepare their appearances with great care. They do it with art. . . . Every page of Caesar's *Commentaries* shows us how much he polished his public gestures. And it is well known that Napoleon always made his public appearances in the most striking way."[7]

De Gaulle counselled the political actor to cultivate an air of mystery — "all cults have their inner sanctums" — and distance — "there is no authority without prestige, and no prestige without distance."[8] He should learn to fascinate the public, at bit like a professional actor: "The leader, like the artist, must have his natural gifts polished by professionalism."[9]

With his cloak of mystery and majestic distance, living in the solitude of the national palace, the hero plays the role of a legendary, sublime character noted for his genius. All this puts him as far as possible from the daily lot of his citizen-spectators, for his objective is to dazzle them in order to strengthen his grip on them.

This technique is the main device of fascism. Mussolini's model was d'Annunzio, the author-actor and warrior-tribune. It was the *Commandante* who marched on Fiume with his nationalist legionnaries to occupy it for a year by sheer rhetoric despite the Allies. With his imperial visage, brassy voice, and Roman salute, Mussolini played his theatrical role with eagles and buskins as props, the whole show evoking Caesar's Rome as seen by Cecil B. DeMille.

Not only does the hero leader adopt his style from the theater, he is also the product of his era's styles of set designing. Thus Hitler's style was marked by expressionism, which was the dominant form of theater during and after the First World War.

---

*Henry Kissinger actually compared himself to her when he left his job as secretary of state on January 19, 1977, saying humorously, "these last few days I've given more farewell performances than Sarah Bernhardt."

Expressionist theater is the medium of violent feeling such as anguish, vehemence, swoons, and ecstatic trances, all accompanied by broad gestures and excessive mime. Its typical actors were Werner Kraus, Konrad Veidt, Alexander Grenach, Max Schreck, and Fritz Kornern, who called himself "a vocal athlete." Describing the expressionist tragedian, Odette Aslan writes: "He must be wildly theatrical, fearing neither the grotesque nor excess nor even caricature. . . . Using his voice and large gestures, he acts on the spectator's senses with both audio and visual bombardments. . . . His movements follow one another without transition, becoming almost caricatural, as jerky as his lines. . . . His palms are either open as a sign of offering or clenched into fists. A grimacing face and twisted mouth accentuate his mimicry."[10]

Anyone reading these lines automatically thinks of Adolf Hitler, with his wild gesticulation, his verbal paroxysms, and his melodramatic declamation. For that matter, Hitler himself told how, after the First World War, he adapted his oratorical style to the needs of vast assemblies: "I acquired the dashing gestures required to fascinate a large hall filled with thousands."

In pre-Nazi Germany, Brecht denounced Hitler's theatricality which lent itself to hypnotizing crowds. He sought to restore the public's critical faculties in order to avoid this Fascist fascination. "At a time when life is becoming tragically theatrical, he is making the theater only too life-like," Brecht wrote. He was reacting against the prince, the chief, the warrior — against the hero, that master of illusion.

ART AND ARTIFICE

There is an evident link between dramatic or political art and the artifice used to obtain the desired effect. The personalization of power, the theatricality of public life is based on insincerity, false sentiments, and simulation. The term *person* derives from the Latin *persona*, meaning a mask used in the theater. And the word *hypocrisy* comes from the Greek for playacting.

In his *Paradoxe sur le Comedien*, Diderot investigated the question of sincerity and true feeling in the dramatic arts. Does an actor really feel joy, sadness, admiration, hate? No. He only feigns them. "Too much real feeling makes mediocre actors; it is the absolute lack of feeling that makes an actor sublime. An actor's tears fall from his head; those of a sensitive man fall from his heart."[11] The same is true of the political actor. "But, you may say, an orator is better when he is emotional, when he is angry. Not so. It is when he imitates anger that he is best. Actors impress the public not when they are furious, but when they project anger well."[12]

Charles Dullin observed that no one has to really feel an emotion in order to show it. Therefore art can reflect falsehood: "I have seen real tears shed, the actor blanche and suffer, carried away by his absolute sincerity, while the public remains unmoved. He was followed by another that pretended pain, and the theater was in an uproar. By his lack of sincerity he achieved the magnification necessary in the theater, communicating not suffering but the mask of suffering. . . ."[13]

Actually, three sorts of attitude are possible. Either the actor really becomes the character he is playing, or he maintains a certain distance from it, or he makes the character assume his own traits.

In the first case, the actor subordinated his own personality to that of the character, or at least to its supposed feelings. This is the method of Konstantin Stanislavski, in which the actor forces himself to "live" the role. Mikhail Tchekhov also advises actors to enter fully into the character's mentality.

It is also the expressionist method, which relies on strong feeling by the actor. Moved by a force that emanates from his own depths, the actor releases a series of emotions. The actor does not merely play a role, or pretend to be someone else, he lives and feels the drama of the play with all his senses.

Brecht reacted against this in favor of a second acting style, that of the Chinese theater, where the masked, impassive actor seems himself to feel none of the emotions affecting the character he plays. He does not resonate to the character's feelings or otherwise identify with him, but speaks his lines almost like a detached observer, distancing himself from the action.

The objective with this style is to keep the spectator from being overwhelmed by the emotion of theatrical illusion. On the contrary, the audience is invited to reflect critically by removing any aura of mystery. In short, by liberating the actor from the need to parody a character's feelings, the spectator is also freed from the fascination and alienation resulting from identifying with a character.

Without this distance, the spectator risks losing touch with the real world to identify with the hero as an ideal and unreal model. This process of projection-identification often leads the spectator to forget his real situation and to assimilate that of his class enemy: "One cannot identify with one's adversary with impunity; identification leaves traces, making you your own enemy."

Brecht favored a lucid spectator who retains his critical faculty, even in the presence of the "positive hero" so dear to Socialist realism and the present Chinese theater: "Man's finest quality is his ability to criticize. . . . He who identifies completely with another man in fact abandons the critical view both of himself and of the other. Instead of being on his guard, he dozes. Instead of doing things, he lets others do things to him. . . . He has the illusion of living, while in reality he is vegetating. Someone is living for him."[14]

This projection of the spectator, this fusing of egos is liable to culminate in the third school of acting, which is the most narcissistic: that in which the actor "becomes" the character.

This is the Lee Strasberg "Method" which was taught at the Actor's Studio, the school that shaped Brando, Dean, and Newman. Strasberg holds that the actor must use his imagination and subconscious, often by undergoing psychoanalysis to find his true personality unclouded by inhibitions and complexes. By drawing on his own personal experience on stage, he makes the character he is playing into himself.*

For the political actor, this means that he combines his personality with his position. He can personalize his job as far as he likes, the way Method actors subjectivize excessively the role they have been given — even if this leads to exhibitionism and an oversized ego.

Carried to the extreme, the *role* of president as cast by constitutional processes becomes less important than the *person* filling it. Like Louis XIV, they can say, *"L'état, c'est moi."* From Bourguiba to Castro, many political superstars encourage this cult of the ego which allows them to shape their position to fit their own personalities, making their official acts subject to their private whims.

The government show put on by such leaders can, through the free exhibition of their emotions, lead to catharsis. As described by Aristotle, this process purges the spectator of his emotions by letting him identify with those of the actor on stage. He thus lives by proxy,

---

*Some say that Giscard d'Estaing has secretly taken Strasberg's course.

with a semblance of life replacing real life. He lets another person live events that he has neither the time nor the means to live. He lets the hero live for him.

Politics today is becoming a theater of illusion, and it is the spectator that is under the illusion, diverted from real problems by the fascinating contemplation of a star actor giving vent to his emotions, some of which are sincere, others ficticious, and all egocentric. How can we deal with this sort of government show? How, except to echo André Malraux's phrase, "To be a man is to reduce the amount of play-acting in one's life."

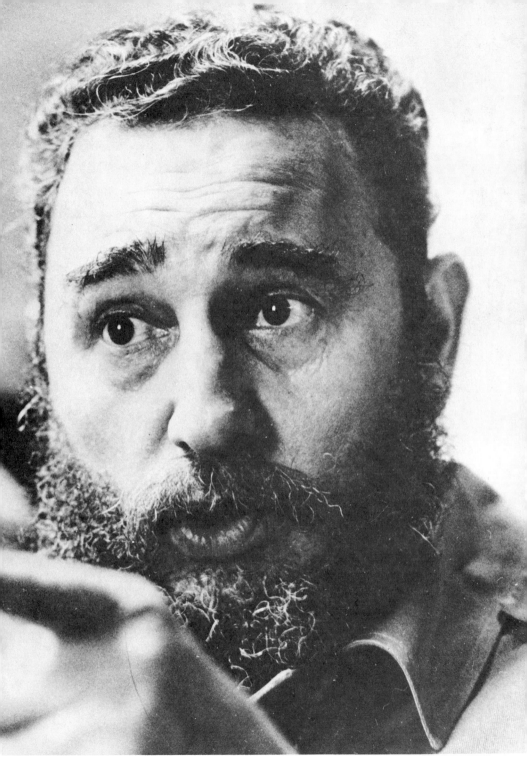

Cuban President Fidel Castro makes a point in Havana while playing host to Senator Frank Church (1977).

Former Secretary of State Henry Kissinger with Constance Towers, who played Anna in the Broadway revival of *The King and I* (1977).

Government as Cinema

*"I have lots of points in common with
Henry Kissinger. We are both concerned
about our egos and the image we
give of them."*
—RAQUEL WELCH

Moviemakers have always been interested in politicians, and
vice-versa. As early as 1912, Raoul Walsh followed Pancho Villa
around, filming his ambushes and executions. Villa even delayed them
by two to three hours so Walsh would have enough light to shoot the
scenes.

In Russia, Sergei Eisenstein made several films at Stalin's request,
including *Alexander Nevski* in 1938 and *Ivan the Terrible* in 1945,
both of which made the new regime appear to be the heir of a glorious
revolutionary tradition. In Germany, the "Mabuse" series from 1922
to 1933 sketched the portrait of a budding dictator, but when Goebbels
as propaganda minister asked Fritz Lang to become the Third Reich's
official film maker, Lang refused.

Hitler himself charged Leni Riefenstahl to film the Nazi rallies at
Nuremberg in 1934. The result was *The Triumph of Will*, which took
two years to make and included oceans of swastika flags, miles of
military parades, stylized eagles, rolling drums, and an omnipresent
Hitler whose profile stood out against the sky.

But the movies soon helped create a political style less stridently
heroic and melodramatic than that inspired by the theater and opera. At
the beginning, of course, early cinema techniques encouraged the
leader to pantomime heavily with excessive gestures and expressions.
The result was similar to expressionist theater. But it soon became
clear that the cinema offered possibilities unknown on the stage; for
example, the close-up, which abolished the distance between the actor

and the audience and made exaggerated gestures unnecessary. With the actor's image enlarged on the screen, even a trembling of the lips or batting of the eyelids would be magnified.

Then the talkies appeared, the theatrical delivery of lines was no longer the rule. A conversational tone — even a whisper — was easily heard by the audience, making actors adopt a more natural style.

Political leaders have adapted their style to this evolution of the dramatic arts. The hero leader necessarily has a style more suited to the theater or silent movies and is less able to use the new tone required by cinema and television, which is more sober, allusive, and elliptical. In this sense, de Gaulle was of the theater generation while Giscard d'Estaing belongs to the cinema and television generation that understands the need for a more nuanced "stage presence."

Another result of the cinema has been to make actors more influential as models to imitate, since they are so much more visible. It was this that gave rise to the star system, which for a long time was virtually the basis of the movie industry.

In a sense, the era of the star system can be broken down into three phases, each corresponding to three main types of stars. Each offered different models to the audience — and to political leaders.

The first phase was from 1920 to 1932, when stars were inaccessible, marmoreal, and inimitable. These were the idols, surrounded by an aura of myth. In short, they were the cinema equivalent of the hero leader.

Then, during the 1930s and 1940s, the star becomes more human. He or she, though still shining brightly, was less exceptional, a bit more like the rest of us. The star became a model that could be imitated — like the charm leader.

The third phase was in the 1950s and 1960s, when stars became virtually the reflection of the spectator if not, indeed, his double. It became more difficult to imitate a star, since he or she was already like everyone else. This corresponded to the political Mr. Everyman.

THE STAR-AS-IDOL AND THE HERO LEADER

In the 1920s and 1930s, movies were vehicles for dreams, and Hollywood was their capital.[1] It was the Hollywood that Joseph Kessel in 1936 called "more fascinating and more universal than all the world's sanctuaries." It was "the enchanted city," the "Olympus of studios," where "gods and godesses, objects of abject veneration" and "passionate devotion" inspired "veritable cults."[2] Two idols in particular reigned over this Olympus: Valentino and Garbo.

With his velvet eyes, catlike walk, and outrageous makeup, Rudolf Valentino[3] incarnated "Latin charm," as befited a Hollywood immigrant from the south of Italy. He moved the masses much as did that other idol of the 1920s and his compatriot, Benito Mussolini.

As Arab sheik, Roman noble, Argentine horseman, Spanish bullfighter, and American aviator, Valentino mined the myth of the seductor. He played it in five successful films: *The Four Horsemen of the Apocalypse* (which was shown in 69 countries), *The Sheik* (seen by 120 million people), *Blood and Sand, Monsieur Beaucaire,* and *Son of the Sheik.*

The hero is the object of a true cult based on periodic contact with the faithful during premieres, swings around the country, etc., somewhat the way a prince occasionally visits his people. His appearance gave rise to scenes of collective delirium, many of which were organized by his agent. Despite manful efforts by the police to protect him, his admirers ripped off his tie or buttons to keep as relics of their idol. Robert Florey, who knew Valentino, recalled the tumultuous crowds that greeted the star during his trips around the United States:

> In New York at the premiere of Young Rajah, the theater was assaulted by the crowd and Rudy had to escape over the roofs. In Louisville, Boston, Philadelphia, Cincinnati, from New Orleans to Spokane and from Washington to Denver, he was received like a king. We traveled at night in a special train, but we had to stop a few times in the Middle West to let Santa Fe expresses go by. Somehow girls in Kansas and Arizona got aboard the train at these stops and hid in the linen closets or toilets. They all wanted to see or kiss Rudy. The poor man had to lock himself in his compartment while I kept his admirers away. That went on for 54 days.[4]

Such idolatry — which political stars, dictators, or apprentice dictators, also provoked in the 1920s — culminated with Valentino's premature death. He had just finished *Son of the Sheik* when he died on August 23, 1926, at the age of 31.

Ten million women mourned him. Hundreds of thousands of Americans filed by his bronze catafalque during the week it stood in the Campbell Funeral Home. Nearly 100 persons were injured in the collective hysteria at his burial in a cemetery on Santa Monica Boulevard. Like the political hero (Stalin, Nasser, *et al.*) Valentino died amid the convulsions of his public, which refused to accept the death of its god. For years, flowers covered his tomb, and fan clubs were organized to keep alive his cult. In 1951, a quarter-century after his death, 70 fan clubs still bore his name. And in 1975 a new one was created in France.*

But it was not only seductors like Valentino or Ramon Novarro, his rival who triumphed in *Ben Hur*, who galvanized the masses. There were also feminine stars in the 1920s — like Greta Garbo.

The Swedish actress made a number of silent films in Hollywood during those years, like Monta Bell's *The Torrent* in 1926 and Fred Niblo's *The Temptress* (in which she played an Argentinian femme fatale). In 1927 it was Edmund Goulding's *Love*. In 1928, Niblo's *Dark Beauty* (in which she was a Russian spy in love with an Austrian officer). In 1929, it was Clarence Brown's *Intrigue's* (about the sacrifice of an English girl), and Sidney Franklin's *Land of Pleasure* (oriental travels and romance with a Japanese prince).

In all these pseudo-sophisticated romantic intrigues of the silent movies, Garbo was above all a face — a marvelous face photographed by William Daniels, her director of photography.

In his "Mythologies," Roland Barthes writes: "Garbo still belonged to that moment of the history of the movies when the impact of the human face on the audience was enormous. . . . A few years before, Valentino's face had caused suicides." Even if sometimes "the makeup was so thick it became a mask; this was not a painted face, it was literally plastered." Thus Garbo tended to imitate the actors of ancient theater who wore masks on stage. She offered her audiences "an archetype of the human face, a sort of Platonic idea of the human being."[5]

---

*Nearly 30 years after Rudolf Valentino, James Dean was killed at the wheel of his Porsche on September 30, 1955, and also became the object of a posthumous cult.

A silent close-up of Garbo partook of magic, of the supernatural. Indeed, she was called "The Divine" from the title of one of her films, *The Divine Woman* that she made in Hollywood with her countryman Victor Sjostrom. A dream creature in the real sense of the term, "The Divine" symbolized evanescent, inaccessible beauty. She was the eternal image of woman, the femme fatale, woman with a capital *W*. She was an enigmatic image created by the rays of a film projector. She was the diva, the goddess who raised womankind to the level of divinity — an idol and idea to be worshipped. To millions of spectators she represented an ideal of beauty which was magnified by the distance that silent movies imposed on faces. As Pierre Leprohon remarks, "the silent movies were not just a show. They were magic. And Greta Garbo was the magician who perhaps created the feminine myth for the last time."[6]

Garbo contributed to this idealization on the screen, on the sets and on the street by cultivating aloofness, mystery, and secrecy — all the devices used by the political hero. Untouchable, distant, inaccessible, she created a barrier between herself and the public, deliberately remaining as enigmatic as possible, the better to fascinate.

Pierre Leprohon notes: "There was a sort of halo around her. She arrived at the studio at 7A.M., before the camera crew, and shut herself up in her dressing room. During the shooting, she was hidden from everyone on the set except the director and cameraman — who were the same for ten years — by screens. She always traveled from her dressing room to the set by car. She lived as a recluse, deliberately ignoring those around her."[7]

She, as the haughty, remote, schizophrenic idol, hidden beneath her hoods and behind her sunglasses, concealed, paradoxically, in order to promote her fame. She, thus, resembled the political hero, lost in the solitude of his power and isolated in his great official residence, riding in black limousines and cordoned off by bodyguards. In both cases, the act is carefully calculated to dazzle the public with rare and much awaited appearances.

"The Divine" corresponded to the mythical, remote, and solemn style of the dictators of the 1920s and 1930s, such as Mussolini, Hitler, and Franco. One can also say that Garbo prefigured de Gaulle, the de Gaulle who applied the precepts of *The Sword's Edge* with its advice to political superstars. Let us not forget: "Such a leader is distant, for there is no authority without prestige and no prestige without distance."[8] Or again, "there can be no prestige without mystery, for people do not respect what they know too well."[9] Or still again, "the great man carefully arranges his appearances."[10]

Then came talking movies. After 1930 Garbo played other roles such as Mata-Hari, Queen Christina, Anna Karenina again, the Dame aux Camelias. Her voice, deep and husky, was what the public expected, but suddenly she lacked part of her mystery and dreamlike quality. The goddess had become a woman. The myth disappeared in the face — and voice — of human reality.

Silence becomes the hero. Here again one remembers the advice in *The Sword's Edge:* "Sobriety of speech accentuates the pose. Nothing enhances authority better than silence."[11]

In 1941 her film *Two-Faced Woman* failed at the box office. And Garbo, at 37, left movies at the height of her glory to become a legend. Even in retirement she continued to nurture her image, just as de Gaulle did following his defeats in January 1946 and April 1969.

THE STAR-MODEL AND THE CHARM LEADER

Then came the second phase of the star system, which began about 1930 and which corresponds in politics to the charm leader.

Movies changed, and stars changed with them. The era of the myth-shrouded, inaccessible idol was over. Certain stars of silent movies had been gods or goddesses with whom no one could identify. But with the talkies, films became more realistic. Their scripts were more believable and their stars began to resemble the spectators, although remaining an idealization. As André Bazin writes: "Close enough to permit us to identify with him, ideal enough to be more than simply a projection of our desires, the modern star is no longer that implacable sun which burned its worshipers."

While still well above the ordinary, the new star could better satisfy the public's affective needs. By combining "the exceptional and the real, the ideal and the quotidian," he could "offer a greater chance of identification."[12]

Like the charm leader, the stars of the 1930s, 1940s, and occasionally even the 1950s combined distance and closeness, superiority and equality, difference and resemblance. They were no longer gods or idols, but men or women who could serve as models to the public. They ceased being objects of hysteria to become examples of behavior.

Thus Gary Cooper was the perfect illustration of the ideal American, the prototype that everyone could hope to resemble, just as everyone in an idyllic and democratic America could hope to rise to the highest social level. Clark Gable, Cary Grant, Gregory Peck, and others filled the same role. And perhaps today Robert Redford, with his imitation of Kennedy in *The Candidate*, is following in that line.

In France, many stars corresponded to this new style: Albert Préjean, Henri Garat, Jean Babinin in his early days, Jean Marais during the war, Gerard Philipe, who died at 37 and was perhaps the last of the romantic matinee idols, and then Jean-Claude Brialy, Jean-Pierre Cassel, and above all Alain Delon.

Ceasing to be utterly inaccessible, these stars represent what everyone would like to be, an ideal to attain. In that they resemble the charm leader, whether the Kennedy brothers, Jerry Brown, Trudeau, Palme, or Schmidt. We have gone from the remote star to the close star, much as we often alternate between a hero type like Franco or de Gaulle and a charm leader like Adolfo Suárez or Giscard d'Estaing. Even if the charmers do have to affect their naturalness with props like rumpled sweaters, coffee cups on the table, or bouquets of flowers in hand.

On the feminine side, the close star becomes the pin-up girl whose obvious sex appeal replaces the unreal attraction of yesterday's goddesses. We have gone through several successive generations of them, from Jean Harlow to Clara Bow, Carole Lombard, Joan Crawford, Norma Shearer, Myrna Loy, Irene Dunne, and Paulette Goddard. Then came Rita Hayworth, Jane Russell, Marilyn Monroe, Jayne Mansfield, and Elizabeth Taylor. In Europe they have been Martine Carol, Gina Lollobrigida, and Sophia Loren.

THE STAR AS REFLECTION OF THE COMMON MAN

The last phase of stardom began in the 1950s and saw the star, after having been an idol and then a model, become a reflection. The actor ceased to be the spectator's hero or even his ideal. He became his mirror.

The star became, in a word, ordinary: the boy (or girl) next door. This corresponded to the evolution of the political leader, who became the common man, more in harmony with the democratic and egalitarian sentiment of today. Both movie and political actors are now like the rest of us. They represent us, in a double sense: the actor represents us as we are on the screen, and the politician represents us in the nation's capital.

One segment of the population that is well represented by actors is youth. In Laszlo Benedek's *The Wild One*, for example, Marlon Brando reflected juvenile delinquency for the first time on the screen. He was followed by James Dean, who faithfully interpreted adolescent feeling in Nicholas Ray's *Rebel Without a Cause*.

Similarly, Brigitte Bardot became the interpretor-reflection of youth's aspirations and impulse to revolt, especially in Roger Vadim's *And God Created Woman* in 1956. With her nonchalance and freedom with her body, Bardot created a style and look that her feminine admirers could immediately imitate.

"The device of remoteness," notes Pierre Leprohon," which was key to Garbo's success and prestige, is reversed by today's stars. Now they achieve stardom by being so real that the spectator can identify with them."[13]

In fact, today's stars help everyone be like everyone else. They are the anti-hero, the anti-idol. Thus American movie stars are most often very ordinary young men who are distinguished neither by their handsomeness nor by any other unusual trait. They are like Dustin Hoffman, with his short stature, heavy features, and hunched shoulders, or like Jack Nicholson, Al Pacino, Elliott Gould, not to mention Woody Allen. French stars have adopted the same style: Jean-Paul Belmondo, Gerard Depardieu, and Patrick Dewaere are typical, as are Annie Girardot, Marlene Jobert, and Miou-Miou.

As actress Anne Vernon notes sadly, "today the theory is that you have to be like everybody else in order to please as large an audience as possible." Without being farfetched, one can also say that this is also the rule of thumb of leaders like Callaghan, Fälldin, and especially Carter with his deliberate effort to be the average American.

THE PUT-ON

Thus does the world of show business influence the world of politics. Show business in this sense includes singers and even boxers as well as professional actors. Indeed, many of today's "idols" are singers who inspire more collective fetishism and frenzy than actors. In boxing, General Mobutu was glad to organize the Ali-Foreman match in Zaire, and Marshal Amin is proud of his past as a boxing champion.

Many leaders, especially in the Third World, act like Rolling Stones of politics or Muhammad Alis of authority. Many of their political rallies resemble singers' fan clubs, and many of their speeches resemble singers' stage performances.

True, today's styles have removed the aura of myth around a star. But rock concerts and movie theaters still run on the star system. No director can find a producer unless he has signed up a Robert Redford, Paul Newman, Marlon Brando, Richard Burton, Elizabeth Taylor, or Barbra Streisand in the lead role. The movie giants are not about to become dwarfs.[14]

So the process of projection-identification continues. Transformed into a voyeur, the spectator lives, loves, and acts vicariously, thanks to the adventures of screen stars, just as he is content to let the political star substitute for his own participation in politics.

This admiration for a star, whether cinematographic or political, thus fulfills a latent function. Unconsciously the spectator — or the citizen — charges the star with giving him the satisfaction that he cannot give himself. He extends himself beyond his personal limits by contemplating the star, living and feeding his self-esteem by proxy, as when El Zorro beats the bad guy or when Idi Amin defies the rest of the world. And this is how alienation as described by Feuerbach comes to affect the individual spectator-citizen. He transfers the best of himself outside himself, to an exterior idol, through a process of myth projection.

As Malraux said: "Marlene Dietrich is not an actress like Sarah Bernhardt; she is a myth like Phryné." But a myth is in fact composed of a complex of imaginary behavior and situations. In truth, these stars, both in the movies and in politics, are false stars, fabricated by masters of illusion — directors or campaign managers — who excell at molding them into the desired form.

The Dietrich myth, for instance, was created by Josef von Sternberg, who took a fairly ordinary German girl and made a femme fatale of her. The Garbo myth began thanks to photographs taken by a magazine photographer named Arnold Genthe. It was developed by Mauritz Stiller, the producer who taught her how to dress, how to play her roles, how to be. There were also Adrian, the MGM costumer who dressed her to best effect, and Daniel Williams, the director of photographer who excelled at capturing the expressions on her face.

Many stars have their favorite cameraman who is expert at producing the best image of them, as well as their favorite lighting and makeup specialists. Cameramen are particularly valued who know how to select the angle that enhances the star's best profile, or makes him look taller.

Then there are all the artifices of makeup to make the most of a face. The Westmore brothers — Mont, Perc, Ern, Wally, Bud, and Frank — reigned over the studios of Hollywood from 1920 to 1950. Today, Frank Westmore has published such sad revelations as the fact that Clark Gable's brilliant smile was due to false teeth and that Shirley Temple's golden curls were a wig.[15] It seems that even Rudolf Valentino was near-sighted, short, skinny, and probably a bit bald. But on the screen he had velvet eyes, a noble stature, and shining, raven-black hair.

Also contributing to the star-product are beauticians, masseurs, hairdressers, costumers, dentists, and plastic surgeons.

Similarly, today's political leaders also have their Pygmalions. There are, first of all, the campaign managers, the political equivalent of film directors, who are expert at modeling plastic politicians. Clem Whitaker, Stuart Spencer, and Joseph Napolitan did as much for their candidates as Stiller and Sternberg did for the stars they created.

Some political actors become no more than malleable marionettes, manipulated by media managers who assure that they get the right spot upstage. In such cases, the perfect political star becomes an empty automation with a manager for a soul. Both movie and political actors thus become, like marionettes, the creatures of those who pull the strings.

Moreover, the rise of television as a political medium has led politicians to imitate movie stars in having their own photographers, lighting men, makeup artists, dentists, and plastic surgeons, in order to project a sparkling smile and generally attractive image. In France, Georges Pompidou was said to have plucked his eyebrows, which were considered too bushy by many voters. In England, Harold Macmillan trimmed a mustache found too old-fashioned by numerous feminine voters. Edward Heath had his teeth arranged. In the U.S., Pat Brown lost 14 pounds in order to compete better with Ronald Reagan's svelte figure. And so on.

Result: the physical and moral image of the leader, like that of the movie star, is often different from reality. As early as 1936, Joseph Kessel wrote of Hollywood stars: "When you see them close-up as they really are, it is impossible not to be disappointed." He was "truly terrified by the difference from the reality and the image. . . . The cameraman, makeup artist, hairdresser, and lighting specialist are no longer there to protect the star, who is reduced to being himself."[16] Thus function those "dream machines" that are Twentieth Century Fox, MGM, Paramount, and Universal.

Today, some campaign management firms which produce political publicity spots are themselves dream machines. They fabricate a physical and especially moral image of a leader that often has little relation to reality. As little relation as Valentino's myth, for example. For the great seducer, in fact, showed little interest in women. And the noble and pure hero was discovered and launched by the script writer June Mathis, whose house he had burgled.

What is a great actor, after all, except a master of disguise? "An actor?" said the French actor Michel Simon, "It's a man who wants to become someone else because he feels ill at ease with himself." Similarly, the political actor plays the hero, the common man, the charm leader, or father figure as does any professional actor, by becoming someone else.

But what does professionalism mean in this instance? Garson Kanin recalls that he's known many amateur actors who thought they were professionals, but Charles Laughton was the only professional actor he knew of who claimed to be an amateur. Laughton said he was proud to be an amateur in the etymological sense of the term; that is, someone who loves what he does. He used to say, "professionals are whores."[17]

SHOW BUSINESS LINKS WITH POLITICS

Actually, show business pros and political pros have a lot in common, as if their common problems gave rise to common solutions and outlooks. Indeed, the two worlds mix increasingly, to the point where some stage and screen stars take part in political campaigns, especially in the United States. In 1960, Frank Sinatra, Dean Martin, Sammy Davis, Jr., and Peter Lawford — who was Kennedy's brother-in-law — actively supported JFK. In 1964 Ronald Reagan, Clint Walker, and John Wayne campaigned on television for Barry Goldwater.

In 1968, John Wayne, Pat Boone, and Connie Francis supported Nixon, whereas Humphrey and Muskie wound up their campaign that year with a TV show on ABC that included 40 show business personalities such as Johnny Carson, Paul Newman, and Nancy Sinatra.

In 1972, Sammy Davis, Jr., and John Wayne were boosters at the Republican National Convention — where Wayne made a speech — that renominated Nixon. On the Democratic side, Warren Beatty gave up movies for two years to devote himself full time to promoting George McGovern. His sister, Shirley MacLaine, supported the same ticket, traveling 20,000 miles and becoming a delegate at the Democratic National Convention.

Dustin Hoffman, who supported the same candidate, nevertheless questioned the position of an actor who gets into politics: "I didn't feel quite right about it. It was a little like doing advertising. It's so easy for someone used to creating characters to do the same in real life."[18]

In 1976 Warren Beatty welcomed Jimmy Carter to Hollywood and gave a party in his honor at the Beverly Wilshire Hotel, which was attended by Faye Dunaway, Diana Ross, and Peter Falk. In June, Elizabeth Taylor, wearing a golden peanut pendent, participated in a fund-raising drive for Carter, who was also supported by Candice Bergen, Jane Fonda, Shirley MacLaine, Bob Dylan, Henry Fonda, Paul Newman, and Robert Redford.

Gerald Ford recruited his supporters among older stars like Yvonne de Carlo, Irene Dunne, and Eva Gabor. Others, like Fred Astaire, Glenn Ford, and John Wayne, went over to Ford after supporting Reagan. And Betty Ford was introduced to the Republican Convention by 72-year-old Cary Grant.

In France, show business stars are more reserved about getting into politics, but the situation is changing. In 1974, Brigitte Bardot, Sylvie Vartan, and Johnny Hallyday publically supported Giscard d'Estaing, whose rally on May 16 at Paris' Sports Palace began with a show by Charles Aznavour, Philippe Clay, Mireille Mathieu, and Michel Sardou.[19] The opposition left was supported by singers Dalida, Jean Ferrat, Juliette Greco, Mouloudji, and actor Michel Piccoli.[20]

But the phenomenon goes beyond mere support, with some show business stars actually entering politics. For that matter, some politicians end up on stage and screen.

In 1974, Vanessa Redgrave ran for election in a London Suburb on the Workers' Revolutionary Party ticket. That same year, Melina Mercouri and Mikis Theodorakis were candidates in Athens. In 1976, the producer Gillo Pontecorvo ran on the Communist ticket in Rome and his fellow producer Damiano Damiani was on the Socialist list.

And we must not forget that Eva Perón was in theater, cinema, and radio before assuming her political role in Argentina; Isabel Perón, or course, was a folk dancer before succeeding her husband as president.

But again it is in the United States that most of this crossing of lines takes place. In 1952, for example, the actor George Murphy was an adviser to General Eisenhower. In 1956, Joseph and Stewart Alsop reported that the Republican party had engaged Murphy "to stage the National Convention in practically the same way a director stages a film."[21] In 1964, Murphy went all the way into politics and beat Pierre Salinger to become a senator from California. In 1966, actor Ronald Reagan became the state's governor, beating the incumbent Democrat Pat Brown who was running for a third term.

Reagan, born in 1911, started his film career in 1937 and made nearly 50 films. In many he was cast as an unrequited lover, despite his good looks.* He referred to himself as "the Errol Flynn of B pictures" and liked to recall that he was usually "the nice guy who didn't get the girl."[22] Reagan married twice, each time with actresses: Jane Wyman in 1940, Nancy Davis in 1952. From 1947 to 1952 and again in 1959, he was president of the Actor's Guild, the powerful film actors' union in Hollywood. That was where he got his taste for politics. He made

---

*In 1940, a sculpture class at University of Southern California chose him to pose as "the Adonis of the 20th Century."

his start in 1964 when he campaigned on television for the Republican candidate for the White House, Barry Goldwater.

Elected governor of California in 1966 and reelected in 1970, Reagan was the ultra-conservative champion of law and order. He ordered the death penalty for the first time since 1963, severely suppressed student riots at Berkeley, and revoked the rector of the University of California. He ran against Gerald Ford in 1976 for the Republican nomination for president. Although he beat the incumbent president in several primaries, he missed the nomination in August 1976, but garnering 1,070 votes to Ford's 1,187. It was a tight race all the way, with even Betty Ford and Nancy Reagan — respectively a former dancer and a former actress — playing their appearances at the convention for maximum votes.

Even the former child star of the 1930s, Shirley Temple, since become Mrs. Black, went into politics. An active California Republican, she ran for Congress but lost before being named by Nixon in August 1969 to the American delegation to the United Nations. Later, in August 1974, she was named ambassador to Ghana.

In France, the actor Roger Hanin ran in 1968 against Albin Chalandon, but lost.

But occasionally the line is crossed in the other direction as well.

In November 1975 the former vice-president Spiro Agnew, who was forced to resign because of alleged corrupt practices, became Frank Sinatra's press secretary. The following year he was one of the few persons invited — along with Reagan — to Sinatra's wedding when he married for the fourth time. Shortly afterward, Agnew published *The Canfield Decision*, a novel about power, violence, and sex.

Another politician got into show business in 1972, when John Lindsay, defeated for the Democratic nomination, became one of the stars of the film *Rosebud*. And in 1976 he too published a novel, *The Edge*, in which the protagonist is an ambitious congressman divided between his wife and his mistress. As the author admitted, "there's a certain obligatory dose of sex in any book."[23]

Sometimes, political leaders still in office make a brief appearance in the world of show business.

There was, for instance, Walter Scheel, who while West Germany's vice-chancellor and minister of foreign affairs in 1973 recorded an old popular song, *Hoch auf dem gelben Wagen*. Profits went to a fund for handicapped children, and there was plenty of money for them when the record became number one on the German hit parade. The vice-chancellor did the song on TV and saw his popularity zoom; a few months later, in 1974, he became president of the country.

Giscard d'Estaing has also had his fling. When he was still minister of finance in 1969, he played the accordion on a TV show. He did it again in 1971 at his party's convention in Toulouse. In 1973 he was on the bill at the World Accordion Festival in Montmorency, and made his historic declaration: "If everyone played the accordion, we would all get along together."[24]

After becoming president, Giscard continued to make an occasional foray into show business, if only for the children of the Elysée staff at the traditional Christmas tree festivities.

Former British Prime Minister Edward Heath likes to indulge his taste for symphony conducting, having led the London Symphony Orchestra in two concerts in April 1975 in Bonn. With wry humor he explains that he has more success leading orchestras than the Conservative party, because "the orchestra has only 120 musicians, but there are 276 Conservatives in the House of Commons."[25]

As a final instance of this intermingling of politics and show business there is the habit of making films of the lives of politicans. Alain Delon in France played Jacques Chaban-Delmas in *Is Paris Burning?* in 1964, and Cliff Robertson played John Kennedy in the film made from Robert Donovan's book, *PT-109*. Kennedy liked the book, which portrayed his wartime exploits in the Pacific. He thought it would make a good film, and his father, Joseph P. Kennedy, put in a word with Jack Warner, president of Warner Brothers, who agreed to do it. In the film's contract John Kennedy reserved the right to approve the script and the choice of actor to play him. "The president," Pierre Salinger tells us, "had definite ideas about the actor he wanted to play his part. It was Warren Beatty."

Kennedy therefore dispatched Salinger by plane to Los Angeles to try to convince Beatty to take the role. He met Beatty at Peter Lawford's, but Beatty refused because he did not get along with Warner's director, Brian Foy. So Warner and Foy ran screen tests on a number of candidates for the role and sent them to the White House. Kennedy and Salinger looked at them and finally chose Cliff Robertson, who got the role.

Meanwhile, Kennedy dismissed Raoul Walsh, the director chosen by Warner, in favor of Lewis Milestone, who was in turned replaced by Lee Martison late in the shooting. As a result of all this, the film's cost went will beyond its budget to $5 million — and still turned out to be one of Warner's worst box office flops.[26]

That episode illustrates the common bonds of feeling and style that link the worlds of politics and show business. Political stars and movie stars share the same preoccupations with their image, and the same exhibitionist tendencies. All of which brings to mind Raquel Welch's remark about the former secretary of state: "I have lots of points in common with Henry Kissinger. We are both concerned about our egos and the image we give of them during our brief moments of glory."[27]

And Robert Altman was really only giving an accurate idea of the similarities between show business and politics when he showed in his film *Nashville* how much a popular music festival resembled the campaign for the White House.[28]

Former Governor Ronald Reagan during an address in Atlanta (1979).

President Franklin Delano Roosevelt who, for all practical purposes, invented media politics.

Mediapolitics

Today leaders adapt their style to mediapolitics, or politics as
deformed and degraded by the mass media. For if the star system has
become the basis of politics, it is largely thanks to the media. Every
politician must know how to be "mediagenic" in order to get the most
out of the mass media which, oddly, are a throwback to ancient forms
of communication. Communication has always been the product of a
given technological and sociological situation. At different times in
history it has been based either on oral or written expression, the two
permanent means — along with images — of communication.

From ancient times until the 15th century, communication was
mainly through voice and gesture, limited to the fundamental
techniques of the orator. But this sort of communication is limited to a
small audience, like that of Demosthenes or Cicero. This drawback
became evident when the city-state became the nation-state, with the
population going from thousands to millions. The time no longer
existed when a speaker could be heard by his fellow citizens gathered
on the Agora or the Forum. There was communication through images,
but its only media were statues, portraits, and coins. In Rome,
statesmen's portraits were engraved on coins, along with a symbol or
slogan. Toward the end of the Roman republic, civil warlords vied
with each other to distribute the most coins bearing their images.
Under the empire, the emperor minted coins with his portrait on them,
as well as a motto. In this way the inhabitants of the immense empire
learned the features of their leader and received from him a political
message, albeit highly condensed.

Louis XVI was the heir — and the victim — of this personalized method of communication, when Jean Drouet recognized him thanks to a coin bearing his features and arrested him as he fled the revolutionaries on June 21, 1791.

But by then we had already entered the second era of communication, for after the 15th century printing began to replace the voice and image. This new technique led to a new kind of propaganda: books, pamphlets, and especially newspapers. Aided by better printing methods and widespread education, the press reached its apogee in the 19th and early 20th centuries. This form of written communication addressed itself mainly to the judgement and critical faculties of the reader. It possessed a great degree of intellectual and rational content, and was less based on the emotions than the preceding forms. It left its mark on styles of propaganda, which had to be less personalized and more carefully programmed. Political debates conducted in the press had to be more about ideas than about persons.

Then came the third and last phase: the return to communication through voice and image. Loudspeakers enabled orators to reach vast audiences, and when radio came along there was no doubt that voice communication was far more important than any other. Photographs began to modify newspaper content, and the image regained its former power through movies and, most importantly, television.

Since then, communication has been dominated by its emotional and personal content, while intellectual and rational content has faded. Books and newspapers, the whole "Gutenberg effect," have yielded to the "Marconi effect" as the audio-visual media emphasize the face and voice, facts and gestures rather than analysis. We have come full circle and are back to preprinted forms of communication.

In many ways this constitutes a regression. Communication and especially propaganda have become more elementary, with less intellectual content. Based on the voice and image of the leader, today's news show put on by the press, radio, and television places the emphasis on emotion rather than rational judgment.

FRONT PAGE

Many great politicians have been journalists. In France, there were Camille Desmoulins and Jean Paul Marat, then Georges Clemenceau, who made his comeback to public life after the Panama Canal scandal via journalism. Jean Jaurès worked at *L'Humanité*, and Léon Blum at *Le Populaire*.

The democratic system aids this, for to govern is to persuade and to move public opinion. But the press can also serve to "sell" persons even more than ideas, and some politicians realized this early on.

The Gazette de France, founded in 1631 by Theophraste Renaudot, became a quasi-official journal of information and propaganda filled with articles by Louis XIII and Richelieu, who wrote under pen names. Later, Napoleon Bonaparte used the press to embelish the facts and to create his own legende. While still in Italy he launched two papers to popularize his campaigns, and later distributed numerous pamphlets vaunting his merits. He took journalists along with him to Egypt and started publishing the *Courrier d'Egypte*.

Back in Paris, *Le Moniteur* became a sort of official political record, with many articles written by Napoleon's cabinet ministers. Other papers had to conform to certain ground rules: "The Emperor," notes one historian, "gradually became a kind of editor-in-chief of the nation's press, indicating which subjects to avoid and which to cover."[1]

These two examples, chosen among many others, show how much interest statesmen take in the press. Some even become journalists in order to promote their image.

Many of their contemporary counterparts do the same. Mussolini started out as editor of the Socialist newspaper, *Avanti*. And Nasser kept close watch on the press, the better to get coverage for himself and the plots prepared against him. As Jean Lacouture writes, "He was always hanging around the pressroom, looking over the paper's makeup, correcting articles, selecting headlines and type faces. One day, Abdel Hadim Amer told him, 'You missed your vocation. You should have been a journalist.' And Nasser replied seriously, 'You're right.'"[2]

Kennedy was also strongly attracted to the press. Once when he was asked what he would like to do after spending eight years in the White House, assuming he won a second term, he replied, "I'd probably like to run a newspaper."[3]

This is often the case with charm leaders, fascinated as they are by speed and change. While he was a student, Olof Palme worked on the Swedish conservative daily, *Svenska Dagbladet*.[4] And in France,

Jean-Jacques Servan-Schreiber used his position as editor of the newsweekly L'Express to launch his political career in 1969.

For that matter, today's press tends to lend itself to the political star system. For a long time — particularly in the 19th century — it was the forum of debate for the great political ideas. With many different papers representing the whole spectrum of political thought, the press of opinion was the medium for analyses and polemics going to the heart of the problems of the day. It stimulated readers to criticize and reflect on politician's ideas.

Then the journalism of opinion declined, much of it disappearing in the face of competition from mass circulation, illustrated newspapers that gave "facts." They also reduced analysis and commentary, devoting the space to photos of politicians.

The motto of Pierre Lazareff, longtime editor of the mass circulation daily France-Soir, was, "explain ideas through facts and the facts through people."[5] One of his former staff members, Jean Ferniot, recalls that Lazareff repeated almost daily, "make your stories interesting, make the characters come to life."[6]

Thus does the press today systematically personify everything, making events comprehensible through the men and women who make news, symbolizing government by those who exercise power. Describing "the cult or rather the illustration of personality by today's press," Jean Ferniot remarks: "Newspapers personalize as often as possible. . . The public is more interested in people than in abstractions. It is more interesting to read 'Kennedy writes to de Gaulle' than 'the United States has sent a message to the French president.'"[7]

Journalists deliberately look for anecdotes, the little touches of personality that go to make up a portrait of a news maker. Their efforts are supplemented by the large amount of space devoted to photos in most papers, except a few rare ones like the French daily Le Monde, which published none at all.

As a result, politics as reported in most papers is reduced to the level of mere anecdote. When elections come, readers have to cast their votes on the basis of a candidate's life-style, having had their attention thoroughly diverted away from the real problems and issues.

By avoiding the fundamental issues and oversimplifying, today's press tends to lull the public to sleep, dulling its critical sense and preparing it to react to its leaders emotionally rather than rationally.

THE GOVERNMENT AND THE FOURTH ESTATE

This favor is returned. While the press is doing all it can to personalize power, politicians are cordially courting its representatives. This has gone on for some time, as Robert de Jouvenel noted in *La République des camarades:*

> No cabinet member would ever refuse an interview, even to a reporter from the least important paper imaginable. At the French National Assembly, even the most powerful politicians of the day stop in the foyer to shake hands with reporters and discuss their projects with them. If a congressman neglects these little conversations for too long, he can be seen wandering sadly through the corridors looking for a journalist who will listen to what he has to say for public consumption.[8]

Twenty years later, André Tardieu bitterly observed the same exhibitionism: "Among parliamentarians, the press holds a very important place due to the publicity it provides . . . They are constantly asking for little favors. 'Be sure to say I was the one who proposed the amendment' one will say. 'Don't forget to mention that I signed the bill' calls another. 'Put it in the headline that I demanded severance of the resolution' says a third."[9]

Today too, those who neglect or mistreat the press often have to pay the consequences. Vice-president Agnew, for example, began a series of attacks on the press in November 1969, calling it out of step with the "silent majority." Later he had to resign when the press uncovered his misdeeds, as of course did Nixon after the press' Watergate coverage.

But others know how to charm the press, like Kennedy who was always very accessible to journalists, giving out information abundantly, about even personal details, and generally creating good rapport with newspeople.

Pierre Salinger, his press secretary, relates how the Kennedy organization won journalists' favor during the 1960 campaign by making their job easier. "We laid on press planes, reserved hotel rooms and made sure that each newsman's bags got to his room, provided buses so they could follow him on the road, and set up press rooms in hotels with extra telephones and telegraph lines."[10]

The press was also aided — and influenced — with biographical material on the candidate, as Salinger put it, "to make it easier to do articles on JFK.''[11] There was immediate transcription and distribution of every remark he made during the campaign.

Newsmen following Kennedy had the full text of his speeches and remarks fifteen minutes after they were made. Thus the reporters could relax and enjoy Kennedy's eloquence, knowing that they would have an accurate transcription handed to them a few minutes later.[12]

The candidate also rotated groups of three newsmen with him on his personal plane to give them the chance to discuss issues freely with him.

Such attention to the press paid off. This amiability, wrote Theodore White, this respect and familiarity with the press influenced all the reporting on the Kennedy campaign, and lack of it influenced reporting in the opposite direction on the Nixon campaign.[13]

Once he had won the election, Kennedy was as attentive to the press' needs as ever. According to Theodore Sorensen, reporters received "twice as much information about the White House as in the past." And through new channels. Salinger gave two short briefings per day to the press, and the president himself often met with the top editors of newspapers and magazines, who were invited to informal press luncheons at the White House. The biggest names in journalism — James Reston, Walter Lippmann, Joseph and Stewart Alsop, Marquis Childs and Joseph Kraft — got special treatment. According to Salinger, if one of them asked to meet the president personally, he generally obtained satisfaction. When there was a crisis, they automatically contacted them to give them the background on the government's attitude. Often the president briefed them himself. Sometimes, for example, he would talk with Lippmann on the telephone or invite him over to the White House.[14]

During Christmas vacation in 1961 and 1962, Kennedy organized several meetings with the 25 accredited White House journalists at Cape Cod and Palm Beach to review the year's events. As Sorensen noted, the annual reviews (which would have been published in any case) thus received better coverage.[15]

Candidates used this same method during the 1976 campaign. In early July, Carter invited over a hundred journalists, relatives, and neighbors to a lunch of fried fish at his mother's house in the woods near Plains. A few days later, Reagen invited 80 reporters and his team of assistants to a Mexican fiesta at his Rancho del Cielo in the Santa Inez mountains 100 miles from Los Angeles. Wearing a western shirt, blue jeans, and boots, and with a Stetson on his head, Reagan shouted with a smile at a television cameraman, "Ready when you are, C.B.!"[16]

PRESS CONFERENCES

Once elected, the new leader's main way of keeping the press informed is the press conference.

Woodrow Wilson inaugurated periodic conferences with the press, holding them twice a week in his office. The presidential press conference lost some of its spontaneity under Harding and Coolidge , and some of its frequency under Hoover. During his first year in the White House, Hoover held one conference every two weeks on average; his last year there he held only one per month.

Roosevelt, on the other hand, gave press conferences twice a week for 30 or 40 newsmen. Under Truman the number went up to 150 for his animated and often controversial conferences. It was at that time that the press conference was transported from the president's office to a room in the State Department, not far from the White House.

Eisenhower also used the Indian Treaty Room at the State Department for the conferences he held for 250 or more journalists, including, for the first time, TV crews. Eisenhower and his press secretary, Jim Hagerty, authorized television to film the conference and to broadcast it later, after the White House had checked it. Kennedy and Salinger did away with the check, allowing live TV coverage. The first of these televised press conferences was held in the conference room of the State Department, which Salinger described thus:

> It was big enough to hold the largest audience we could possibly hope for. But thanks to a system of mobile partitions in the back, we could reduce the room's size on days when fewer newsmen showed up. That way, the president's press conferences were always standing room only — and that is the only concession to TV show business that I admit to.[17]

For that matter, Kennedy never drew less than 400 reporters and photographers at each of his 62 press conferences in Washington, or an average of 21 per year. This compared to 83 for Roosevelt, 24 for Eisenhower, 21 for Johnson, and 7 for Nixon.[18]

On the eve of each press conference, Kennedy's aides tried to imagine the 20 or 30 questions that would be asked the next day, and prepared appropriate documentation on them. Salinger passed this to Kennedy late in the afternoon, and he studied it before going to sleep that night.

At breakfast the next day he rehearsed with his chief advisors. "I sat opposite JFK," Salinger reports, "and while he ate his ham and eggs I riddled him with questions phrased the way I expected the newsmen to ask them." The president took a nap after lunch to be in good shape. "Bundy, Sorenson and I woke him at 3 P.M. and gave him additional documentation while he dressed."[19] The press conference began at 4 P.M. at the State Department.

Whenever he could, Kennedy screened the press conference afterward. He was often critical of himself, exclaiming, "I could have got out of that one better," "What awful lighting!" or "That camera angle is killing me!"[20]

This free-swinging, spontaneous tone contrasted sharply with the atmosphere in press conferences given by other Western leaders at the time. As Sorensen has mentioned, before each conference got under way, Kennedy would say half-seriously that he did not particularly like confronting journalists, that he envied General de Gaulle, who held only two press conferences a year and accepted only questions carefully prepared in advance, and for which he had learned the answers by heart.[21]

Salinger underlined this same contrast: General de Gaulle's press conferences were always carefully orchestrated in advance. His aides went over questions ahead of time with pro-government juournalists, and *Monsieur le President* rehearsed his answers in detail.[22]

The Gaullist press conference was in fact a long monologue, interrupted àrtificially by journalists who agreed to play the game. With him they were complaisant, deferential, and reverent:

> About a thousand journalists were seated on the Elysée's ballroom to take part in this sort of ritual ceremony. . . . The

subjects to be covered were naturally dictated by circumstances. My views on each topic were well prepared, and my press secretary had insured beforehand that questions would be asked about them.[23]

With the complicity of the press, de Gaule denatured the institution of the press conference. In the United States, it is a spontaneous and often tense meeting, for example those with Nixon, who did not like them and had as few as possible. Under France's Fifth Republic, on the other hand, it was turned into a conventionalized rite, a theatrical spectacle with all the necessary elements: protagonist, setting, audience.

The Elysée's ballroom was transformed into a sort of theater with a thousand seats to handle about 600 journalists and 200 to 300 guests such as members of the National Assembly, diplomats, and officials. Everyone was seated beneath the crystal chandeliers, ready to listen and applaud. Television and newsreel cameras were on the stage and in the four corners of the room. At 3 P.M. sharp, the red curtain parted and de Gaulle appeared. One was almost surprised that there was no master of ceremonies to announce his act.

Pierre Viansson-Ponte has explained how this "high mass, this important rite" with its "official questions" was carried out:

> All the questions were asked at once, in no special order. The general then put them in categories and declared that he would proceed to handle such and such subjects in sequence. Then he asked the "author" of each subject he intended to cover to repeat his question. Thus he avoided any bad surprises and insured that only questions he wanted to reply to were considered.[24]

This way, he avoided spontaneous questions by any newsmen who might have slipped between two "official" questioners. By going along with this game — which continues in a slightly different form under Giscard d'Estaing — the press accentuates the personalization of power and its similarities to show business. But this is nothing compared to the way the audio-visual media tend to degrade public life into a show.

HIS MASTER'S VOICE

In the days of antiquity, the word was all-important. Orators like Demosthenes or Cicero reigned by virtue of their voices and the speech that most of their fellow citizens, gathered at the Agora or the Forum, could hear. Then the city-state became the nation-state, and went from a population of a few thousand to several million. Limited to an audience that had become ridiculously small in proportion to the nation's total population, the spoken word's influence declined, to be replaced by the written word as magnified by the printing press.

But in the 20th century, radio rehabilitated the spoken word. Paradoxically, modern techniques have given renewed importance to ancient rhetorical techniques. For long, the direct contact with the orator had been considered archaic because the size of modern states kept the voice of Stentor from reaching the outer extremities of the city. Listening had become less important than reading. But the invention of radio reversed the situation by removing the audible limits of the spoken word and made it more important than the written word. And soon television restored the power of physical presence to the orator.

Does this return to the origins of oratory mark the progress or the regression of political communication? In some ways — and especially under certain conditions — there is definite regression.

First of all, radio is an instrument for repersonalizing power. By restoring the influence of the leader's words and voice, it risks giving rise to all sorts of affective attitudes toward the government. By establishing — or seeming to — direct contact between the leader and the listener, it can create attraction or repulsion, sympathy or antipathy, none of which have anything to do with rational judgment.

Similarly, radio can be the instrument of a certain deprogramming of the individual's critical faculties. Whereas a printed manifesto or speech lends itself to rational examination and analysis, thanks to the possibility of re-reading it, a purely oral declaration may be thin in content and address itself primarily to the listener's feelings rather than to his or her reason and critical sense.

Much depends on the political context in which radio is used. Sociologists who have studied the question find that the political impact of radio is strongest in a totalitarian situation. Indeed, Marshall McLuhan considers radio to be the very essence of totalitarian technique. As a "hot medium," it is the tool by which despots can impose any message they want, since the opposition has no opportunity to use government-controlled radio stations to broadcast its views. In a sense, Nazism was born of the loudspeaker and the radio.

"The fact that a Hitler was able to exist politically is the direct result of radio and public address systems," McLuhan says. What the Führer actually said was not as important as the means he used to say it: "Radio led to the first mass experience in the electronic 'implosion.'"[25]

And McLuhan adds: "Radio is a hot medium. It spreads the Hitler phenomenon and brings a society to the boiling point. It is madness to authorize radio stations in under-developed countries like China, the Moslem world, and India. It is like pouring gasoline on a fire."[26]

From the Nuremberg of yesterday to today's Third World, radio serves dictators well by transmitting the only official line and creating an unreal — even surreal — climate. We have only to recall Orson Welles' radio adaptation of H.G. Welles' *The War of the Worlds* in 1938. The broadcast set off nationwide panic, with hundreds of thousands of listeners mistaking the radio drama for reality and believing that Martians had actually landed. As McLuhan puts it, "Hitler did the same thing, but he was not play-acting."

McLuhan's remark is right in a sense, for Hitler had a good grasp of the advantages of the oral over the written word. He himself wrote in *Mein Kampf* that "all the great events that have shaken the world have been provoked by the spoken word, not by writings." Radio enabled him to spread gross, mindless propaganda more easily than he could have through writing. A veritable sorcerer of this "language of the masses," Hitler also wrote that "propaganda must always situate its intellectual level so as to be understood by the most simple-minded person to whom it is addressed."

But McLuhan's thesis goes too far in its generalization. To be sure, Hitler owed much of his success to public address systems and radio, and he cleverly used and abused the inherent strength of this "hot medium." But he never would have been able to attain the success he had if his broadcasts had been made in a climate of freedom and political competition. Such an atmosphere would have enabled citizens to compare Hitler's speeches with those made by other leaders from other parties. Confrontation with reality via objective and independent information would have led to a critique of Hitlerism rather than to the Hitler myth.

Thus it is true that radio can be a dangerous weapon in the hands of a European dictator following the First World War, or of a current Third World despot. And this is all the more true in an age when the transistor radio enables radio broadcasts to reach a wider audience than television. But such a "radiocracy" can no more exist in a pluralistic regime than a "teleocracy" can, for such a society allows all varieties of political opinion to be heard. Indeed, radio can even promote democracy by getting more people interested in politics than more costly and less accessible printed matter can.

Still, radio does establish a special rapport between leader and listener, and it thereby promotes the personalization of politics. Even if the listener does not feel that it is "his master's voice," as in the case of dictatorships, he has an impression of familiarity with leaders that leads him to pay more attention to their personalities than to their political programs. After all, a person's voice is one of the first things that makes a good — or bad — impression when meeting a stranger.

THE PRINCE OF RADIO

In some ways, the 1933–1945 presidency of Franklin Roosevelt, the longest in American history, was a form of rule by radio. The new medium enabled FDR to "project" his charisma and insure his influence over the nation. He was the acknowledged master of this new communications technique whose appearance coincided with his presidency.

The number of homes equipped with radios doubled in the United States from 1932 and 1943. Thanks to this, President Roosevelt's broadcasts reached a much larger public than those of President Coolidge. The following figures show the relationship between presidential elections and the rise of radio in the U.S.:

Election	Total radios in use
Harding (1920)	400,000
Coolidge (1924)	3,000,000
Hoover (1928)	8,500,000
Roosevelt (1932)	18,000,000
Roosevelt (1936)	33,000,000

Even before reaching the White House, Roosevelt experimented with radio while he was Democratic governor of New York. He quickly saw in it a powerful instrument for rallying public opinion to his side by establishing direct rapport and short-circuiting the state legislature and written press, both of which were dominated by the Republican party. It was during his first term as governor that he hit upon the method of the informal "fireside chat" to speak directly to New Yorkers.

During his 1932 presidential campaign, candidate Roosevelt also made frequent use of radio, for the same reason: to neutralize the opposition from the Republican-dominated press. Estimates were that 59 percent of the daily newspapers and 55 percent of the weeklies were against him.*[27]

Once he was in the White House, Roosevelt continued to use radio. From March 1933 to January 1934, for example, he went on the air 84 times. During his entire presidency, Roosevelt made 28 fireside chats, each reaching an estimated 80 million Americans. This was one of his key techniques in getting around obstinate congressional opposition to his reforms.

FDR's radiogenic talent, his "incomparable radio personality and voice," cannot be overestimated in understanding his success. As one analysis said, with his fireside chats Roosevelt made governmental affairs interesting and personal; on a variety of issues he created a public opinion that few congressmen could afford to overlook.[28]

Roosevelt's personality, as projected via his fireside chats and the intimate person-to-person rapport he thereby established, were his most important political weapon. This was borne out by a 1938 poll by the American Institute of Public Opinion, which showed that 80.3 percent of those questioned said they liked Roosevelt's personality.[29]

GOVERNMENT BY THE WORD

In France as in the United States, radio became an important means of political communication in the 1930s. President Gaston Doumergue

---

* From 1958 to 1969, President de Gaulle used radio and television in the same way. His press secretary Alain Peyrefitte went so far as to say before the National Assembly that local TV served to balance off local newspapers alleged to be hostile to de Gaulle.

spoke directly to French citizens on March 24, 1934, and Socialist Léon Blum afterward complained: "President Doumergue's use of the first person singular is becoming a bit too much."

In 1937 and 1938, Édouard Daladier and Paul Reynaud used radio as well, often to announce their decisions directly to the country. Thus the prime minister made his declarations on foreign policy and the finance minister discussed his economic plan publicly before submitting them to the National Assembly.

When the War and then the Occupation came, there was a virtual battle of words between Vichy and London on rival frequencies. Using military command methods, Marshal Pétain made "calls" and transmitted "messages" intended to impose his presence as chief on public opinion.

"In the beginning was the Word," and that phrase seemed to apply especially to de Gaulle on June 18, 1940, when he spoke on the BBC for the first time: "Tomorrow, as today, I will speak on Radio London." His eloquence made a BBC microphone in his hand a powerful weapon of war. He again made use of this radio charisma during the troubled moments of May 30, 1968, preferring radio to TV in the hope of acquiring greater resonance.

Under the Fourth Republic, Pierre Mendès France systematically made radio addresses, just as Antoine Pinay had already used the medium in 1952. Their common objective was to garner public support in their struggles with the National Assembly.

Beginning a series of weekly Saturday evening talks, Premier Mendès France declared on June 26, 1954: "My intention is to speak regularly to you to talk simply of what the government — your government — is doing and thinking. . . It would be encouraging and promising for all concerned if we could establish a sort of affectionate intimacy between the government, the nation's elected representatives, and public opinion."[30]

But what the Fifth Republic began in 1958, television had begun to replace as the prime mode of political communication, just as it had done earlier in the United States during the 1952 presidential election campaign.

Still, radio retains its usefulness in a complementary role to reach certain segments of the public who tend to use it more than others: motorists, housewives, elderly persons, and young people with transistors. Also, in countries where parties have to pay to make broadcasts, radio time costs less than TV. Hence it is often used as a supplement in American campaigns, for example Goldwater's in 1964 and Nixon's in 1968.

Nonetheless, even when combined with radio, television has now become the main standby of mediapolitics and of the political star system.

Soviet Party Leader Leonid Brezhnev (left) and Former President Richard Nixon at welcoming ceremonies on the south lawn of the White House (1973).

Man in the Public Eye

*"It's not the mirror's fault if you've got
an ugly mug."*
—GOGOL

In the 1950s, television replaced newspapers and radio as the main source of information. About 97 percent of American homes possessed at least one radio, and 7 percent a TV set in 1950. In 1957, the respective figures wer 98 percent and 82 percent. Twenty-seven million Americans could follow the presidential election campaign on TV in 1952, making it the first "TV election," just as 1932 had been the first "radio election."

If it had not been for television, Richard Nixon would not have been elected vice-president in 1952. And without it, he would not have been beaten by John Kennedy in 1960, when nearly nine homes out of ten had at least one TV set. Television was to Kennedy in 1960 what radio had been to Roosevelt in 1932: the means to victory. In 1968, Nixon finally was elected president, thanks largely to a very effective TV campaign. And the Ford-Carter TV duels were the high point of the 1976 campaign.

In France, the proliferation of TV sets at the end of the 1950s also heavily influenced political life. For Charles de Gaulle, back in power in 1958, TV was to be what his broadcasts from London had been during the war. And the TV debate between Giscard d'Estaing and François Mitterrand was an important turning point in the 1974 election.

The politician's ideal is to get included in normal TV programming, whether on a political discussion show or otherwise. The best time slot is naturally the evening news, which always draws a large audience. But another favorite is the news panel show like NBC's "Meet the Press," CBS's "Face the Nation," or ABC's "Issues and Answers."

Next in line are the popular variety shows, to reach a big segment of the audience that does not watch discussion shows. Thus Richard Nixon, Robert Kennedy, and John Lindsay got good exposure on Johnny Carson's "Tonight" show, Joey Bishop's "Nighttime Venture," and the "Merv Griffin Show."

Similarly, French political leaders gladly participate in talk shows or variety programs, happily rubbing elbows with show business stars. Besides these regular programs, there are also special shows for politicians, either those already in power or those on the campaign trail. These are of several types.

THE SPEECH

The most classic example is the straight speech. Generally seated alone at a desk, the leader addresses the TV audience directly. Often the result is mediocre, especially if he is obviously reading his speech. That was the problem with Italian Premier Aldo Moro, who always read his text in a droning voice without ever lifting his eyes to the camera.

In his first TV address on June 13, 1958, de Gaulle made every mistake in the book: his face practically covered by enormous horn-rimmed glasses, he kept his eyes fixed on the text, which he held rigidly at face level. A few months later, however, all these faults had been corrected, and de Gaulle had become a virtual TV pro. This miraculous change was due to advice from Marcel Bleustein-Blanchet, president of the Publicis advertising agency and, reportedly, diction lessons from an eminent member of the Comédie Française.[1]

De Gaulle's speeches, usually 20 minutes long, were filmed for TV at the Elysée, using a cardboard backdrop that looked like a study. In his memoirs, de Gualle describes the care with which he prepared each speech:

> Whereas in the old days I had always made speeches without referring to notes, it was my habit when speaking in a studio to read from a prepared text. But now the audience was watching de Gaulle on television. To be faithful to my persona, I had to speak to a nation as if I were looking each person straight in the

eye, without either glasses or text. Still, my speeches to the nation were "ex cathedra" and destined to be carefully scrutinzed, so I wrote them out in detail, being sure during the filming to say exactly what I had prepared. . . That evening, the show was on the world's biggest stage.[2]

Other politicians, less willing to make the effort to memorize their speeches, use the technique of TV news commentators. They read their text on a teleprompter, which lets them read it without the text being visible to the audience, the words running along a screen just below the camera. Thus they can look the audience straight in the eye without even consulting a note, giving the impression of having mastered perfectly their material.

But the teleprompter has been known to break down. It happened once to Eisenhower, who yelled into a live microphone, "How the hell does this thing work?"[3]

THE CONFESSION

A subspecies of the TV speech is the TV confession. The most famous one was that made by Richard Nixon on September 23, 1952, which bears the name of his dog: "The Checkers Speech." Accused of accepting funds illicitly and using campaign money for personal purposes, the candidate for the vice-presidency laid himself bare before the public:

> Now, and this is without precedent in the history of American politics, I am going to give you a complete financial history of everything I have earned, everything I have spent, everything I owe.
>
> I own a 1950 Oldsmobile; a $3,000 equity in the house in California where my parents live; a $20,000 equity in my house in Washington; I have $4,000 in life insurance. I owe: $10,000 on my house in California; $20,000 on my house in Washington; $4,500 to the Riggs National Bank; $3,500 to my parents; $500 on my life insurance. That is all. It is not much. And I would like to add this: Pat does not have a mink coat. She has a respectable Republican cloth coat. And I would also

like to say that we did receive a gift after my nomination. I mention it so that no one can criticize me for not telling all. A man in Texas had heard Pat say on the radio that our children would like to have a dog. Believe it or not, the day we set out on this campaign we received a message from Baltimore saying that there was a package for us. Do you know what it was? A little cocker spaniel in a cage that had just arrived from Texas. It had black and white spots, and our little girl Tricia, who is six, gave him the name Checkers.[4]

When the broadcast was over, mothers all over America were dabbing at their eyes, and Darryl Zanuck telephoned to say, "that was the most extraordinary show I've ever seen." Later it was learned that this speech, so touching in its evident spontaneity, had been worked over during eight days of rehearsals.

Twenty years later, on February 15, 1972, Jacques Chaban-Delmas also chose to defend himself, after the press had published his income tax returns, by making a TV confession, assisted by an interviewer, Pierre Desgraupes. Today he says of it:

That broadcast remains one of the worst memories I have. Besides the painful nature of the subject and being in the impossible position of defending myself from false charges, I was haunted by the feeling that maybe I had chosen neither the right tactic nor the right means. All during the broadcast it was as if I was outside myself, listening to myself speak with a thin voice, unable to really be myself. I would never wish that on my worst enemy.[5]

DEBATES

This brings us to the dialogue format, the most spectacular form of which is the televised debate between two political adversaries, especially when they are running for the same position.

The challenge to a TV debate has become a ritual in the United States. It had its greatest vogue during the 1960s, when there were debates between John Kennedy and Hubert Humphrey during the West Virginia primary in 1960, Kennedy and Nixon during the 1960 presidential election, Pierre Salinger and George Murphy during the California Senatorial contest in 1964, Ronald Reagan and Edmund "Pat" Brown during the California gubernatorial race in 1966, Reagan and Robert Kennedy on CBS's "Town Meeting of the World" in 1967, Eugene McCarthy and Robert Kennedy during the California primary in 1968, and so on.

The most famous debate, of course, remains that between John Kennedy and Richard Nixon during the 1960 presidential race. Four debates were organized — on September 26 in Chicago, October 7 in Cleveland, October 13 in Los Angeles, and October 21 in New York — alternating among the three major networks. Each one drew an estimated audience of between 65 million and 70 million people.

The ground rules called for a panel of journalists to question the two candidates; not once did they directly question each other. They were given two and a half minutes to reply and 90 seconds for rebuttal.

In all four debates, but especially in the first, form was more important than substance, for both the "actors" and the spectators. And despite the best efforts of the show's organizers, Nixon had several setbacks, particularly on September 26.

Before this first debate his assistants set up two small 500-watt lamps to light his face to best effect. As Ted Rogers, his media consultant, explained, he does not come across well on TV; there is too much contrast between his pale white skin and his jet-black hair. But press photographers who were admitted on the set just before the broadcast unwittingly jostled the lamps out of position.

Moreover, Nixon's face was drawn due to a recent illness, and he refused to use makeup, except for a light application a Lazy Shave on his dark beard. This Max Factor cosmetic gives a pancake makeup color to the skin that a man can use to cover up five o'clock shadow. But under the bright lighting on the CBS set, that was not enough: close-up shots showed every whisker on Nixon's face. The Chicago *Daily News* went so far as to ask in a headline, "Was Nixon sabotaged by the TV makeup man?"

For the following debates Nixon was persuaded to wear theatrical makeup to overcome this handicap. Later, during the 1968 campaign, he applied a thick paste to his face, inspiring Kurt Lang to crack, "after following this campaign, I'm forced to conclude that Elizabeth Arden has replaced Thomas Jefferson as the patron saint of universal suffrage."

The last slipup affecting Nixon in that first debate in 1960 concerned his suit. Notified that the set's backdrop would be number five on the gray scale, Nixon wore a light gray suit designed to strike the right note of contrast. But under the strong lighting on the set the suit appeared a lighter grey than expected, and Nixon blended into the background, losing valuable stage presence.

As Mrs. Rose Kennedy, JFK's mother, put it after the debate, "I felt very sorry for Nixon's mother than night."[6] As to the Democratic candidate with his sharp awareness of how to dress for TV, he wore a dark gray suit and blue shirt, and had a healthy tan.

After Kennedy won by the narrow majority of 113,238 out of over 68 million votes cast, Douglass Cater, one of the journalists who questioned the candidates, remarked that a pessimist might wonder whether it wasn't, in fact, the Republican candidate's pale skin more than his positions on issues that caused his defeat.[7] Theodore White also underscored the fatal result of the camera shot that showed the vice-president leaning forward, his Lazy Shave powder streaked with sweat, the deep shadows of his eyes, his cheeks and face hollow with fatigue.[8]

Indeed, the audience did seem to judge the candidates more on the basis of their faces than their ideas. After the first debate, a pollster, Sam Lubell, reported that the immense majority of those interviewed mentioned the way the candidates handled themselves rather than the issues debated. Another poll, by Elmo Roper, also revealed that style was more important that substance in the debates.[9]

In any case, with Kennedy and Nixon having only two and a half minutes for their answers, they had to keep things moving with the speed of an intellectual tennis match. Each time they were tempted to voice an idea that was too new or too profound to be developed within that time limit, they chose not to mention it.

In sum, this sort of televised duel encourages voters to form their opinions on the basis of other factors than the logic of the candidates' positions. Their style of presentation, the appearance and their superficial debating talents become just as important, if not more so. There is a visceral reaction to a voice, a face or a look in the eye that has nothing to do with the debate's content.

The candidate's themes and the intellectual content of their answers do come across on TV, but they fade from the spectator's memory even faster than when the debate is on radio. For that matter, the same debate can give different results, depending on whether it is followed on radio or TV.

Polls taken after the Kennedy-Nixon debate bear this out. Persons who listened to it on radio found that the two candidates scored about evenly. But those who followed it on TV thought that Nixon did very badly. The difference in public opinion was thus based on image, and on image alone.

Unlike radio, TV transmits images more than ideas. We have all noticed this while trying to follow an explanation closely. Our attention tends to be diverted by details: facial expression, hair style, crooked shirt collar, or an element of decor are inevitably distracting. In these circumstances, a good closeup is more effective than a long speech. As La Rochefoucauld said, there is no less eloquence in the tone of voice, the eyes and general appearance of a person than in his choice of words.'' Which is, after all, a good definition of what we mean by ''telegenic.''

A person's ''fourth dimension'' appears on the screen, creating an intuitive feeling of sympathy or rejection in the spectator which is independent of logical argument. The image transmits messages to his unconscious, giving rise to attraction or repulsion that are hard to define except by phrases as ''He's got class,'' ''He seems nice,'' or ''He looks shady.''

For voters *watch* TV more than they listen to a candidate's remarks, and they therefore judge him on his style and what they can infer from his temperament. As Philippe Braud notes, ''the image short-circuits the verbalization of political options. It is anti-discourse.''[10]

And a French politician, Robert Fabre, confides, ''it's significant that people always say 'I *saw* you on TV,' not 'I *heard* you.' While paying more or less attention to what is being said, they are more interested in the program's presentation, decor and clothing. I have often been told, 'You didn't look well last night on the program,' or 'Your tie didn't go well with your suit.'''[11]

The image can even go so far as to substitute for language. As Enrico Fulchigoni observes, it is easier to memorize the image than the speech that accompanies it.[12] The televised image produces an immediate reaction in the subconscious — irrational, quasi-biological — of empathy or hostility. Then the conscious, rational examination of the message's content triggers reactions based on education and cultural stereotypes which may reinforce or destroy the first impression given by the candidate's image.

To be sure, a candidate's telegenic qualities act within a rather narrow margin, but they can amplify or interfere with his message, which is an important consideration. Thanks to that, a TV debate is liable to contribute little to the rational examination of a platform or program. It tends to encourage a sentimental judgment about the politicians involved.

THE JERRY AND JIMMY SHOW

During the 1976 presidential campaign three TV debates were organized between Gerald Ford and Jimmy Carter. Each lasted an hour and a half, during which the two candidates answered questions posed by three journalists under the direction of a moderator.

As in 1960, the candidates did not address each other directly, unlike the Mitterrand-Giscard debate in France in 1974. They limited themselves to answering the journalists' questions and to commenting on each other's answers without ever entering into a real dialogue.

Each had three minutes to answer the question, two to rebut his adversary's position, and another three to sum up his viewpoint.

The three debates were prepared and staged like a TV show. First, both candidates screened the Kennedy-Nixon debates to look for good and bad points to adopt and avoid. Thus it was that Ford's advisers told him not to imitate Nixon's manner of looking all over the set during his rival's remarks. It was better, they said, to watch the moderator, the newspeople, or Carter himself.

Then, each candidate prepared for the debates with his team of specialists. On the Republican side this included the debate supervisors Mike Duval, Alan Greenspan, and William Seidman. On the Democratic side, there were issues advisers such as Stu Eisenstat, political consultants like Ted Van Dyk and speech writers like Theodore Sorensen and John Stewart. The objective on both sides was to be able to reply easily on any subject that might come up.

Carter went through several question-and-answer rehearsals, facing a crossfire of questions from his assistants. Ford went several rounds with a sort of sparring partner, Don Penny, a former actor and TV producer who vaguely resembled Jimmy Carter and who imitated a Southern accent.

Before the show went on, the two principal's representatives carefully went over last-minute details, with Ford's winning on two points: the decor was to be blue to minimize the president's bald spot, and the two candidates would stand side by side behind podiums only five feet apart. This meant that the audience would notice that Ford was taller and larger than Carter.

But Carter's men obtained satisfaction on the question of Ford's podium, which would not bear the usual presidential seal. They also insured that the podiums would be only waist high. As a Democratic adviser put it, "Jimmy uses his hands and body well," whereas "the president is no good at body language."[13]

Naturally, the Republicans were concerned about makeup, recalling the problems Nixon had with Lazy Shave in 1960. Aware that Ford disliked cosmetics, a TV veteran, Carruthers, advised the president to use a sun lamp two or three minutes every day during the week preceding the debate or to get a natural tan — not too natural, though, for Ford had a tendency to peel rapidly after too much sun.

Carter received his advice from Barry Jagoda, a former CBS producer, and publicist Gerald Rafshoon counselled him to exchange his big smile, which appeared forced, for a "humble smile," meaning "smile with the lips nearly touching." For "Jimmy has his good smiles and his bad smiles."[14]

Everything was rehearsed and checked down to the last detail; makeup and facial tics, lighting and color of decor, cameras and sound quality — despite the fact that the sound broke down for 28 minutes during the first debate.

On September 23, 1976, nearly 100 million Americans followed the first debate on the three TV channels. It was to be on the subject of domestic politics and the economy, with Edwin Newman as moderator and ABC's Frank Reynolds, the *Wall Street Journal*'s James Gannon, and *The New Yorker*'s Elizabeth Drew as panelists.

Media pros decided that the first round was boring. But to the general surprise, Ford, clearly at ease and poised, beat Carter on points, the latter appearing tense and speaking too fast. Carter hit his stride only in the last third of the debate.

Afterward, a Gallup poll found that 56 percent of those questioned judged Ford's performance good, against only 50 percent for Carter.

Even when the pollsters asked about the candidate's positions on a given question such as inflation, abortion, etc., their answers were couched in such phrases as "he looked thoughtful and well informed," "he seemed too aggressive," "he did not appear sure of himself," and so on.[15] In other words, most questions concerned the surface of the debate and not its substance.

On October 6, the second debate concerned foreign policy. This time, the polls favored Carter, who showed greater agility and pugnacity, and generally took the initiative. He looked especially good in contrast to Ford, who stated that Eastern Europe is not dominated by the Soviet Union.[16]

The third debate was on October 22 in Williamsburg, Virginia. It was a dreary affair with both candidates attempting mainly to avoid making mistakes, even if Carter did go out on a limb and say he would not intervene if the Soviet Union invaded Yugoslavia. Still, he appeared more relaxed and self-confident than Ford. The Roper poll gave him victory with 40 percent of the public favor against 29 percent for Ford, with 31 percent saying it was a draw.

As if to underline their place in show business, the Ford-Carter debates were held in theaters: on September 23 at the Walnut Street Theater in Philadelphia, October 6 at the Palace of Fine Arts in San Francisco. Even the Robert Dole-Walter Mondale debate between the two vice-presidential candidates was held on the stage of the Alley Theater in Houston.

Once again, form was more important than matter, the answers to questions less important than the manner in which they were made. Indeed, a few days before the first debate, anthropologist Margaret Mead telephoned Rafshoon, Carter's counsellor, to advise, "Style over substance! Style over substance!"[17]

DEBATING IN FRANCE

Television debates have also caught on in France,* especially thanks to programs like *À Armes Égales* produced by Alain Duhamel and

---

* Other debates to be noted have been between Palme and Fälldin in Sweden in September 1976 and the Schmidt-Kohl debate on September 30, 1976, in West Germany.

Michel Bassi and *L'Évenement* put on by Henri Marque and Christian Bernadac, and Jean-Marie Cavada's *C'est à Dire*.

On May 10, 1974, 20 to 25 million French citizens watched the hour and a half debate between Valéry Giscard d'Estaing and François Mitterrand in their race for the Elysée Palace. Irresistibly, the mass media turned the debate into a match where personal performance counted for more than political platforms. Thus radio station Europe I had a polling agency question 400 persons by telephone about the candidates' qualities and faults. Result: Giscard was found to be more appealing, more interesting, more sincere, and more dynamic, whereas Mitterrand was seen to be more at ease, more human, and more loyal.

Not only is the public's attention oriented toward personalities rather than programs, but indications are given as to what to think about the candidates. It is as if it were more important to judge their style and presentation than their ability to think cogently.

One can only agree with Mitterrand's criticism: "On television, what is said is less important than what is seen." Everything incites the public to observe the two adversaries as if they were athletes: "They treated me as if I were a boxer in the ring," Mitterrand writes, "although despite the sporting language used in newspaper articles, I did not have the impression of being in a match."[18]

But whatever Mitterrand may have felt personally, his televised debate on March 2, 1976, with Finance Minister Jean-Pierre Fourcade was treated in the same sporting metaphor by the press.

In the final analysis, French experience in this field confirms what has happened in the United States. Polls taken after such TV debates are always disappointing to political scientists. The audience always answers that so-and-so "won" what is always considered to be a contest, with individuals typically replying, "he really had him on the mat." But when it comes to commenting on the ideas exchanged and the candidates' respective positions, nothing has been retained by the public mind.

THE MAN IN THE ARENA

Another form of TV debate utilizes a larger number of questioners. This is the so-called "man in the arena" formula invented by Roger

Ailes, Richard Nixon's TV manager during his 1968 campaign. Here the objective was to project the image of a "new Nixon" full of spontaneity and warmth that would make him more attractive.

The first of these ten broadcasts of one hour each was done inChicago. Standing on a circular platform six feet in diameter and two feet high, Nixon faced his eight questioners, who were seated around him in a semicircle. About 300 spectators, carefully selected by Republican party officials, were seated behind Nixon.

The "arena" effect — with its echo of a martyr in the lion's den— tended to put the spectators on the side of this isolated man surrounded by hostile forces. By applauding Nixon's replies, the studio audience communicated to the TV audience the impression that he had not only charm, but authority and all the other qualities required of a president.

As to the questioners, they varied from six to eight. This time there were eight, carefully picked to make up a balanced panel representing the American voters: a black, a Jewish judge, the president of a Polish-Hungarian association, a suburban housewife, a businessman, a farmer, and, to make the panel seem more authentic, two journalists.

Advice given by the Fuller, Smith, and Ross advertising agency for recruiting these panel members: The group should give the general impression of youth. Try for example to have three persons in the 25 to 35 year-old age range and three between 35 and 50, preferably about 40. It should be four men and two women, or at most three and three. They should be fairly good-looking and as typical as possible of the average American voter.[19]

This broadcast and those following were a great success at giving an impression of direct communication between Nixon and the public, via his representative questioners. They created suspense and mobilized support from the TV audience, whose sympathy for the underdog standing alone on the platform was aroused.

In France, Giscard d'Estaing tried a similar experiment on February 1, 1977, but he enlarged the formula. Sixty men and women selected by the Sofres polling agency to represent the entire French electorate were gathered in the Elysée ballroom to question the president on live TV for three hours.

The 60 guests were seated at 12 oval tables, each table being assigned a series of questions on a single theme such as domestic policy, agriculture, and so on. The president went from one table to another to answer the questions.

Five days earlier, on January 26, Giscard had participated in a similar show, though it was less spontaneous. Labeled "Women's Questions," it included filmed questions from 14 French women, which Giscard watched while seated on a sofa at the Elysée and then answered live.

TELEPHONE AND TELETHON

There exists still another, similar formula: the broadcast using telephone questions.

Under these ground rules, the politician offers to answer live, on radio or TV, any question asked by any person who calls in. Actually, such a broadcast uses a team that filters the questions and puts them through on the air in a certain order. This gives an illusion of spontaneity, but insures that the politician will be asked only the questions that enable him to elaborate on his favorite subjects.

In 1960 during the West Virginia primary, Hubert Humphrey bought a half-hour of TV time. But due to limited resources, he had to accept an authentic telephone program without the filtering team.

The broadcast opened with Humphrey alone at his desk. In front of him was a phone with buttons for two lines. The TV audience heard both the question and the reply.

The first question was "What makes you think you are qualified to be president, Senator Humphrey?" After this abrupt beginning came the heart-felt cry of an old woman: "Get out of West Virginia, Mr. Humphrey, get out!" A bit later there was a courteous voice saying "Senator Humphrey, I just want you to know that I apologize for that lady who told you to get out. We do not all feel that way here in West Virginia, and I am very sorry she said that." The candidate cut off this long-winded digression with brief thanks. He had barely begun to answer the following question, when an operator broke in to cry "Get off the lines, get off the lines, we've got an emergency!" As Theodore White notes slyly, from then on, the broadcast lost all cohesion, proving only one thing, that TV is not a good medium for a poor man.[20]

Many candidates therefore prefer to avoid improvisation by having questions sorted out and categorized as far as they can without actually cheating. This is often done in the "telethons" that often wind up presidential campaigns.

In 1968 on election eve, Nixon taped two telethons of two hours each on NBC, one for the East Coast and one for the West Coast. In the studio, 125 operators — including his daughters, Julie and Tricia — took the calls. The operators had been recruited by local Republican party officials, as had been the studio audience that applauded the candidate's every reply.

Nixon's one-man show was interrupted a few times: once was to interview Julie and Tricia as they took the calls, another intermission showed David Eisenhower reading a message from his grandfather, and a third included a short conversation with Pat Nixon.

Hubert Humphrey broadcast his own telethon that same evening. He had Nancy Sinatra, Johnny Carson, and Paul Newman as moderators. Nixon also had his show business representatives on hand, with Jackie Gleason opening the show. For that matter, as early as 1960 Nixon had ended his campaign with a four-hour telethon on ABC which ranged from the discussion of complex problems to a conversation with Ginger Rogers.

SPOTS

At the opposite pole from such long telethons are the short advertising spots of a few minutes or, more often, 20, 30, or 60 seconds, which present the candidate and his merits exactly the way commercials advertise any other product.

Behind this idea is the conviction that most of the TV audience does not like political talk shows and are liable to change stations when one comes on. But they can stand a short spot slipped in between two popular shows, provided it is only 30 to 60 seconds long. Such spots thus reach many more voters who are opposed to the candidate or undecided and let him get his arguments across, even if he has to sneak them in.

This is how "quickie" politics is developed. Instead of elaborating his position on serious problems of government, the candidate uses these short spots that only serve to project a personal image.

In 1952, an advertising man named Rosser Reeves recommended an Eisenhower TV campaign based on a large number of short announcements, with the general appearing in each one. Fifty spots of 20 seconds each were prepared. They contained only very general statements, the objective being to maintain the candidate's image of well-meaning sincerity, with questions and answers such as this:

"Mr. Eisenhower, what do you think of the cost of living?"

"My wife Mamie complains about it too. I tell her that our job is to change all that on November 4."

Ever since, advertising spots have been an integral part of any politician's campaign. Like many others in 1968, Nixon taped several spots that were not over a minute long, acting on advice from his TV counsellor, Harry Treleaven, who learned how to use them while at the J. Walter Thompson advertising agency. The spots were produced by Eugene Jones, who did the "Today Show" on NBC for eight years. Objective: To show Richard Nixon as a man of his times, a man of heart and imagination, without his having to say anything at all substantial.[21]

Hubert Humphrey's advisers also produced a series of spots, including the one they called "the 20-second laugh." This one opened on a TV set with a sign on its screen saying "Agnew for Vice-President." The audio accompanying the image was a long burst of laughter, followed by the statement, "It would be funny if it weren't so serious."[22]

The same barrage technique was used in the 1976 campaign, with President Ford being filmed at the White House, speaking to the Congress, on an official trip to Peking, and so on. The number of spots broadcast increased toward the end of the campaign, becoming a virtual audio-visual bombardment costing about $10 million.

Jimmy Carter also used TV commercials, including many done by media consultant Tony Schwartz, who had done anti-Goldwater spots for Lyndon Johnson. But Carter owed one new idea to Gerald Rafshoon: the use of five-minute TV spots as the backbone of the campaign. Whereas Madison Avenue had always considered a product hopeless if it required more than 30 to 60 seconds to sell it, Rafshoon's new technique succeeded in making his candidate look different and even profound with the longer spots. Everything is relative.

As Hamilton Jordan, Carter's campaign manager, put it: "You need five minutes to look thoughtful. But if you spend over 40 seconds on a given subject, the spectator will get up to go drink a beer. So the solution is to handle five or six subjects per message.''[23]

As can be seen, the candidate's advisers are still far from respecting the wishes of John O'Toole, president of Foot, Cone, and Belding, one of the largest American advertising agencies, who said in 1972: "I ask ad men not to confuse candidates for the presidency with a deodorant, or the White House with an armpit."

DOCUMENTARIES

The last of the standard advertising formats, and also the longest and most costly — but no richer in content — is the documentary. This is usually a film of about 30 minutes designed to give a more complete portrait of the candidate.

This technique has even become common in gubernatorial campaigns. In 1966, when actor Ronald Reagan ran against the outgoing governor of California, Edmund "Pat" Brown, Brown had Charles Guggenheim produce a film entitled "A Man vs. an Actor." The objective was to ridicule Reagan by mixing film clips of political news with segments of Reagan's old westerns and TV commercials, especially those for cleaning products. "And here's exciting New Boraxo waterless hand cleaner," went one, "New Boraxo waterless hand cleaner removes the toughest dirt or stains. Gets hands clean and smooth fast anytime." At the end, the voice over proclaimed, "Vote for a REAL governor, not an acting one: Pat Brown."

But this satire had a boomerang effect, with the TV audience siding with Reagan against such attacks. That same year, Charles Guggenheim produced a more successful film, a 30-minute documentary for Milton Shapp, candidate for the office of governor of Pennsylvania, entitled "The Man Against the Machine." The idea was sparked by a poll done by Joseph Napolitan, Shapp's adviser, which showed that many voters considered the Democratic party to be run by a network of old professional bosses.

In order to win the Democratic nomination, Shapp therefore chose to go over the heads of the state's Democratic organization and address himself directly to voters. He became the candidate who dared challenge the party machine, hence the title of the TV documentary, which was produced by Shelby Storck.[24] Shapp won the Democratic nomination, lost the race to his Republican opponent that year, but was finally elected governor of Pennsylvania in 1970 and re-elected in 1974.

In 1968, Hubert Humphrey had a half-hour film produced which was entitled "The Mind Changer," showing him in a variety of informal situations. He was seen bowling, fishing, wearing a funny hat, and struggling to get his line back when it became tangled on the bottom. Even the fact that one of his granddaughters was mentally retarded was played up.

The idea was to show Humphrey as a profoundly human person, sweating, laughing, weeping, and loving the out-of-doors. This was to distinguish him sharply from the mechanical side of Richard Nixon and make Nixon appear heartless. As the film's voiceover put it: "You can't fabricate humanity. You either have it or you don't. Hubert Humphrey is brimming with it. Not everyone can say the same."[25]

During the 1976 campaign, a 30-minute recorded TV film made to resemble a political discussion showed President Ford responding well to prepared questions put by a pseudo-reporter who was actually NBC's sports commentator, Joe Garagiola. This "Joe and Jerry Show" was broadcast in five key states on election eve.

MEDIA CONSULTANTS

Special advisers for TV use now hold a central position in American campaigns. It began in 1952 when Rosser Reeves did Eisenhower's TV spots, and continued in 1956 when Eisenhower engaged actor Robert Montgomery as adviser for his television campaign.

In 1960, Richard Nixon went so far to avoid criticism for using Madison Avenue's services in his campaign that his TV advisers, chosen from among the best New York ad agencies, had to take up quarters in an anonymous office on Vanderbilt Avenue, a block east of Madison Avenue.

But soon media use for political propaganda became a regular profession, and its specialists are known as media managers. Their job is to oversee television advisers, producers, and directors.

The profession now has its stars, like any other. There is Charles Guggenheim, who works for the Democratic party, and who has done films for Brown ("A Man vs. an Actor"), Shapp ("The Man Against the Machine"), and Humphrey ("The Mind Changer"). There is also Bob Squier, who produced the Humphrey telethon in 1968.

On the Republican side, the star is still Harry Treleaven, who spent 18 years with the J. Walter Thompson agency, leaving it as a vice-president after having managed the advertising budgets of Pan Am, Ford, RCA, and the like. In 1968 Treleaven ran Nixon's TV campaign from his office at the Fuller, Smith, and Ross agency.

For Nixon, Treleaven created the Media and Publicity group with Len Garment and Frank Shakespeare, who had spent 18 years with CBS. He also hired Roger Ailes, production director of the "Mike Douglas Show," to produce panel discussion programs like the "Man in the Arena" show.

The Tennessee senatorial race in 1970, for example, was particularly interesting not so much because Republican William E. Brock III ran against Democrat Albert Gore, but because their respective media consultants were Harry Treleaven and Charles Guggenheim. When the vote was in, Brock had beaten Gore — or if you prefer, Treleaven had outclassed Guggenheim.

In 1976, Treleaven served as Reagan's adviser, and did some spots in which, as he confessed, there were some "faults and technical imperfections to make them look more real."[26] Under the supervision of Treleaven and Ruth Jones, both veterans of the Nixon campaign, these spots were prepared by Marc Ball, a film producer from Nashville.

As for President Ford's commercials, they were produced under the direction of a 32-year-old ad man named Bruce Wagner, by an agency called Campaign '76 Media Communications, Inc.. The agency was directed by Peter Dailey, a Los Angeles ad man who did similar work for Nixon in 1972. Ford also used Don Penny as media consultant.

On the Democratic side, the Lois Holland Callaway agency worked for Senator Henry Jackson, while Rafshoon concentrated on producing a Carter image that made him the candidate who was "not from Washington — a man of honesty and sincerity." His films showed Carter running peanuts through his fingers or leaning against a fence of his farm and declaring that the government should be as good and honest and decent and faithful and competent and compassionate and also as full of love as the American people are.[27]

THE POLITICS OF IMAGE

These specialists do not think of their job as one of informing, educating or persuading. For them, television is above all to produce a visual effect enhancing the candidate's personality. This is done with impressions and feelings more than with reasoned judgment. Their principle: personalize the campaign to the maximum. Their theory: in winning votes, the candidate's image is infinitely more important than his platform or party label.

Thus has been born the politics of image, which today takes the place of politics based on platforms and parties. The candidate's profile serves as his platform and his image replaces ideology. It is as if the media consultants had read a bit too much of Marshall McLuhan's writings on television.[28]

A Canadian sociologist, McLuhan considers that "the medium is the message." The important thing is not so much content as the medium through which the content is transmitted. For a communication technique, far from being neutral, shapes ways of thinking, feeling, and acting. It transforms our modes of apprehending and perceiving exterior reality.

Thus is was that printing tended to fashion a universe that was at once analytical, rational, abstract, and categorized. The exterior world was fragmented and organized according to a perfectly linear order, rather than being perceived globally through the immediate and multiple experience of human sensibility.

But this linear, abstract notion of reality declined along with printing itself, as the Gutenberg Galaxy was supplanted by the Marconi Galaxy; that is, by radio and television. Television in particular requires a multisensorial participation, mobilizing our entire psychological and sensorial equipment.

So the mutation of the media led to the mutation of the message. In the age of the print shop, graphic communication imposed a reasoned, linear pace on written thought. Today, submerged by the multisensorial, simultaneous assault of the electronic media, the individual acquires a global mode of perception.

Moreover, television is a "cold" medium thin in information content. It carries an incomplete message which is mainly suggestive. In this it is different from the "hot" media (like printing or radio) which, being rich in information, carry a complete message and require no creative participation.

As a "cold" medium, television depends heavily on involvement by the receiver of the message, who has to reconstruct it through creative perception. The television message is incomplete the way an abstract painting or a Rorschach test is incomplete. The television image, says MacLuhan, obliges us constantly to "fill in" the blanks with a convulsive sensorial participation.

Its "weak" definition makes the viewer continuously rearrange the few sketchy points it delivers into a sort of abstract work. He therefore participates in the creation of a reality that is presented to him only in outline form. At the limit, this is the same as an individual who projects his own fantasies onto ink spots which represent nothing in particular.

McLuhan's analysis means two things in terms of politics. First, certain leaders seem to have taken literally the idea that "the medium is the message." For them — especially for charm leaders, so careful of their image — form is much more important than substance, the way something is said more important than what is said. Style can replace a platform. In his way, Giscard d'Estaing is not far from falling into this trap. At least he was until he published *Democratie Française,* the book in which he attempted to outline his political philosophy.

Second, these leaders have grasped the notion that television lends itself better to a flux of images than to the battle of ideas, to multisensorial participation than to rational examination. The confrontation of contrasting positions, the debate of ideas does not come across well on the tube. On the other hand, TV is ideal for transmitting an incomplete or only suggestive message that can then be reconstructed by the viewer.

So these leaders keep their political messages down to simple sketches. They incite the viewer to complete as he will these indistinct, imprecise, and summary ideas. Is not this exactly what Jimmy Carter did in 1976? Used with skill, this "cold" medium handsomely repays ambiguity and even political vacuity.

THE TELEPOLITICIANS

With McLuhan as their prophet and media consultants as their guiding lights, a new generation of politicians has appeared. They have assimilated the rules of television art — which is more often artifice — so well that they might be called *telepoliticians*.

The telepolitician's first technique is to create a gap between image and reality, projecting an image of himself that bears little relation to the truth. As Machiavelli put it in *The Prince*: "In general, men judge more with their eyes than with their hands, for everyone has the opportunity to see, but few can touch. Everyone sees what you seem to be on the outside, but few have any feel for what is inside. And those few dare not contradict the opinion of the majority. The common man judges only by what he sees."[29]

In 1968, Ray Price sent Richard Nixon this note: "The voter reacts to the image of the candidate and not to the man himself, with whom 99% of the population has never had and will never have any direct contact. It's not what exists that counts, but what is projected. . . We do not have to change the man, but the impression received of him."[30]

In both 1968 and 1972, voters supported the "new Nixon," the one that had been fabricated by his media consultants: natural, spontaneous, poised. But before long they discovered that "the old Nixon," also known as "Tricky Dick," was with them. The Watergate affair broke open and the real image replaced the artificial one which had been built up with such care by the television specialists.

The telepolitician's technique is to keep politics on an emotional, rather than rational, level. Harry Treleaven wrote in 1968 that we will not have many opportunities to persuade by logical arguments — and this is just as well, for those who vote for irrational and sentimental reasons are infinitely more numerous.[31]

William Gavin, another member of the Nixon team — he entered the White House in January 1969 as presidential speech writer — thought along the same lines. He said that the voter is fundamentally lazy, and they cannot expecte him to make the least effort to understand what is said. Reasoning calls for a high degree of discipline and concentration; it is much easier to go by impressions. Reasoning can put off the TV audience by making it either agree or disagree, but an impression can envelope it and invite it to acquiesce without making any intellectual demands on the individual.[32]

The telepolitician does not want to argue, plead, or try to convince the TV viewer through rational processes. Rather, he attempts to stir emotions and give rise to an impulsive feeling of confidence in him. He does this by speaking to the viewer's instincts — so easily abused — rather than to his reason, to his senses instead of his conscience.

The Humphrey camp also preferred such "emotional appeals" to "logical dissertations." As Joseph Napolitan put it, television can be the most emotional of our media, and he sees nothing wrong with using emotions. More people vote with their heart than with their head. Elections are won and lost by emotion, not by logic.[33]

The last technique of the telepolitician is to substitute form for content, strictly applying McLuhan's dictum that "the medium is the message." As an assiduous reader of the Canadian sociologist, Gavin says of TV viewers, and especially of the young who form the TV generation: "We leave blanks to fill in in their minds, elementary concepts based on emotion without any need to worry about analysis or reasoning. . . This must always seem to be uncalculated, spontaneous and incomplete. Incomplete — that's the key word."[34]

COOL

We must keep McLuhan's formula in mind: television is a cool medium, weak in definition and relatively poor in information. It provides an incomplete message that is unfinished or simply suggestive. It invites the participation of the viewer, who has to perform a reconstruction through creative perception. This leads him to complete the message as he sees fit, projecting his own expectations on it.

This cool medium requires cool personalities, unlike radio, a hot medium that lends itself to slogans, emphasis, and well-defined declarations. The mock-heroic style of a Hitler is more suited to radio than to TV, which works against strong personalities and flamboyant oratory. In this regard it is significant to note the decreasing part played by lawyers in political leadership, for their practiced eloquence appears too emphatic on the tube. They articulate their messages rather than only suggesting them.

This was evident, for example, when Nixon, the argumentative lawyer, faced a cool Kennedy and lost. Eight years later, the "new Nixon" had adopted the proper style of expression for the cool medium. He had learned one of McLuhan's prime rules, not to "heat up the cool medium."

Well before Nixon's experience in 1960, the first victim of TV was probably Senator Joseph MacCarthy, the witch-hunting chief of the Senate's Permanent Investigations Subcommittee. When the subcommittee's hearings were televised in April 1954, he thought he was greatly increasing his popularity. But the result was the opposite of what this virulent orator expected. Instead of appearing to the nation as an uncompromising patriot, he gave the impression of being a rude bully. The televised hearings that were to have been his triumph turned out to be his political death warrant.

Generally speaking, the oratorical style suited to a parliament or a political rally does not work on TV. Since it is normally watched by a small family group or persons alone, it requires a more intimate, less bombastic tone. It makes no sense to address people, comfortably seated in their living rooms, the way a politician addresses a crowd. The vehement approach would simply make them feel ill at ease.

Moreover, TV magnifies any faults in a speech. As the writer François Mauriac noted, "The least lack of tact on television reverberates like a thunderclap." And on the tube, standard oratorical devices look much too obvious.

That is why Hitler would never have lasted in the TV age. The grotesqueness of his grandiloquence and his gesticulations would have been apparent immediately. For television's close-ups call for a measured tone and simple, relaxed style — whether real or feigned. The manner must be as underspoken, direct, and intimate as a private conversation.

The hero image is therefore difficult to project in the TV age, at least in political systems that subject the would-be hero to competition from other politicians. De Gaulle's heroic style worked from 1958 to 1965 mainly because he had no competition. Air time on TV was reserved for his monologues. This changed during the presidential election campaign of 1965, when all candidates had access to TV. As a result, the general had to change his usual haughty style and use a relaxed, more spontaneous tone.

But if TV serves "heroes" badly when there is competition, that is usually not the case in the Third World. There the hero leader can bend TV usage entirely to his will. General Mobutu, for example, uses TV to reinforce his image. Since he has a monopoly on TV, viewers have no way to make a comparison.

But in pluralistic systems, TV often precipitates the decline of the hero. On the other hand, it favors the cool style of the ordinary man (or of the ordinary father figure), as long as his style is not too banal. This was Senator Jackson's problem in 1976 during the race for the Democratic nomination, when the press's comment was "he looks gray even on color TV." To acquire a less dreary image, the senator consulted with television producers and film directors like David Wolper, but in vain.

Ford did not come across very well on television, either, appearing ill at ease. The exception was his acceptance speech at the Republican Convention in August 1976. To be sure, that text had been very carefully prepared over a space of several weeks by White House writers under the direction of chief speech writer Robert Hartmann and his assistant, Robert Orben, along with Media Consultant Don Penny, a former actor and TV producer.

Television does favor the charm leader much more than the ordinary man. For he is the very prototype of the calm, moderate personality whose "weak intensity" produces "strong participation" on the part of the viewers.

The model of the cool leader as early as 1960 was John Kennedy, who was a master of television. As Theodore Sorensen remarked, Kennedy's style corresponded admirably to this medium. His spare eloquence, the absence of emphasis and gesticulation, the nuanced gravity of just the shadow of shyness suited the intimacy of TV perfectly.[35]

Kennedy often repeated that TV was his best weapon. Indeed, it is a moot question whether his close victory in 1960 over Nixon — by only 113,000 votes out of a total of 69 million cast — was not largely due to his attractiveness on TV. After all, it was known that four million voters decided on the basis of the TV debates, and 75 percent of those voted for Kennedy.

All the world's charm leaders have the same relaxed spontaneity, the same simplicity and project the same cool image. This is true of

Trudeau, Palme, Carter — so like a charm leader in this respect — or Giscard d'Estaing, who says he hates "turgid grandiloquence." Affecting poise and calm, avoiding anything that might "heat up the cool medium," these telepoliticians often avoid another danger: overexposure.

OVEREXPOSURE

To keep his appearances from becoming commonplace and tiring TV viewers, the political leader must limit the duration and frequency of his "exposure" in the studios. Thus Roosevelt meted out his speeches and in the middle of an economic crisis, he gave only four fireside chats. Even that was a record, for he made only four others in the three following years.

Other presidents tend to overdo their use of the media. Thus Giscard d'Estaing celebrated his first year in office in May 1975 with a virtual media festival, day after day.

On May 19, 1975, there was a 25-minute filmed retrospective broadcast on France's channel 3, which gave an enthusiastic accounting of one year of "reform."

On May 20, there were several media events. That morning, *Le Figaro* published an interview with him. Then he received his cabinet ministers at the Elysée and spoke to them for over a half hour. At 1 P.M. Philippe Bouvard questioned him on Radio Luxembourg. That same evening the president dined with his faithful supporters from Ringeldorf, in Alsace, while France's Channel 1 broadcast a documentary on his first year in the Elysée.

For 90 minutes, viewers could see the president as he went through his daily routine at the Elysée, in his office, the living room, the garden, playing the piano. He was shown with the cabinet, his advisers, the Elysée staff, as well as with his dogs. He presided over a meeting, ate breakfast while going through the morning newspapers, and dined with his family. The inquiring camera was shown everything from the Elysée kitchen to its linen closets. Sèvres porcelain, Aubusson tapestries, and lawns.

On May 22 it was the turn of another channel to focus on Giscard. This was in part due to a suggestion from him that he be interviewed by

Jacques Chancel, one of French TV's top interviewers, on the theme of how a year in office had affected him.

Thus does Giscard d'Estaing continue to work at touching up his official portrait via TV, while the opposition complains about "brainwashing," commandeering the state's information media, and the president's self-glorification.

A poll taken during Giscard's first anniversary week showed that he recorded his best popularity score in a year, with fully 59 percent of his countrymen satisfied with him — 6 percent more than in April 1975, despite rising unemployment and prices. Clearly, he had been able to shape public opinion independently of the country's real situation. It was as if he was actually substituting his image for his policies.

But this excessive use of the media can lead to public lassitude through overexposure. On radio and TV it is necessary to pace oneself. As Franklin Roosevelt observed, the public cannot long stand being hammered at constantly with the same shrill note.[36]

Giscard's book, *Democratie Française,* was published on October 11, 1976. He granted an interview to France's Channel 2 the evening before, and another to Channel 1 on the 14th. On the 17th he was on a radio panel show on one station, and replied to listeners' letters on another station on the 25th. There was a radio interview with him on the 27th, in addition to countless articles in magazines and newspapers and serial prepublication of his book in the newsweekly L'Express.

But despite all this media coverage, a poll taken at the time showed a surprising decline in the presidential popularity: in November, 44 percent were unhappy with his leadership compared to 42 percent who were pleased; in December, the respective figures were 47 percent and 39 percent. Who knows? Perhaps politics and marketing do not obey the same laws after all.

TV SHOW POLITICS

Still, assuming a leader avoids such overexposure, TV show politics can be effective. To be sure, television is not the absolute weapon of political combat, at least not in an open society. Liberal democracies do not tolerate a telecracy. But studies do show that those voters who are the least interested in politics are the most open to influence from TV, especially if it dramatizes the issues and uses the star system.[37] [38] Even if more politically aware voters are less impressionable and the TV effect on them is only marginal, it nonetheless exists. And it can alter the result of an election by changing only a few of the more sophisticated minds.

It is well known that campaign managers concentrate their TV tactics mainly on the undecided voters who generally do not hold strong political views and who are more influenced by the staging of the political show. Since the majority of the public has already made up its mind, the TV campaign aims deliberately at the 25 to 30 percent of the electorate who is still hesitating. It is made up of those who are less informed, who care little about platforms and issues, and who get interested in politics only when it becomes a spectacle. They like an election to resemble the shows they are used to following every week on the tube.

Telepoliticians are good at exploiting the tendency of such viewers to prefer diversion to information, who see TV as a medium of escapism through the complex process of identification or catharsis.

For them, TV is the main source of distraction and entertainment. To reach them, the political leader must become, if not an entertainer, at least an accomplished performer or showman. Otherwise he will fail to capture their attention — and their vote.

For that matter, TV professionals exphazise this tendency. As Roger Ailes, the former producer of the "Mike Douglas Show" who was hired by Nixon to handle his TV debates in 1968, puts it, "candidates of the future will have to be real hams."[39]

And Jean-Luc Leridon, who produces a political talk show on France's Channel 2, says, "the excitement is just as great as filming a great ham actor. On my program, the guest politicians are in virtually the same situation as if they were on stage. There is an audience, a well-defined theme, filmclips as stage props, and, above all, the revealing of his character that often comes as a surprise both to him and to the audience. It all lends itself perfectly to show business techniques."

As for the politicians that he calls "the new stars," he notes: "They ask us for advice about makeup, lighting, what suit and tie to wear, and all the rest. Two of them, Michel Jobert and Jean Lecanuet, even showed up with several ties and asked me which was best."[40]

"Many people," write L.A. Dexter and D.M. White, "listen to great orators, preachers and professors not to learn from them, but to be diverted, moved, amused or consoled."[41] To this list may be added telepoliticians.

This is especially true if we are to believe the theory of "communication play" or "communication pleasure" advanced by William Stephenson, who writes: "Communication pleasure gives the feeling of amusement, contentment, serenity or enchantment that we associate with the theater, art, conversation, social life, and so on. To participate in it is to obtain a certain increase in the pleasure of living."

Just as we take pleasure in observing the spectacle of life on the stage or the screen, so also do we like to watch the spectacle of politics on the TV tube. This can be in the form of a televised senate hearing, a political convention which nominates a candidate for the White House, coverage of election night, or a presidential speech.

The mass media enable citizens to engage by proxy in the political game — or the election game, as it is crudely called by Joseph Napolitan, one of the leaders of that political persuasion industry that we might call political show business.

Former President John F. Kennedy during the Kennedy-Nixon debates (1960).

Former President Nixon at the G.O.P. convention in Miami (1968).

The Political Show Business Industry

"Sell your candidates the way business
sells its products."
—LEONARD HALL, CHAIRMAN OF
THE REPUBLICAN NATIONAL COMMITTEE

Like the theater, politics has its stagehands to move scenery and create special effects. These technicians belong to the fast-rising profession known as the persuasion industry, not to say the political show business industry.

Propaganda, so overused in dictatorships from the 1920s to the 1940s is linked in the public mind to authoritarianism or totalitarism. Thus, after 1945 aggressive propaganda techniques yielded before the new, smoother techniques of persuasion, at least in Western pluralistic societies.

Unlike totalitarian propaganda, persuasion derives from modern advertising methods which are more suited to a political "market" characterized by competition.

In a democracy a candidate cannot be imposed on the country by the sort of crude brainwashing upon which propaganda relies. He has to be "sold." Neither is the public assaulted by brutal frontal attacks. It is suavely, smoothly, and insidiously seduced.[1] This is done by modern methods of motivational research, marketing, sales promotion, public relations, and advertising.

Today the candidate-product has to win the election-market and get the most vote-sales. As the president of Young and Rubicam in France says, "the candidate is a product. He is packaged with his physical appearance, his way of speaking, smiling, moving. His platform determines his market definition and position."[2]

Similarly, political parties become brand names. Attachment to a party resembles fidelity to a given brand of goods. Today's political campaigns are organized like advertising campaigns. They are based on initial studies of the political "market," complete with polls and surveys — the gathering and analysis of all relevant factors; on in-depth study of the public image of parties and candidates in the race; on psychological research into voter motivation; on simulations of all possible tactics to be used; and so on.

THE STRATEGY OF POLITICAL DESIRE

In these "scientific" campaigns the primal question is, of course, how to make the voter-consumer buy the candidate-product. Thus the importance of motiviational research created by Ernest Dichter, a psychiatrist who emigrated to the United States in 1938 and founded the Institute for Motivational Research. The Institute's objective: to determine buyers' hidden motives in order to orient them better toward a given product. As Dichter puts it, to find the "why" of behavior and then determine the means of guiding it.[3]

For Dichter, these hidden motivations derive more from emotion than from reason. For if as he says, rationalism is a 20th-century obsession, pure irrationalism is often the key to understanding our conduct. It is therefore necessary to plumb the unconscious.

Another great "motive analyst," Louis Cheskin, director of the Color Research Institute of America, professes the same opinion:

> Motivation research looks into what determines the choices people make. It uses techniques that go deep into the unconscious or subconscious mind because preferences generally are determined by factors of which the individual is unaware. . . Actually, when the consumer makes a purchase he generally acts emotionally and compusively, unconsciously reacting to the images and designs associated in his subconscious with the product.[4]

With regard to this, Dichter discovered that the link between the consumer and a product is not only economic, but also essentially psychological. It symbolizes a way of being or appearing. In 1939, Dichter observed this in a study done for the company that makes Ivory

Soap, in which he developed the concept of a product's "image" or "personality." Soap is not judged, Dichter claimed, so much on its price, appearance, foam, or color as on all these qualities plus one, which is imponderable and almost evanescent, and which Dichter called the soap's personality.[5]

In sum, what incites an individual to want one product rather than another is the satifaction of deep needs of which he is himself unaware. To sell merchandise successfully, therefore, it is necessary to find out what these subconscious desires are — through in-depth interviews or psychoanalysis — and adapt sales strategy to them.

This leads to "behavior strategy," which examines the client's deepest motivations in order to better manipulate him and influence his conduct. That is why Vance Packard considers the actions of these "hidden persuaders" to represent regress rather than progress for man in his long struggle to become a rational and self-guiding being.[6]

But motivational research is not limited to the commercial world of advertising people. For politicians also are interested in getting the most appropriate messages to their electoral customers. So they have the same sort of research done into the subconscious motives involved in the political "purchase" in order to better influence consumers of political "products."

Dichter admits that politicians, businessmen, or advertising people who, leaving aside appearances, recognize the basic irrationality of humans and understand their needs and desires, have a better chance of success.[7]

In reality, "implicit communication" counts for more than "verbal communication." He has observed, Dichter notes, in surveys taken during electoral campaigns that the public pays much more attention to the gestures, expressions, and smiles of candidates than to the sense and content of their speeches. Finally, Dichter gives his advice on how to sell a new product to a public which is often traditionalist. First, say that the product is new, but that it fulfills a traditional function. Avoid claiming that it breaks with the past, in favor of saying that it lasts better than former products. Second, show that the new product does not break with the past, but that it is the natural result of evolution.[8]

Reading such advice, one has the impression that it must have been written especially for Georges Pompidou and Giscard d'Estaing, who respectively proposed, in 1969, "a new departure with continuity," and, in 1974, "continuity and change."

ADVENT OF THE ADVERTISING MAN

Political advertising appeared at the same time as motivational research, in the 1930s. Following its new defeat in the 1928 presidential election, the Democratic party created its own advertising department. Four years later, with Roosevelt in the White House, this department provided him with a public relations service. In 1936, the government employed at least 146 publicity people full time and 124 part time.[9]

The Republican party did the same. In 1936 it decided to transform the presidential election campaign into a virtual "national sales campaign." As Ralph Casey explained, it amounted to an intense, skillful, and highly organized commercial effort to disparage President Roosevelt and to sell Governor Landon and his "common sense," which would be heavily advertised.[10]

The Republicans called on sales technicians as well as advertising and public relations specialists. For the first time, the job of public relations director appeared in the party's organizational chart. In previous campaigns, the party had simply listed an advertising director.

From then on, the commercialization of politics increased in both parties at each election. Especially from 1952 on, candidates systematically engaged all the services advertising agencies have to offer: creative teams, buying time and space in the press and on radio and TV, production of advertising spots similar to commercials, public relations activities, and so on.

In 1952 the Batton, Durstine, and Osborn agency organized Eisenhower's TV campaign, including Nixon's famous Checkers Speech.

In 1956, Leonard Hall, chairman of Republican National Committee, told all the party's state committees to engage a full-time public relations consultant to insure Republican victory in Congress to match Eisenhower's in the White House. The Republican party would win because it had a great product to sell, Hall said. Sell your candidates the way business sells its products.[11]

In 1960, Nixon also used Madison Avenue's services, while the Democratic campaign was run by Lawrence O'Brien, who was an advertising and public relations man before joining the Kennedy team in 1951.

In 1968, the New York agency of Fuller, Smith, and Ross worked for Nixon in cooperation with Harry Treleaven, a former vice-president of J. Walter Thompson. And once he was in the White House, Nixon surrounded himself with advisers who in many cases came from the world of advertising, such as Erlichmann, Haldeman, and his press secretary, Ronald Ziegler, who also came from J. Walter Thompson. They were all there to "sell" his policies, often through less than commendable tactics.

That same year, the Doyle, Dane, and Bernbach agency, which had already worked for Johnson in 1964, was engaged by Humphrey, while the Papert, Koenig, and Lois agency helped with Robert Kennedy's candidacy in the Democratic presidential primaries.

President Ford's advertising spots were prepared in 1976 by Campaign '76 Media Communications, Inc., directed by Peter Dailey, a Los Angeles advertising man who had done similar work for Nixon in 1972. Ronald Reagan was advised on such matters by Harry Treleaven. On the Democratic side, the Lois Holland Callaway agency worked for Senator Jackson, while, as mentioned earlier, Gerald Rafshoon of Atlanta assisted Jimmy Carter.

The political use of advertising agencies has also reached the local level. In 1966, for example, Jack Tinker & Partners advised Nelson Rockefeller on his New York gubernatorial campaign and produced his TV advertising spots.

In Europe, many parties use the same methods, starting on the national level and quickly adapting them to the local level. Britain's Conservative party used an advertising agency, Coleman, Prentiss, and Varley, for the first time in 1959, under the direction of Ronald Simms, the party's head of advertising services. The Labour party soon followed that example.

In France in 1965, Jean Lecanuet engaged an agency called *Services et Méthodes* to help run his campaign for the presidency. The agency was headed by Michel Bongrand, who had made a name for himself by promoting a series of "James Bond" products in France. The agency gave a highly personalized tone to what many called an "American-style" campaign.

As the press reported Lecanuet's predicament: "It was rumored that he had been unable to block all the agency's mistakes, such as having pinup girls distribute roses to workers at Renault automobile plants.

Lecanuet had also stopped the use of documentary films showing him washing up at home in pajamas."[12]

In 1967, the same agency contributed to the Gaullists' narrow victory. In 1974, it helped beat Chaban-Delmas in the presidential race. Earlier, Chaban-Delmas had engaged Roger Vaurs, a public relations specialist trained in the United States, to brush up his image.

CAMPAIGN MANAGEMENT

Beyond the activities of advertising or public relations agencies, there is a whole industry devoted to political persuasion that developed in the United States. Campaign management, as it is called, handles the direction, coordination, and organization of campaigns, and it is a fast-growing business.

It consists of supervising all aspects of a campaign, including planning, strategy, research and analysis of information, media use, and so on, by coordinating the work of different specialists, from pollsters to speech writers, political advisers to TV producers.

In this field we have gone from amateurism to highly sophisticated professionalism. In the old days, the campaign manager was most often a friend belonging to the same party and working voluntarily. Today, he is usually a professional who is engaged and remunerated by the candidate. Often he belongs to a campaign management firm specialized in running campaigns and furnishing diversified services from advertising to fund raising, electoral marketing to making documentary films.

It is necessary to distinguish the campaign manager from the campaign consultant. The former works full time on the campaign and is charged with its overall direction. The latter renders a more limited, specialized service such as speech writing, media consulting, or strategy planning.

Still, some political consultants are generalists and resemble independent campaign managers. Thus Joseph Napolitan considers himself a political consultant. In 1968 he created the International

Association of Political Campaign Consultants with Michel Bongrand, which held its first conference in Paris in March 1969.*

In the beginning, this new service was basically public relations, an activity developed in the United States in the 1920s when big business began coming under fire and turned to public relations experts to improve its image.[13]

The political situation in California in the 1930s gave these experts the chance to apply their techniques to public life, for three reasons. First, due to the progressive movement, the state organized numerous elections, referendums, and the like. Second, the Depression sent thousands of people to the state who no longer had any definite political allegiances. Finally, the state's political parties had been weakly organized.

Thus in 1933 in San Francisco, Clem Whitaker, a lobbyist and public relations expert, and Leone Baxter, head of a local chamber of commerce, founded Campaigns, Inc., the first professional campaign management firm. In 1938 they institutionalized their relationship even further by being married.

From 1933 to 1955, the firm won 70 of the 75 campaigns it managed. One of its clients was Earl Warren, who was governor of California from 1943 to 1955 before becoming Chief Justice of the U.S. Supreme Court. The agency experience one of its rare losses when it was tardily engaged in 1967 to advise former child actress Shirley Temple Black in her bid for a seat in the House of Representatives.[14]

The two partners finally decided to get out of politics and sold the agency's political department to their son, Clem Whitaker, Jr.. By then, however, they no longer had a monopoly on campaign management, not even the dominant position in California.

That belonged to the Spencer, Roberts, and Associates agency, which was created in 1960 in Los Angeles by Stuart Spencer and William Roberts. The firm had about 60 campaigns to its credit, including Senator Kuchel's reelection in 1962 and Nelson Rockefeller's campaign in the 1964 California presidential primary, which was narrowly won by Barry Goldwater. In 1966 it managed Ronald Reagan's win in the California gubernatorial race against Edmund

---

* Its headquarters are at 9, rue Alfred de Vigny, Paris.

Brown, presenting Reagan as a citizen-politician running against a political pro, thus making a virtue of his lack of political experience. Reagan won by a million votes and was reelected in 1970, again with help from the same agency.

The firm had a few losses that year, however, and handled no major campaigns in 1972. In 1974, William Roberts was ill and sold his part of the agency to Stuart Spencer. Interestingly enough, Gerald Ford hired Spencer to run his campaign in 1976 after losing several primaries to Reagan; Spencer guided Ford to victory over his former client.

Another big firm, also in California, is Baus and Raus, whose cofounder, Herbert M. Baus, owed his training to Whitaker and Baxter. Baus and Raus advised Nixon in 1960, Goldwater — in the California presidential primary of 1964, — and Governor Edmund Brown in 1966. In the last two cases mentioned, the agency was face to face with its rival, Spencer and Roberts. So the question is, was it really Reagan who beat Brown in 1966, or was it Spencer and Roberts who beat Baus and Raus?

Other California agencies specializing in campaign management include Robert McGee National Directors and Hal Evry's Public Relations Center. But if California remains the state with the most such firms, other states are not without their services. For after 1945, many of the factors that had influenced California politics began spreading across the nation.

All states, for example, were increasingly affected by population mobility, weakening social structures, and changes in traditional allegiances. Moreover, progressive reshaping of election districts and an influx of new residents meant that politicians were often unknown to local voters. To get across to this public, politicians tended to use specialized agencies rather than the weakened party organizations.

In the 1960s, campaign management thus became a nationwide service industry at all political levels. The agencies were employed not only by candidates to the White House or to Congress, but also to win governorships and seats in state legislatures.

A study done by the *National Journal* in 1970 indicated that out of 67 Senate candidates, 62 had used advertising agencies, 30 engaged media consultants, 24 used national polling firms, and 20 hired campaign management firms. Only five candidates did not use the services of such specialists.

David Lee Rosenbloom tallied nearly 60 professional campaign management firms in the U.S. in 1972. Besides these, another 200 agencies offered campaign management among their various services. Among them, scattered throughout the country, we might mention important ones like Civic Service, Inc., in Missouri, which worked for Senator Robert Dole of Kansas in 1968. Then there is Matthew A. Reese and Associates in Washington and Kansas City, who have helped several Democrates including Senator Thomas Eagleton of Missouri. Campaign Consultants, Inc., has its offices in Boston and Washington, and has helped Senator Edward Brooke of Massachusetts and Spiro Agnew when he was governor of Maryland. Real-Poland, Inc., in Texas worked for Governor John Connally in his 1962 and 1966 campaigns. There is Publicom, Inc., in Washington. And U.S. R&D, run by two former assistants to President Kennedy, William Haddad and Robert Clampitt, is one of the main firms used by the Democratic party, along with Joseph Napolitan Associates.

Along with Clifton White, Lawrence O'Brien,* and Hal Evry, Joseph Napolitan is one of the country's most famous campaign consultants, having scored, for instance, 15 wins out of 17 campaigns in 1972. In 1960 he worked with Lawrence O'Brien for John Kennedy in the New Hampshire, Wisconsin, and West Virginia primaries. In 1964, the same team worked for Lyndon Johnson. In 1966 Napolitan advised Shapp, who just missed the Pennsylvania governorship, and in 1968 he worked for Humphrey, who narrowly lost to Nixon.

The largest agencies, which have up to 250 staff members, offer complete campaign management services, with specialized departments, and a client can hire all or part of them. Smaller ones with only a dozen or so members do not handle all services themselves. Depending on what is required, they subcontract with specialized firms or independent professionals.

The list of specialists used in today's campaigns is surprisingly long: public relations experts, advertising men, advance men, fund raisers, marketing men,[15] demographers, statisticians, psychologists, social psychologists, political scientists, computer programmers, mailing

---

* Lawrence O'Brien was in the unfortunate position of being campaign manager of three unlucky candidates in 1968. First there was President Johnson, who decided not to run, then Robert Kennedy, who was assassinated, and then Humphrey, who lost.

experts, speechwriters, radio and TV producers, film makers, media consultants, makeup people, artists, pollsters, and on and on.

In addition, there is campaign research, which deals with everything related to gleaning a maximum of information on voters' desires. This way, the candidate does not simply declare a platform based on what he thinks is right, but on what his potential constituency wants.

Many of these activities, such as statistical analysis, vote projections, simulations, polls, and so on, rely on scientific techniques. The director of research is therefore usually a political scientist.

After engaging Walter D. DeVries as director of research in 1962, George Romney was elected governor of Michigan three times, thanks in good part to the quality of his research team's polls. DeVries returned to academe in 1967 to teach political science at Calvin College.

POLLS

The first public opinion polls date from the 1930s, and were used for the first time in a national election in 1936.* They were begun by Elmo Roper and Paul Cherington (Fortune Surveys), George G. Gallup (The American Institute of Public Opinion), and Archibald Crossley (The Crossley Poll). Other masters of the trade include Joe Belden, Mervin Field, Robert Coursen, Glenn Roberts, and above all Louis Harris, who worked for John Kennedy in 1960. In 1976, Ford and Carter engaged Robert Teeter and Pat Cadell, respectively.

The first political poll at the local level dates from 1946, when Elmo Roper did one for Jacob Javits, then candidate in New York's 21st Congressional District. Many have been made for local elections since then, despite their high cost.

According to Louis Harris, over two-thirds of Senate candidates, probably three-quarters of gubernatorial candidates, and about one out of ten of those running for the House of Representatives had recourse to polls.[16]

---

* The French Institute of Public Opinion was created in 1938.

Polls give a complete picture of a voting district: age, sex, educational level, and income of voters; the candidate's strong and weak areas within it. They indicate what the public thinks of him. And they reveal which are the most important issues for the voters and what their opinion on them is. They can even measure public reaction to a candidate's platform before he has put it in final shape, enabling him to adapt it where necessary to obtain a more favorable reception.

Joseph Napolitan used such polls during Shapp's campaign for governor of Pennsylvania in 1966. Shapp was initially in favor of raising the minimum age for a driver's license from 16 to 18, and also of lowering voting age from 21 to 18. "We did some polls," Napolitan recounts, "and we discovered that a strong percentage of voters were favorable to raising the age for driver's licenses, but were against lowering voting age. So in our campaign material that year we underlined his position on driver's licenses and ignored his position on lowering voting age."[17]

This sort of feeling out the situation can make for plastic politicians without either ideas or convictions, ready to model and adapt their platforms to match voter's preferences. With no firm position on the issues, such a candidate becomes a mere mirror of the prevailing opinion.

It is here that image specialists and those involved in research join forces. For the main objective of the image makers is to know what the voters want in order to shape their candidate's personality around that.

Before putting a new product on the market, advertising men use market studies to find out what the consumers would like to have and to make the product appear to conform to their desires. Before promoting their candidate, image makers use polls to find out what sort of politician voters want.

Before doing a documentary film on Shapp for use in the Democratic gubernatorial primary, Napolitan commissioned four polls. They revealed that voters associated the Democratic party with a political boss system whose main occupation was siphoning of public funds. Napolitan therefore decided to present his candidate as a man outside machine politics, and Charles Guggenheim's film was entitled, "The Man Against the Machine."

Another problem with polls is that when published during the campaign, they may influence the vote, thereby creating public opinion as much as they measure it.

This can produce a bandwagon effect, with hesitant voters deciding in favor of the candidate most likely, according to the polls, to win. That gives them the satisfaction of identifying with a winner, and also of going along with the majority.

Thus many voters are tempted to abandon their initial choice to jump on the bandwagon. This appears to have happened in France in 1974, when it worked against Jacques Chaban-Delmas and in favor of Valéry Giscard d'Estaing.

Polls can therefore represent an instrument of manipulation and pressure by creating a feeling of unanimity or at least a trend in favor of a given candidate. They can tend to "normalize" voter behavior, encouraging individuals to conform to the mainstream opinion.

Another effect of polls is to create the underdog effect. This occurs when voter sympathy flows toward the candidate said to have least support by the polls. Some voters will shift to his side to keep him from being too bady beaten.

Actually, however, there have been few systematic and empirical studies done of the effects of polls on voter behavior. The ones that have been done point largely to the bandwagon effect. After reviewing the literature on the subject, Joseph T. Klapper concluded that there was no absolute proof that publication of polls effects or does not effect voting results. Personally, he does not believe that either the bandwagon or underdog effect is of significant size, but he refrains from rejecting the possibility of some effect. [18]

Harold Mendelsohn and Irving Crespi also think that the effect of polls is probably insignificant or minimal. [19] They claim that if such effects occur (and it would not be reasonable to exclude that possibility on some individuals), the incidence is so small as to be impossible to measure. [20]

Still, Columbia University has done two studies that give credence to the bandwagon effect. One concerns the presidential election of 1940 when Roosevelt beat Wilkie. [21] The other covered the Truman-Dewey race in 1948. [22]

Louis Harris also believes that polls can influence voter behavior to some extent. "On the whole," he writes, "we do not believe that polls can modify an election result by more than three or four [percentage] points, but since most elections result in a nearly 50-50 vote, it would be less than candid not to admit that they can affect the outcome. More precisely, a candidate who uses polls skillfully can change the outcome." [23]

The clever candidate can, for example, hide poll results unfavorable to him and publish only the positive ones. Rather than information, polls then become propaganda instruments, or perhaps ''pseudo-events.''[24] Publishing poll results is one way of getting the media to mention a candidate whose name might otherwise not pop up in the press that day. So it can be seen that the use of polls is often an attempt to make ''news'' and influence the voter rather than inform him.

THE COMPUTER

Campaign technology became even more sophisticated — and costly — with the introduction of computers.

At one point, the leader in the field was Arkansas Governor Winthrop Rockefeller, brother of Nelson Rockefeller. He has been described as the only politician in America who kept his own private computer for his political work and who maintained, out of his own pocket, a team of experts to run it.[25] It was estimated in 1967 that this IBM computer cost $10,000 a month to rent. Governor Winthrop Rockefeller's team was doubtless the first to have an Electronic Data Processing card for such a vast district: the entire state of Arkansas.

Computerized information facilitates door-to-door canvassing in each precinct as well as voter registration. It has made a science of mailings, especially for fund raising, by addressing personalized and diversified letters to voters.

Joseph Napolitan confided that computers introduce a delicate, personal touch to the mailing campaign, for example by repeating the voter's name in the third or fourth paragraph to give the impression that the letter is personal and not part of a mass mailing.[26] Moreover, the candidate's signature can be reproduced mechanically so well that it looks like a true longhand signature. In these mailings, the candidate matches the content of the letters as closely to the desires of each voter, going so far as to adapt his remarks to the addressee's age, sex, profession, and so on.

With such numerous and detailed capacities, the computer is obviously a valuable tool in campaign management, and it is hardly surprising that Spencer and Roberts has acquired a minority holding in Datamatics, Inc. — especially since the computer also can produce sophisticated simulations. A simulation is an imitation of real life processes. Its key words are *what if? What if* the candidate takes a certain position on inflation? *What* will happen *if* he supports — or condemns — more liberal abortion laws? Long before the election, simulation procedures enable him to measure the impact of different strategic or tactical options. The likely result of each can be predicted on the basis of input to the computer.

The first political simulation was done in 1960 for Kennedy by the Simulmatics Corporation, a group of social scientists (Professors McPhee of Columbia, De Sola of MIT, and Adelson of Yale) and Democratic businessmen. It was done in cooperation with Elmo Roper's Public Opinion Research Center which possessed much of the data required. The main question asked of the simulation specialists: what attitude should Kennedy, a Catholic, have on the question of his religion, which was sure to be raised by his opponents? After 480 calculations, this answer was communicated to Kennedy on August 25, 1960:

> If the campaign becomes rough, he will lose relatively more Protestant votes to Nixon, but he will gain votes among Catholics and minority groups. Sharp anti-Catholicism during the campaign will provoke a backlash favorable to Kennedy among Catholics and others offended by this prejudice.[27]

As a result, Kennedy chose to face the religious question squarely, and many postelection analyses concluded that he had made the right decision.

ADVANCE MEN AND SPEECHWRITERS

Guided by simulations and polls, often adapting his position to conform to their results, the candidate uses still other artifices to win votes.

There are advance men, for instance, who precede him wherever he goes to arrange the trip, organize rallies, and brief the candidate on local problems and leaders. This way, the candidate can refer to them in his speeches, thus giving the impression of a good knowledge of local affairs. Advance men are commonly used in presidential campaigns, but Edward Kennedy was one of the first to use them in a Senate race.

Other campaign technicians include speechwriters, who prepare the candidate's declarations and addresses for him. John Kennedy hired such speech writers as Arthur Schlesinger, Jr., a Pulitzer Prize-winning historian, Ralph A. Dungan, special assistant adviser, Richard N. Goodwin — who later served as Lyndon Johnson's speechwriter — and Pierre Salinger.[28] But his most favored adviser, his "intellectual blood donor,"[29] was Theodore Sorensen, who worked closely with him for ten years.

In his memoirs, Sorensen recounts how Kennedy and he meticulously prepared wisecracks, quotations, one-liners, and so on. The result was far from spontaneous improvisation:

> Kennedy took down the better jokes told by other speakers for later use. I had a large "humor file" that kept on getting larger. Since the texts of his speeches given to the press usually had anecdotal material removed, we could use it in other speeches. . . . Besides our humor archives, we kept a collection of conclusions, usually quotations from famous persons or allusions to historical events that, accompanied by a brief peroration, could serve as the ending to any speech on any given subject.[30]

In 1976, Sorensen worked on the acceptance speech given by Carter at the Democratic National Convention, which had been mainly written by his chief ghost writer, novelist Patrick Anderson. Thus do successive Democratic presidents, like so many actors, "interpret" the sonorous speeches of Ted Sorensen, official playwright and permanent prompter of the White House.*

The same thing goes on, of course, in the Republican party. President Ford even officially hired a White House gagman to spice his speeches with witty asides and opening jokes.

The preparation of Ford's acceptance speech at the Republican National Convention in Kansas City in 1976 was especially laborious. Well before D-Day, Robert Hartmann, White House adviser and chief

---

*In January 1977, Carter appointed Sorensen director of the CIA, but he renounced the job in the face of strong Senate opposition.

speechwriter, went to work with five writers from his team. Two weeks before the convention, Ford and Hartmann began to meet for several hours a day to shape the speech and adapt it to the president's oratorical style. Phrases were recast, syntax simplified, complicated rhetorical turns deleted. On August 8, Hartmann had a long work session with Ford at Camp David.

One week before the day of the speech, Ford began working on his oral delivery. First he read the speech to an audience of three persons: Robert Hartmann, his assistant Robert Orben, and media consultant Don Penny, a former comic actor. Then he recorded it on video tape and went over it several times to polish his presentation. All this time, his advisers worked hard to get him to cut down on his favorite rhetorical tricks of lowering his voice to a melodramatic whisper or using grandiose flourishes.

The president took the tape with him to Kansas City to practice with it up to the last minute. Result: a performance so good that his team decided to buy a half-hour of TV time in September to broadcast it as part of his campaign. Hartmann's comment: "If I had two weeks to work on every one of his speeches, they would all be that good."[31]

With such hyper-preparation and utter lack of spontaneity, the candidate becomes almost an actor, practicing his lines under the critical eyes of the playwright or director, who supervises his interpretation of the role down to the least detail.

Such a comparison is not excessive, for professional campaign managers act like impresarios, always on the lookout for new talent and lining up engagements when they find it. Indeed, political leaders are fabricated much the same way as show business stars.

A STAR IS BORN

Certain campaign professionals use talent scout techniques to discover promising performers and incite them to run for election, using their services.

It was professional campaigner Roy Day who discovered Richard Nixon. In 1946, Day, then president of the Los Angeles Republican Committee, created the "Committee of One Hundred" to find a candidate for the House who could beat the incumbent Democrat, Gerald Voorhis. The Committee made a call for prospective candidates that was carried on page one of 26 newspapers. Nixon answered the call and appeared before the Committee, which chose him for the job.[32]

Such pros always look over their potential clients carefully and avoid accepting automatically just anyone with political ambitions who wants to hire them. They consider that their professional reputation depends on how many elections they win; consequently, they refuse to work for candidates who are obviously not "saleable products."

In 1965, Ronald Reagan asked Spencer and Roberts to handle his campaign for governor of California the following year. The agency's executives held several sessions with him to determine whether he had an attractive personality. Reagan submitted to several interrogations by them before finally demanding in exasperation, "now, by God, I want a few answers from you guys! Are you going to work for me or not?" After a few days more of thinking it over, they agreed to take the job.

Once a client is accepted, the professional manager takes him in charge, right down to the smallest details of dress, or "costuming."

If we are to believe Napolitan, Shapp wore awful brown socks that were always too short, leaving his shanks bare when he sat on a platform. Despite his adviser's insistence, Shapp refused to wear any other socks. After his loss in November 1966, Napolitan sent him a Christmas present of a half-dozen loud, reddish-brown socks with the note, "to hell with it, now you can wear whatever you want!"[33]

Shapp finally was elected governor of Pennsylvania in 1970, but history has not recorded whether by that time he had changed his taste in socks.

Napolitan had similar problem with Charles Ryan, the former mayor of Springfield, Massachusetts who in his first campaign wore white knit tennis socks: "I suggested to him that he wear something more traditional, and he did it."[34]

With such attention to detail, professional campaigners — especially those specialized in television campaigns — behave with their candidates like film directors with their stars. Like Pygmalion, they fabricate new — and artificial — personalities for them. Treleaven did it for Nixon in 1968 and later, in 1976, for Reagan; Napolitan did it for

Humphrey in 1968. In all cases, they did for their candidates what Mauritz Stiller did for Garbo or Josef von Sternberg did for Dietrich.

The perfect star is an automaton with a soul in the image of his or her director. And political stars similarly become puppets whose strings are pulled by their campaign managers or their media consultants.

In 1964 as in 1968, with Roy Day as with Harry Treleaven or Frank Shakespeare, Nixon's success was due to professional campaigners. The Nixon discovered by Day and the "new Nixon" shaped by Treleaven are both triumphs of astute political management. Let Nixon stray from the advice given him by such experts and the result, in 1960 and 1974, was failure. In the absence of adequate stage setting and direction, the artificial image gives way to reality.

Richard Nixon's political death was due to having become himself once again, none other than "Tricky Dick." He made the mistake of casting aside the image so carefully created for him by those masters of political stage direction, Treleaven, Shakespeare, and Ailes. Thus is born — and dies — a star.

For that matter, these campaign professionals can be as unfaithful to their candidates as film directors sometimes are when they discover a new star to replace the old one. As we have seen, Stuart Spencer fabricated Reagan's image in 1966 and 1970, getting him elected governor of California. But in 1976 he advised Ford, Reagan's direct rival for the Republican presidential nomination.

And although accepting only Republican clients, Spencer and Roberts advised the liberal wing — Rockefeller in 1964 — the right wing — Reagan in 1966 and 1970 — and the center — Ford in 1976. Actually, Spencer and Roberts seems to side with the Republican who pays the best.

Similarly, Civic Service, Inc., works only for Republicans, as does Robert Walker or F. Clifton White. White's particular specialty is organizing conventions, and he helped Nixon in 1960, Goldwater in 1964, and Ford in 1976. Generally speaking, it appears that such professional managers are used more by the Republican party which can better afford their costly services.

Nonetheless, some professionals work exclusively for the Democrats, such as Matthew A. Reese and Associates, Real-Poland, or Publicom, Inc. As for Napolitan, he writes: "I am a Democrat. In the United States, I work only for the Democratic candidates that I like.''[35] But abroad, he is less consistent. In 1969 he worked for the reelection of President Ferdinand Marcos of the Philippines, who is seldom considered a liberal.

Less scrupulous agencies work for both parties. Baus and Raus, for instance, ran Nixon's California Primary campaign in 1960 and Goldwater's in 1964, but shifted easily to Democrat Brown in the 1966 California gubernatorial race.

In France, the Services de Méthodes agency advised Jean Lecanuet in his try for the Elysée against de Gaulle in December 1965. But it worked for the Gaullists during the National Assembly and Senate elections in March 1967.

New campaign managers came to the fore during the 1976 presidential race in the U.S. First there was Hamilton Jordan, 31, who served as Carter's campaign director. A former political science student at the University of Georgia, Jordan had worked for Carter for ten years, first as his youth coordinator (at age 22) during Carter's unsuccessful bid to become governor of Georgia in 1966. Next he was Carter's campaign manager in 1970, when they won. As early as 1972, he sent Carter a memorandum on how to win the White House in 1976. When the campaign officially got under way in September 1976, Jordan supervised a team of 700, including 302 in his Atlanta office.

Ronald Reagan's campaign manager was John Sears, 36, a former legal aide to Nixon and whiz kid of the 1968 presidential campaign. Gerald Ford had several managers. Businessman Howard Callaway was replaced in March 1976 by former Commerce Secretary Rogers Morton. But Morton proved more affable than effective, and he was in turn replaced, after the Republican Convention, by James A. Baker III, 46, a bright Houston lawyer and former Under Secretary of Commerce. But from March 1976 on, the professionals took over. Stuart Spencer moved in to become Ford's de facto political director, while Clifton White and William Timmons were hired as convention managers.

These pros meticulously organized the Kansas City convention, paying special attention to liaisons — via telephone and walkie-talkie — with the convention floor. They even found time to give whimsical names to the principals: President Ford was referred to as Tarzan, Mrs. Ford as Jane, Nelson Rockefeller was Superman, and Rogers Morton was Batman.[36]

CAMPAIGN EFFECT

The exact impact of such campaign methods remains to be seen. Clearly, even the most successful campaign is not going to dictate every voter's choice.

First of all, many voters make their decision even before the official campaign begins, or just as it is getting under way. According to Kurt and Gladys Lang, from 50 to 84 percent of voters have made up their minds beforehand.[37]

Analysis of American presidential elections from 1948 to 1968 reveals the same thing: about one-third of all eligible voters determine how they will cast their ballot well before the candidates are officially designated at the party conventions, one-third decide during the conventions, and only the last third make their choice during the campaign.[38] But this last third is often the decisive factor in an election, especially a close one like those in 1960 and 1968.

Studies of French presidential elections give the same results. On May 27 and 28, 1969, for example, when the country was between two rounds of balloting, the Sofres agency did a poll. "Have you made up your mind, or might you still change it between now and next Sunday?" the agency asked. Analysis of the answers showed the 68 percent knew exactly for whom they would vote, whereas 32 percent admitted they might change their minds.

This large percentage of undecided voters shows how important the "floating" vote is, and how much the outcome of an election can be influenced by a good campaign.

The question remains of why more of the public is not affected by campaign efforts. The answer is to be found in the various factors that predetermine an individual's political choices.

First, there is party loyalty, especially in a bipartisan system. According to Angus Campbell, three out of four persons in America consider themselves either Democrats or Republicans, and habitually vote for their party's candidates. But this is less important in primary elections, where party identification is the same for all.

Next comes the individual's feeling of belonging to a given social group. That person is not an isolated atom, but belongs to various groups with their own norms, standards, and opinion leaders, all tending to orient the voter's decision. Also, the voter's socioeconomic status often weighs in the balance.

Finally there are the individual's political attitudes, predispositions fashioned by experience of politics, which limit a capacity to change both opinion and vote.

Due to these factors, many voters will only have their attitudes and convictions crystallized and reinforced by the campaign. Often they subconsciously practice "selective exposure," retaining only elements of the campaign that confirm the choice they have already made. Overall, then, all the candidates' campaign efforts actually affect voter decisions only marginally, as several sociologists have concluded after systematic studies.[39]

But can influence over one-third of the voting public really be considered marginal? The campaign will not make the majority change their minds, but it does affect importantly the undecided vote. And it is often this third of the electorate that determines the outcome.

Actually, a campaign is always directed at two publics. The first is made up of voters who have strong political views. Their attitudes are stable and unchanging, and resist all efforts by the professional persuaders.

To be sure, these citizens who take politics seriously follow the campaign attentively in the newspapers and on radio and TV to obtain a maximum of information. But analysis of election results shows that these people have, in fact, already made their choice. They made it before the campaign began, and it can only confirm and reinforce their attitudes. Paradoxically, the voters who pay most attention to politics are also those who are the least disposed to change their minds.

On the other hand, there is a second public composed of persons who do not pay much attention to politics. Their attitudes are unstable and weak. They do not identify with a party and are therefore impressionable.

It is this second public that forms the target for the persuasion industry. For it does not attempt to change the attitudes of those who have strong political motivations, but aims instead at voters who do not much care one way or the other.

These people are particularly responsive to the form of a political message, rather than to its content. With them, it is important to be equivocal, to keep the messages ambiguous enough to correspond to widely varying expectations. As one study notes, a campaign theme will be particularly effective if it can seem to convey a number of different meanings.[40] And the message — often a TV spot — should be repeated often to get the attention of these voters who do not habitually pay attention to anything political.

To attract this segment of the public the mass media are most effective, especially television, since such persons look to the media not for information but for entertainment and diversion. This "play function" of the media is one of the central concepts of mass communications.[41] It represents escape from the unpleasant world of duty and responsibility, a moment of freedom and fantasy, an interlude in the work day. Much of the public look to the media for the gratification and satisfaction of a brief respite, and campaign professionals know how to manipulate this desire. They know that for this segment of the public, composed of citizens with little political motivation, politics is only something to chat about once in a while, and then only when it has entertainment value. What they expect from the media during a political campaign is not information, but diversion.

Distract, captivate, amuse: these are the objectives of the campaign professionals. That is why they particularly like to use TV debates which increase the excitement and drama of a campaign by giving it a semblance of combat — entertaining combat. This they aim at the less motivated voter, the one who wants both communication and pleasure from the media in his or her role of spectator.

Thus does the political show depend on its public for success. For nothing about it — neither skilled political actors, nor media complaisance, nor the sophisticated techniques of the persuasion industry — would be effective if the public did not go along with it.

PART THREE
The Public

Politics, we have seen, tends more and more to become show business, more often than not a one-man show. But there can be no show without spectators.

If power has become personalized, it is not only due to those who exercise it. Those who submit to it or who support it are also responsible. For it could not long exist without a public willing to accept it, without the public's complicity.

We must, therefore, look into the reasons why this political show is so successful with the public. We must ask the why and wherefore of the personalization of power.

Former Algerian President Hourai Boumediene (left) and Libyan strongman Moammar Khadafy at the fourth summit of nonaligned nations in Algeria (1973).

Why Star System Politics?

"The people are happy when attending a spectacle; this is the means by which we hold their mind and their heart."
—LOUIS XIV

Why is it that today's leaders have become stars? How has this personalization come to be? What has it produced? On what ground, on what substrata has it developed? If this phenomenon has been successful with the public, that means it must have roots that go deeper than mere chance.

We must therefore examine everything that supports this political deviation by analyzing the historical, economic, social, psychological, cultural, and institutional conditions that form the "environment" of the personalization of power.

CRISIS AND PEACE

Historical analysis shows that times of crisis produce super-personalization. To meet exceptional perils, the public turns willingly to a man who symbolizes and often concentrates power — someone like a Roman dictator.

Danger of civil war or conflict with a foreign nation constitutes a major crisis. In such situations, an anxious citizenry often look for salvation to a father figure, preferably a heroic one. In France, this has been Thiers in 1871, Clemenceau in 1917, Doumergue in 1934, Pétain in 1940, de Gaulle in 1958.

Could de Gaulle have staged his comeback without public fear of a civil war? A savior requires a dramatic situation to serve as his vehicle. If necessary he provokes it or exaggerates it, depicting the dark dangers that threaten the country and offering himself as the only bulwark against chaos — real or imaginary.

Such a savior is often a military figure who presents himself as the shield of national unity, the war-tested protector. It is a Bonaparte, a Boulanger, or a Pétain.

Today, military power often rules in Latin America, the Middle East, and Africa with this pretention of incarnating national unity. The list runs from Marshal Amin (Uganda) and Bokassa I (Central African Empire) to Generals Mobutu (Zaire), Lamizana (Upper Volta), Eyadema (Togo), Habyalimana (Rwanda), Sida Barre (Somalia), and Nimeiri (Sudan), to Colonels Boumediene (Algeria), Qadaffi (Libya), Traoré (Mali), Kountche (Niger), Bagaza (Burundi), and Opango (Congo).

In such countries, crisis can take the form of affirming national independence. This requires a liberator, a "historic chief" who throws off the colonial yoke. He is followed by a successor who carries on the anti-imperialist fight and around whom nationalism crystallizes. Thus since the 1950s has the history of the Third World singularly favored the personalization of power.

Crises can also be economic and social. In 1932, Roosevelt was elected to deal with the Great Depression. In 1933, Hilter was the product — quite different — of a profound crisis that shook Germany. A similar crisis seized Italy and produced Mussolini in 1922.

These two dictators used their crisis-generated authority to protect a threatened socioeconomic system. But crisis can also be the agent of social change. This is the case of the revolutionary leader — Lenin or Mao — who uses crisis to accelerate the movement of history toward a radical transformation.

When the crisis is over and peace returns, routine authority replaces crisis authority. This does not always mean that power is depersonalized, but there is usually a transition from the hero figure to the ordinary man figure.

The end of the crisis is also the end of the idol. Public opinion rejects the prestigious leader who is identified with difficult times. It longs for calm after the storm. It therefore turns away from the great man in favor of more ordinary leaders, considered better adapted to ordinary times. As we have seen, it was not by mere chance that Attlee followed Churchill, Khrushchev followed Stalin, and Pompidou followed de Gaulle.

Unlike the personalization of power in times of crisis, peacetime personalization requires a leader with the Everyman image. But it can also work to the advantage of the charm leader if the public perceives him as a relief from charisma. Many charm leaders — Kennedy, Trudeau, Palme, Giscard d'Estaing — accede to power at a moment when their country is or seems to be in a period of calm and economic peace. A secure atmosphere creates confidence in the future and favors candidates who represent a "change."

On the other hand, in periods of ecnomic crisis or international tension, voters reject inexperience, youth — even relative — and the desire for change. They prefer the protective father figure to the innovative, audacious brother figure.

The public willingly turns over the helm to a young sailor when the sea is calm and there are no clouds on the horizon. But let a storm come up, and the old captain is more reassuring. An uncertain atmosphere tends to incite the public to look for security in an authority figure.

THE ECONOMICS OF PERSONALIZATION

Besides the historical situation, are there certain economic conditions that favor personalized authority, that even shape the historical situation itself? Is there an economic side to the personalization of power?

The Marxist answer is well known. The state is only "a machine for the oppression of one class by another," even if it pretends to be an impartial arbiter in the class struggle.

"In exceptional circumstances," Engels notes, "there are periods when the classes in their struggle are so close to equilibrium that the power of the state as a pseudo-mediator maintains a certain independence from them. Thus the monarchies of the 17th and 18th centuries kept the nobility evenly balanced against the bourgeoisie and the bourgeoisie against the proletariat.

Basing himself both on Marx and on the *18 Brumaire de Louis-Napoleon Bonaparte*, Gramsci attributes Caesarism, Bonapartism, and fascism to social blockage. When neither the haves nor the have-nots are in a dominant position, whether it be in 1922 or in 1851, the providential man must come forth to arbitrate a situation that leads to paralysis.

Bonapartism is therefore the product of equilibrium between the classes. In order to maintain this fragile balance, the bourgeoisie consents, while keeping its economic power, to delegate its political power to a "great man" in the form of a national hero or victorious general. This gives the state a relative autonomy, enabling it to serve the dominant class without appearing to be its slave, all the while being supported by the dominated class. Thus Louis-Napoleon Bonaparte was made president, then emporer, by the public will.

De Gaulle, in turn, received the support of the masses in a very complex class configuration. By skillful use of universal suffrage, he governed to the profit of the dynamic bourgeoisie and to the detriment of the traditional notables who were the product of the peasantry and the former middle class. In this way he instituted a state adapted to neocapitalism.

The ideal of liberal capitalism was that of an unobtrusive state, of the "night watchman state" that Gramsci talked of. But neocapitalism requires a strong, activist state to administer the economy, modulate consumption, keep an eye on salaries, encourage investment, and so on. It has to support and occasionally subsidize the large private groups that attempt to discipline the market.

This strong, activist state needs leaders of undisputed legitimacy who, strengthened by universal suffrage, can act to change traditional economic structures and social classes and bring about a restructuring favorable to the monopolistic bourgeoisie.

In a word, periods of equilibrium or quasi-equilibrium between the classes favor a strengthening of the power of the state as pseudo-arbiter, and the consequent personalization of power. Thus came about the tyrany of the Greek city-states of the seventh and sixth centuries B.C., as well as the dictatorships of the Roman Republic of the first century B.C.. In both cases there was a paralyzing balance between the new classes and those that were traditional.

Today, under-development gives rise to over-power, as if the nations of the Third World, often tormented by ethnic or tribal divisions and handicapped by economic backwardness, were attempting to compensate for these obstacles with an excess of political authority — as if a unified and concentrated government were better suited to impose national unity and economic modernization — as if the economic deficit could be offset by a political surplus, if only the hyperactive government could automatically bring progress in its wake.

SOCIETY AND MASS COMMUNICATIONS

But in its way, over-development also favors personalized power, if not personal power. For it creates a technicized, robotized, standardized society. A "mass society" demographically more numerous, more bureaucratic, where the individual has the feeling that he does not count.

In ancient times, when society was composed of primary groups, the population was in personal and direct contact with its leaders. Today the individual is less and less integrated into a family or village community and he therefore loses his identity in an abstract, bueraucratic universe reminiscent of Franz Kafka's *The Castle*.

The dehumanized, mechanized society, which suppresses or distends personal relationships, sometimes provokes a compensatory phenomenon in the form of the personalization of power. It is a sort of backlash attempt to retain, at least at the summit of public life, a minimum of human contact and a bit of the human warmth that has disappeared at the base.

Thanks to the mass media, which everywhere reproduce the leader's voice and image, the citizen has the impression of a direct contact. And the leader deliberately plays on this need of affective relationships, even if they are illusory. Thus does the irrational reappear in the over-developed countries. Thus does charisma assume its importance in great anonymous societies.

Indeed, if government by star system is to be a corrective to the ills of mass society, it must first of all develop those ills. Hannah Arendt has shown how the totalitarian system — whether under Hitler or Stalin — deliberately sets out to destroy all social and family relationships. It replaces them with a single large and shapeless mass which is unable to resist it. Totalitarian movements are massive organizations of atomized and isolated individuals. The very root of totalitarianism is, according to Arendt, the completely isolated human being without any social relationships with family, friends, comrades, or simple acquaintances. The individual obtains the feeling of his or her usefulness only by belonging to a movement, to a political party.[1] And this, of course, requires a prestigious leader.

Star system government has always existed although it was less obvious in the past. In the 19th century, government was strongly personalized at the local level: mayors and other local notables had great power as a result of the relative lack of communications.

Today the mass media have "nationalized" this tendency. The press, radio, and television have transferred personalized power from the local to the national level. Now each citizen has the impression — even if illusory — that he or she knows the head of the national government as well as everyone knew the village mayor before. Modern information methods have not created this phenomenon. They have simply put it on a different level and accentuated it.

THE PSYCHOLOGY OF PERSONALIZATION

But star system government also has its psychological roots. In its way, it reproduces the alienation that Ludwig Feuerbach analyzed in religions. "Religion," he wrote, "is a loss of man's substance. He projects it onto a 'divine being' exterior to himself which is the product of his consciousness. He invests the idol that he has created with the virtues and potentials that are the substance of humanity itself."

Through this mechanism of projection, man perceives in the exterior world, in other beings, the affective qualities that are uniquely his. Thus is born an idol that he creates from his substance and from the best of himself that he contemplates and adores as a being apart.[2]

This "alienation of man in a divine being" has its equivalent in the alienation of the citizen in the political idol. Here too he endows an exterior figure with all the virtues he amputates from himself. He transfers to the hero everything he would like to be or do himself. This Olympian figure serves as a medium for the projection of the individual's aspirations and dreams.

There remains the possibility of identifying with this ideal political being. In his analysis of the affective identification with the Führer,

Wilhelm Reich observes that this tendency is the psychological foundation of national narcissism; that is, of a feeling of pride deriving from the "grandeur of the nation." What counts is the exhilarating idea of belonging to the master race and being led by a genius.[3]

Glorying in the leader they have chosen, the masses feel flattered and proud. Just as, Feuerbach notes, a servant derives dignity from that of his master, thanks to his master's honor, he satisfies his own need of honor.[4]

In this way the citizen feels greater value and dignity in his own life by proxy, thanks to the hero figure or charm leader. For it is easier to effect the necessary projection-identification by voting for a young, handsome leader — in the image of the Kennedy brothers, for example — and thereby feel the gratification of self-glorification. The voter projects his desire for heroism or adventure on a leader and puts himself unconsciously in his place to the point of living a dream.

This leads us to question whether the psychological base of personalized power is not what has been called "the instinct to obey," as if the individual had a need to be mastered.

"Machiavelian" sociologists answer in the affirmative. For them, democracy is only an illusion or a mystification. The masses everywhere have always been dominated by a small minority resembling Pareto's "elite," Mosca's "leadership class," and Michels' "oligarchy."[5]

For Michels, "the iron rule of the oligarchy" rests not only on the tendency of the leadership class to perpetuate itself, but also on the inertia of the masses, who prefer to be led by political "professionals." In short, the taste for power is complemented by the taste for submission.

This submission to personalized authority appears to have its psychoanalytical roots. Analyzing "the concept of the great man," Freud remarks that "most human beings feel the imperative need of an authority to admire, to kneel down before and by which to be dominated and sometimes even mistreated."[6]

Reich also observes this "hunger for authority" that underpins the ideology of the Fascist Führer. But he does not consider it natural and inevitable. The idea that "man needs authority and discipline" or "discipline and order" is grounded in the antisocial structure — but only a reactionary would hold that structure is eternal and immutable.[7]

SUBMISSION CULTURE AND SHOW BUSINESS CULTURE

Even more than from psychology, the personalization of power springs from culture, in a double sense.

First of all, institutional democracy, "legal-rational" authority is only viable if the citizenry possesses a minimum of culture in the broad sense of education and the corresponding capacity for abstraction. Thus the cultural under-development of France in 1848 favored the election by universal suffrage of Louis-Bonaparte, who proclaimed, "the name Bonaparte is itself a political platform."

In the Third World today the same general lack of education produces the same willingness to accept personalization. According to UNESCO statistics dating from August 1971, the illiteracy rate was 73.7 percent in Africa and 46.8 percent in Asia.

The term *culture* can also be used in a political sense, meaning a complex of political attitudes, biases, and inclinations to react in a certain manner to certain political situations.

According to Almond and Powell,[8] these attitudes, which trigger off certain behavior, are composed of three elements: cognitive (knowledge), affective (feelings), and evaluative (values). Political culture amounts to everything one knows, feels, and believes. The cognitive element is made up of what we know, or think we know. The affective element comprises our feelings of attraction or repulsion, sympathy or antipathy that go beyond rational judgment: these are the things personalized power is based on. The evaluative element includes our values, beliefs, and ideologies.

Depending on which elements dominate, a political culture will be more or less "secularized." Almond and Powell define "cultural secularization" as the process by which individuals become more and more rational, analytical and empirical in their political action. Reason dominates the emotions and ideology; rational judgment prevails.

It would therefore appear that a weakly "secularized" political culture constitutes the most favorable terrain for personalized power.

On the basis of this analysis, the authors distinguish three main sorts of political culture. First there is a "parochial" culture in which individuals have little feel for the national whole; ignoring the nation-state, they are concerned only with a political subsystem such as the village, clan, or tribe. Next there is the submission culture in which citizens are aware of the political system, but remain passive with regard to it. They feel it to be both exterior and superior to them. They hope to benefit from the services it can offer, they fear its demands or decrees, but it does not occur to them to participate in it.

Finally, there is the participation culture. Its "subjects" become veritable "participants," true citizens. They act on the political system, orienting its direction through various means such as elections, demonstrations, etc.

This analysis can provide us with a key for interpreting personal or personalized power. Certain peoples of the Third World, especially in Africa, have scarcely grown out of a "parochial" culture and are still in a state of submission. They do not participate in politics, but remain deferential witnesses of power who are simply invited to admire, fear, and obey.

The same submission culture explains the success of Stalinism in the Soviet Union. Stalin's cult was built on an absence of solid democratic traditions in a country which had barely emerged from despotism. For centuries czarism had habituated the people to its absolute rule. This "cultural" situation made an immediate transition to freedom unlikely.

But this does not explain personalization in countries with long traditions of democracy, whose citizens have long considered themselves "participants" and not "subjects." Is this the result of a regression back toward the submission culture? It would not seem so.

Such citizens continue to believe themselves active participants in the political system, freely deciding the national destiny with their votes. In fact, the alienation has been unconscious and insidious, operating like an anesthetic. Fascinated, the individual no longer takes part in the normal course of public life. He contemplates — captivated, dazzled — leaders who act in his name, who "represent" him in a double sense — in the juridico-political sense of exercising the rights of another, and in the show business sense of representation, that is, a dramatic production or performance.

Thanks to the power of the audio-visual media, we must therefore add "show business culture" to the three types analyzed by Almond and Powell, one that is much more dangerous than the submission culture. For the latter is based on bald domination and overt violence, whereas the show business culture is all simulation, artifice, and parody. It is the false representation of democracy, a simulacrum of participation culture. The individual believes himself free, active, and influential. He thinks he is an actor in the political system, when he is only a spectator, gulled and taken in by the "political game" played on the TV tube and in voting booths.

How could he revolt against this when he has the impression that he is a full-fledged citizen participating in the exercise of national sovereignty? But in truth he does not participate in it any more than a stadium spectator is playing football or a movie-goer takes part in the amorous activities of a pornographic film. He has simply paid the price of admission — whether it be a ticket or a ballot — to watch others act or love in his stead.

Thus does show business culture insidiously replace participation culture, and political voyeurism replace democracy.

THE FETISHISM OF POWER

Fetishism must be included, as well as voyeurism, for here and there power remains the object of a quasi-religious cult. This semisacred power demands fullest adherence and an almost sacramental participation. It imposes an attitude of devotion and fearful submission on its citizens. In such a case, opposition becomes sacrilege and criticism a heresy.

Considered a God-sent priest or sorcerer, the leader of such a land enjoys veneration unadulterated by rational judgment. It takes his very person as its object, since he is the symbol of supernatural forces. The magical or religious basis of such power provides a solid basis for its personalization.

In ancient Rome, the cult of the emperor was established by Augustus, and every emperor became a god when he died. Some like Caligula and Domitian even became divinities before their deaths. As St. Paul said, "Non est potestas nisi a Deo." Like good theocrats, French sovereigns had themselves anointed and proclaimed "kings of France by the grace of God." At Bossuet's urging, Louis XIV elevated himself to the level of a divinity — at least until Massillon declared beside his coffin, "God alone is great, my brothers."

Napoleon took the purple, the crown, and the papal anointment at Notre Dame Cathedral to proclaim his legitimacy. Wanting to be considered greater than a king, the emperor disdained to be anoited merely by the archbishop of Rheims. Henceforward, his birthday became a religious feast day and the church became his propaganda organ. He summed up his own attitude when he said, "a society without religion is like a vessel without a compass. Only religion can give the state firm and durable support."

Later, Franco became "Caudillo of Spain by the grace of God." Today still, several hereditary monarchs claim divine right, such as Morocco's Hassan II, a descendent of Mohammed and Commander of the faithful, and Saudi Arabia's Khalid, Imam of the faithful and Guardian of the Holy Places of the theocratic tradition of Islam.

Occasionally black Africa also places governmental authority firmly on the foundation of ancentral religion. In a study of its traditional political systems, Jean Ziegler notes, "in Africa, authority admits of no subdivision into religious, symbolic, economic, or spiritual. It is all one."[9] Here the multifunctional aspect of a political structure reaches its acme, and from Nkrumah to Mobutu it derives its religious aura from the most diverse sources.

But paradoxically, even athiestic systems find a functional substitute for religion in the cult of their national glories, which are venerated as much as any god, whether living or dead. There was Lenin, there was Stalin, there was Mao. Complete with embalmed cadavers, crystal coffins, and grandiose mausoleums, the New Russia and the New China continue the political and religious rites of the age-old empires they follow.

POLITICAL SYSTEMS AND PERSONALIZATION

Certain political systems also favor personalzied or personal power. Besides hereditary monarchies, they are, in order, regimes based on plebiscites, presidentialist and presidential regimes, parliamentarian with a majority, and parliamentarian without a majority.

A regime based on plebiscite is one in which government authority is based on the personalized referendum. In France, this democratic Caesarism has taken the form of Bonapartism and Gaullism. Both transform the plebiscite into a vote of confidence in a single person.

Napoleon Bonaparte organized four plebiscites. One approved the Year VIII Constitution in 1800, another his status as Consul for Life in 1802, another the creation of the Empire in 1804, and a final one the *Acte Additionnel* in 1815. His nephew Louis-Napoleon held three referendums: in 1851 to ratify the coup d'état of December 2, in 1852 to re-establish the empire, and 1870 to ratify the constitutional reforms effected ten years previously.

De Gaulle used the referendum periodically, giving it the character of a plebiscite. Rather than being the occasion for the people to express themselves freely on a political problem — as is done in Switzerland, for example — a referendum can become a means of pressure when the chief executive demands that the nation manifest its confidence in him. He can do this at the moment of his choosing, using whatever pretext he likes.

Other than the referendum to approve the new constitution on September 28, 1958, the general used this technique four times to go over the heads of the National Assembly and the parties and reach the people directly. On January 8, 1961, it was to approve the Evian agreements; on October 28, 1962, to revise the system for electing the president; and on April 27, 1969, to approve the reform of the senate and regional reorganization. Each time he transformed the referendum into a question of confidence in him personally, saying on television that he would not remain in office if the vote was negative.

In his speech on January 6, 1961, for example, he said: "Citizens of France, you know that it is to me that you are replying with your vote . . . That is why I turn to you, bypassing all intermediaries. As everyone knows, this question is between each of you and myself."

And in his speech on October 18, 1962, he said: "If you answer is no, or even if an affirmative vote is weak, mediocre, and dilatory, it is obvious that my duties will be terminated immediately and irrevocably. For what could I accomplish without the cordial confidence of this nation?"

In his interview with Michel Droit on April 10, 1969, he said: "The continuation of my tenure in office or my departure depend on the answer that the nation will make to the question I have asked." Summing up the other calls he had made to the nation, de Gaulle added: "On each of these occasions, with confidence in the nation I have asked it if it had confidence in me."

At the end, this extreme personalization of each referendum led to failure. On April 27, 1969, the result was 53 percent *non* and, as promised, the general submitted his resignation.

His departure showed his respect for universal suffrage, but it did not erase the past. The Gaullist referendum always became a plebiscite accompanied by a threat to resign. It was an attempt to force adherence to his policies, rather than an opportunity for the country to express its opinion freely, without pressure, on a given national issue.

Consulted by its "guide" whenever he wants, however he wants, on the subjects and in the manner he thinks best, the "sovereign" people can reply only with monosyllables. It is impossible not to see this as a caricature of popular sovereignty and a denaturing of the referendum, with the people only asked to ratify and applaud, not really to decide freely.

Another system that lends itself to personalization is the presidentialist regime, a distorted copy of a true presidential regime, which balances the authority of the president elected by universal suffrage by checks from an active parliament. The presidentialist regime, characterized by an accumulation of powers by the chief executive and a taming or domination of the parliament, is often seen in the Third World.

In Latin America, laws prohibiting the immediate reelection of a president at least insure that his time in office will be temporary. In Africa, on the other hand, presidents are generally indefinitely eligible for reelection and are frequently voted back into office. This creates great stability of the presidential office; for example, Presidents Senghor of Senegal, Houphouet-Boigny of the Ivory Coast, Sékou Touré of Guinea, or Ahidjo of the Cameroons (who won his last election with 99.99 percent of the vote).[10]

Certain African presidents have themselves proclaimed presidents for life, guaranteeing a long stay in office, such as Presidents Habib Bourguiba of Tunisia, Jean-Bedel Bokassa of the Central African Empire,[11] Francisco Masie Nguema Biyogo of Equatorial Guinea, H. Kamuzu Banda of Malawi, or Idi Amin of Uganda. Of course, this does not grant the beneficiary immunity from a coup d'état.

Next on the list of political regimes which favor personalization of power is the authentic presidential regime like that in the United States.

Its dominant trait, election of the president by universal suffrage, makes it a more personalized regime than a parliamentary system in which the head of government is only an elected representative among others. In this latter case, the people have not mandated any power to him personally, and he can only run a collegial government as *primus inter pares*.

Personalization can exist, however, in a parliamentary regime with a majority, in which the chief executive has a stable and coherent majority as the result of legislative elections.

By voting for a given party or coalition in legislative elections, the citizens determine the direction the government must take. This often happens in countries with bipartisan politics. When each party or coalition has a recognized leader, the election is transformed into a duel between the two party leaders. This is the case in Great Britain, Canada, New Zealand, Australia, Federal Republic of West Germany, Austria, Sweden, and so on.

The British or West German voter knows that the queen or president will automatically designate as head of government the leader of the winning party. British subjects who voted in 1974 for the Labour or Conservative candidates were expressing their preference for either Wilson or Heath as prime minister. And German citizens voting in 1976 for either the Social Democrat or Christian Democrat candidate were indicating whether they preferred Schmidt or Kohl as chancellor.

The parliamentary aspect of such systems and the absence of a direct election of a president should not, therefore, be taken to mean that a majority-parliamentary regime does not personalize power. For elections under such a system in fact become unofficial presidential elections.

For that matter, campaigns for legislative elections in those cases resemble presidential campaigns in which two leaders are running for the highest office in the land.

The Ford-Carter debates or the Mitterrand-Giscard d'Estaing debate occurred under presidential or semipresidential regimes. But they were not so different from the Wilson-Heath debate in 1974, or the ones between Trudeau and Stanfield in Canada in 1974, Whitlam and Fraser in Australia in 1975, Kreisky and Taus in Austria in 1975, Palme and Fälldin in Sweden in 1976, or Schmidt and Kohl in West Germany in 1976.

Even more than 1969 and 1972, the 1976 legislative campaign in West Germany was ultra-personalized. Party platforms and machines were in the background, well behind their leaders and advertising agencies. The SPD posters carried Schmidt's portrait with the caption, "Work with us. Vote for Schmidt," or "Schmidt must stay as Chancellor." The CDU posters showed Kohl and proclaimed, "For the love of Germany; Helmut Kohl, German Chancellor."*

We have yet to mention the parliamentary regime without a majority, or the sort known in France before 1958, in Italy, the Netherlands, and so on, in which the government is not directly determined by the election results and does not benefit from a stable and coherent majority to support it.

Here we find the traditional characteristics of the parliamentary regime that brakes personalized power. Designated by the parliament and responsible to it, the head of government can be overturned at any moment by his peers, in particular if he attempts too personal an exercise of power. As *primus inter pares*, he is no more than his colleagues' leader in the cabinet or congress. He therefore must work hard to satisfy the demands of the people's elected representatives.

In this system, there are many parties, each headed by rival leaders, and they do not admit of any but the most narrowly limited personal power. Any politician who goes beyond that is exiled from government the way the ancient Greeks banned Themistocles, Aristides, Comon, Megacles, and Hyperboles, whose excessive popularity threatened democracy.

Following the personal power of Napoleon III and, later of Pétain, France's Third and Fourth Republics had constitutions that limited the personalizations of power. The French had learned that unfettered government authority can become a monster that is better to cage in advance.

The reasoning behind these constitutions was that a leader who becomes too popular is going to abuse his power. They therefore encouraged the selection of drab, self-effacing prime ministers. If one happened to acquire a certain charisma, he was turned out of office, whether he be Adolphe Thiers or Antoine Pinay, Léon Gambetta or Pierre Mendès France.

---

* Ultra-personalized posters date from the 1950s in Europe. Labour's in 1955 said, "You can have confidence in Attlee." The CDU's in 1957 showed Chancellor Adenauer with the caption, "Let him work."

The rule was, he who gains favor with the public loses his position of power. To stay in office a prime minister had to possess the parliamentary skills par excellence: amiability, discretion, flexibility, procedural tact. It was the escence of routine authority, of the ordinary man, and of anonymous power.

In September 1949, President Henri Queuille was congratulated by friends on the first anniversary of his premiership. His suitably humble reply: "I may seem very demanding, but I have still not reached my goal. That will come if, after having spent a few years here, I can stroll down the street without anyone's recognizing me. I would like to be able to speak to a passerby, exchange a few remarks with him, ask him who was premier of France, and have him say, 'I don't know.'"[12]

This depersonalization of power also held for the office of president, with the parliament avoiding leaders with too much personality in favor of more modest, inoffensive presidents. "Anyone smart enough to avoid creating a scandal can become president," a journalist remarked when Sadi Carnot reached the Elysée Palace in 1887. At about the same time, Clemenceau defined his policy: "I always vote for the stupidest candidate." In 1920, Clemenceau was beaten in the race for the Elysée by a parliament that applied his policy to the letter: it elected as president Paul Deschanel, who later had to resign because of mental disorders.

De Gaulle made several revealing remarks about these modest presidents of the Third and Fourth Republics. Describing his meeting on October 13, 1944, with President Lebrun, he wrote: "I shook his hand with compassion and cordiality. After all, he had only two problems as chief of state: he was not a chief, and there was no state."

And after the funeral of the last president of the Fourth Republic, the first president of the Fifth Republic stated: "In recalling René Coty's personality, one is reminded of the phrase of La Bruyère: 'Modesty is to merit what shadows are to the figures in a painting: they lend it force and relief.'"

Actually, it was inevitable that de Gaulle would follow Coty as president. For depersonalization also has its risks. It leads, in times of crisis, to the explosion of a desire too long held in check: the call for the providential man. Both Bonapartism and Gaullism followed regimes that were utterly without personality. Too much continence can lead to perversions.

PARTIES AND PERSONALIZATION

Besides a country's political institutions, its party system also influences the personalization of power.

A tightly structured party made up of numerous committees and local notables, each concerned about his autonomy and equality with the others, often inhibits personalization. Both Clemenceau[13] and Mendès France were victims of these tendencies within their own Radical party.

Mass parties, on the other hand, with their great numbers of members, lend themselves better to personalization. Their dimension and centralization often create a bureaucratic-oligarchic situation that favors its leaders, particularly the top man, who may become the object of a personality cult.

Lenin, Stalin, Khrushchev, and Brezhnev all powerfully personify the Soviet Communist party. Even the French Communist party had this tendency under Maurice Thorez, as could be seen on his 50th birthday, when the party sent out special membership applications that began, "Dear Maurice Thorez, I wish you long life and good health, and on your fiftieth birthday I join the FCP . . ." At the top, the application bore the heading: "I join the party of Maurice Thorez" instead of "the Communist party."[14]

Today, although he is not the object of a personality cult, Georges Marchais strongly symbolizes the party, which did personalize its propaganda in 1969–1970 with a campaign entitled, "Tell me, Mr. Marchais . . ."

Similarly, certain leaders of Socialist parties are closely identified with their organizations. Formerly such Socialists as Stauning, Branting, Vandervelde, Guesde, Jaurès, and Blum enjoyed this status. Today it is Brandt in West Germany's SPD and Mitterrand in France's Socialist party.

Then there are catch-all parties which often have leaders whose personality is as important as their platforms, allowing them to attract members of various political inclinations.[15] Often these leaders are brought in from outside the party to assume its moral direction, as Pompidou did with the UNR and as de Gaulle did with the same party previously.

As the general put it after the elections of 1962 in speaking of the successful UNR candidates: "They were elected in my shadow."[16] Many of them had in fact substituted references to de Gaulle for coherent political platforms. As early as 1959, at the UNR national convention, Habib-Deloncle admitted as much: "We won thanks to equating the UNR with de Gaulle, This means that we have an unconditional duty of fidelity to the general personally and to his policies."[17] De Gaulle was everything, the UNR party was nothing — certainly not a major party practicing internal democracy. It was only a grouping of faithful vassals who had pledged allegiance to a charismatic chief.

Without going to such lengths, many catch-all parties also make their leader's personality their main element of attraction. This is true in West Germany of Adenauer's CDU and Schmidt's SPD. It was long true of Wilson's Labour party in Britain.

In general, a tightly structured party produces depersonalization, a mass party relative personalization, and a catch-all party hyper-personalization.

Not only does the type of party inhibit or accelerate personalization, but the type of party system also plays a role, depending on the relationships among the various parties of a given country. We can almost formulate a sociological law to the effect that the personalization of power is inversely proportional to political competition.

A multiparty system creates a maximum of competition and counters personalization. A government backed only by unstable parliamentary majorities must necessarily be a coalition government. It is headed by leaders who are unable to shape it in their image. This was the case of France's Third and Fourth Republics, and is the case in Italy today. A bipartisan regime produces the relative personalization of a two-leader debate, as in Britain, West Germany, and Austria.

When there is one clearly dominant party that stays in power for a long period, its leader becomes identified with national political power and this leads to strong personalization. This happened with Indira Gandhi and the Congress party even before she proclaimed the state of emergency.

In the ultimate phase of this sort of personalization, all political opposition disappears and the leader of the remaining party often exploits the situation to become head of state for life and to establish a virtual personality cult.

This is obviously true of Fascist parties, which overtly practice hero worship of the leader himself, not just of his position. Here, the *führer prinzip* replaces elections as the source of political legitimacy.

In under-developed countries of the Third World, the one-party system encourages adulation of the head of state, who often is also its founder.

Despite their claims to collegial leadership in conformity to Leninist thought, many Western Communist parties also assume an attitude of veneration of the supreme leader, whether he be Stalin, Mao, or Kim Il Sung. Even the Romanian Communist party, which has not gone to the excesses of its Soviet or Chinese counterparts, is devoted to its secretary general, Ceaucescu, who is at once president of the Council of State, president of the Republic, president of the Council of Defense, and president of the Higher Council for Socio-Economic Development.

All these factors tend to explain why power becomes personalized. Now we must try to see what functions it fullfils that make it appear useful to the nation.

President Mobotu of Zaire greeting the crowd prior to the Ali-Foreman fight in Kinshasa (1974).

The Goals of Star System Politics

"People! Listen to the poet!
Listen to the holy dreamer!"
— VICTOR HUGO

To what uses is personalized power put? To what needs does it correspond? The question of its causes aside, what are its functions?

We might define a function as "the contribution an element makes to the organization or the activity of a whole of which it is part."[1] In this sense, the notion of function is derived from biology and all the analogies observed by Herbert Spencer and others between a living organism and "the social organism."

Just as there are functions vital to the human body such as breathing, digestion, and so on, some functions are indispensible to the social body. Like a biological organism, society forms a whole whose interdependent constituent elements insure certain functions corresponding to fundamental needs.

But, as Robert King Merton has noted, there exist dysfunctions as well as functions. If functions contribute to the adaptation or the adjustment of the system, dysfunctions interfere with the adaptation or the adjustment of the system.[2]

In terms derived from Freud, Merton offers still another distinction. That of manifest functions, which contribute deliberately to the functioning of the system, and latent functions, which are equally important but involuntary and unconscious.

Manifest functions are the objective consequences which, contributing to the adjustment or adaptation of the system, are understood and willed by partcipants in the system. Latent functions are, correlatively, those which are neither understood nor desired.[3]

This notion raises several questions. What are the objective and observable consequences of the personalization of power? What contributions does it make to the organization or to the action of the political system? In short, to what needs — evident or not — does it correspond? What functions — manifest or latent — does it fullfil? And what also are its dysfunctions and its risks for the political system where it develops?

Is personalization helpful or harmful to the political system? And what, precisely, are its advantages and disadvantages as seen with scientific objectivity?

The following functions may be considered as positive contributions of the personalization of power: integrating function, stabilizing function, mobilizing function, support function, pedagogical function, cultural function, erotic function, representation function, play function, and occultation function. In reality, these last few "functions" constitute deviations. They amount to dysfunctions.

INTEGRATION, STABILIZATION, AND MOBILIZATION

First, personalization can exercise the function of integration by promoting the unity of the organization (nation, party, etc.) where it appears.

Prestige is not only a social absurdity that satisfies the ego. It also fulfills a unifying function. Thus it can serve to unify a nation that has just achieved independence and which is in search of its identity.

When a recently decolonized people begins the search for its identity, they willingly identify with a prestigious chief, a founding hero who already speaks for the national identity and unity, especially in relations with foreign countries.

"The greatest common denominator," writes Jean Lacouture, "is at once a proof of individual and collective existence and the certainty of cultural identity and political unity . . . The leader is both the geometrical center and the polestar of the group."[4]

He incarnates and expresses the nation, bonding it together with his prestige. As president of a country comprised of 450 tribes speaking 250 languages or dialects, General Mobutu has said, "The people of Zaire know that Mobutu is the unifier because national unity did not exist before he took over. They consider him a peacemaker because he has brought stability. His actions and his teachings have enabled us to be what we are.'' [5]

This unifying function is often fulfilled at the party level by a prestigious leader. Just as Kenyatta was Kenya or Mao was China, so Leon Blum was the French Socialist party and Maurice Thorez was the French Communist party. Today in a Socialist party with several tendencies, François Mitterrand plays the role of synthesizer and unifier, thanks to his prestige.

In all these cases, personalization becomes a factor of order and coherence by mobilizing esteem, admiration, and goodwill which are conducive to obedience and discipline. Thus does the leader's influence reinforce the organization's cohesion.

Not only does prestige fulfill a unifying function in a given group, but it also tends to stabilize its power structure.

A prestigious leader often enjoys a very stable and durable power position, his prestige shielding him from criticism and therefore from attempts by rivals to challenge him.

By definition, a personality cult precludes all criticism, whether it be of Stalin, Mao, or Kim Il Sung. Everyone is obliged to bow before the glorious leader, who is often reputed to be infallible and irreplaceable. He can even be proclaimed president for life, as in Yugoslavia, Tunisia, or Uganda.

If the cult does not go this far, the chief can be regularly confirmed in his functions by successive presidential elections, like Presidents Senghor in Senegal, Houphouet-Boigny in Ivory Coast, [6] Ahidjo in the Cameroons, or Ould Daddah in Mauritania, who belong to the first generation of African leaders which reached power in the framework of the 1956 Deferre Law. Until now their prestige appears to have consolidated their positions.

Moreover, prestige functions as a mobilizer as well as an integrator and stabilizer. It polarizes attention, excites argument, and channels energies. Under such a leader's guidance, the masses accept discipline and the individual limitations necessary for the common good, especially in underdeveloped countries. This sort of personalized power possesses a great capacity for mobilizing [7] human and material resources to accomplish a nation's goals, the prestige that attaches to it favoring mass participation in a common project.

Indeed, such mobilization is a way of satisfying people's need for a sense of participation. At least it gives the illusion of participating, but without giving individuals any real power. The "mobilist party"[8] can thus modify public attitudes, fill a pedagogical role, and prepare the people for authentic participation later.

TEACHING AND SUPPORT

Star system leadership can, then, contribute to increasing the political sophistication of a people. It marks a transition in the process of helping individuals interiorize certain values, orientations, and attitudes toward the political system.

Childhood is of course the period when this inculcation of political culture is the most intense, and several studies, notably that of David Easton and Jack Dennis, have offered a model for the political instruction of children.[9]

Teaching politics to children in such cases is done by using certain easily identifiable key figures. In the United States, the main one is the president. This is the first element learned, the first link the child uses to build up his conception of the political system as he progressively adds more and more elements and comes to discern the different functions of each.

Easton and Dennis divide this process into four periods. First there is politicalization, an increasing awareness of politics. Then comes personalization: certain authority figures serve as contact points between the child and the system. Then there is idealization of political authority, when the child perceives it as perfectly benign or malevolent and learns to love or hate it. Finally comes institutionalization, when the child goes from a personalized conception of the political system to an institutional impersonal one.

This outline is, to be sure, neither universal in its application nor without its shortcomings. But in a sense, the political development of the adolescent peoples of the Third World is not unlike this model.

The charismatic chief of a young nation resembles the authority figure who serves to crystallize the first political feelings around himself. Then comes the institutionalization, when the people have finished their political apprenticeship and are ready for a full political life.

In this light, the Great Teacher, whether it be Stalin, Mao, Nasser, Bourguiba, or Mobutu, corresponds to a temporary phase of "mobilization," preparing the nation for authentic "participation."

This preliminary phase serves to create national unity, to develop the sense of national identity, to establish the state's authority and to get the citizens involved in the political process. It represents the learning of democracy under the tutelage of a Leader-Teacher who explains his policies to the people. In this way the personalization of power fulfulls a teaching function. It is the school of political participation for a young nation.

Moreover, star system politics often maximizes the support for the system. As Easton[10] sees it, this system is involved in an exchange of input and output (decisions and actions) with its environment. There are two sorts of input: demands and support. To cope with the demands made on it, which may tend to overload it, the political system is reinforced by certain forms of support.

This support can be of three kinds. There is support for the entire political community formed by the nation itself. There is support for the political regime; that is, the constitutional and legislative ground rules. And there is support for those in positions of authority.

In charismatic systems, the support to the authorities is so great that it takes the place of support for the regime. In such cases, personalization of power is such that political fidelity is directed more at individual leaders than at institutions.

The constitutional facade remains, but it has no substance. Sometimes there is not even the pretense of respecting the formalities: constitutions are ignored, parliaments suppressed or suspended, parties neutralized, and elections forgotten.

The regime no longer counts for anything; only the supreme authority and the prestige surrounding it are important. To use Max Weber's terminology — not David Easton's — this is the essence of charismatic authority. This contrasts with the "legal-rational" authority incarnated by a bureaucracy, which reposes on the rule of law: each person in authority is backed by constitutional and legal rules that have been rationally established to assure that the office is more important than the person holding it.

Star system government is always concerned with the problem of support. For its support — whether it is addressed to persons in authority, to the regime, or to the community — is always threatened either by erosion or collapse. The latter occurred in France in May 1968, when the public became aware of de Gaulle's failures and diminished prestige, leading to his leaving the Elysée 11 months later.

When support is given to the supreme authority rather than to the regime, it is both more intense and more precarious. It is liable to be fragile and ephemeral, lacking the durable solidity of support based on laws and institutions that go beyond a single man.

Public disappointment can in the end be as great as the expectations that the leader initially aroused. If he experiences setbacks and failures, support for him often disintegrates abruptly, for authority founded on prestige and the illusion of permanent success and infallibility cannot survive failure.

That is why many dictators go from the height of glory to the depths of ignominy with surprising speed. It happened in 1945, when Mussolini, fleeing in a German uniform, was arrested by partisans. He was judged summarily and executed with Clara Petacci in a country lane in Bonzanigo. Their cadavers were taken to Milan, where a crowd hung them by the heels on the wall of a garage in the Piazza Lareto. In Italy, the Tarpean Rock is never far from the Capitol.

THE CULTURAL FUNCTION

But star system government often fulfills a sociocultural function by serving as a model or pattern. The leader gives rise to imitations and shapes the public's political behavior, the way the public imitates a film star's mannerisms and gestures.

In such cases the political leader exercises a profound cultural influence on his nation. Its citizen-spectators mimic his life-style and way of speaking as if he were the ideal archetype. They feed on his substance.

This process of identification with a model, this "mimetic current,"[11] this projection-identification can be particularly strong among the young nations of the Third World.

Colonization and decolonization seriously upset the social structures and culture of the group in such countries. They led to social trauma and an almost complete absence of traditional social values and relationships. Former norms of behavior disappear, without being replaced by a new system of any coherence. This "de-cultured" society without social structures and standards of conduct is in a state of *anomie*.

Created by Emile Durkheim, the concept of *anomie* refers to a condition in which norms are inexistent or contradictory, leaving an individual — or a society — uncertain as to how to behave. Such a crisis of beliefs and mores naturally makes a charismatic leader more attractive.

As Bertrand de Jouvenel writes: "The phenomena of social and moral disharmony favor the spread of absolute power. Uprooted men facing a new way of life find no behavior patterns to guide their new persona."[12] This is fertile ground for leaders who would formulate new behavior rules to produce social cohesion.

He resembles the poet as seen by Victor Hugo: wise man and clairvoyant, guide of people who makes "the future flame:"

> People! Listen to the poet!
> Listen to the holy dreamer!
> In your night, incomplete without him,
> Only he bears the light.[13]

The charismatic leader sees higher and farther. He enlarges the horizon. This "holy dreamer" provides his fellow citizens with projects and visions. As Napoleon said, "you can only lead a people by showing it a future: a leader is a merchant of hope."

Recently decolonized nations searching for their own identity are especially susceptible to this National Poet, this State Wise Man. From the viewpoint of pscyhoanalysis, Erik Erikson has remarked that the masses can be "starved for charisma," particularly when they are suffering the anxiety of an "identity vacuum." The charismatic chief's functional role is then to offer safeguards, identity, or ritual to the group.

After the cultural alienation of colonization, a decolonized people begins its search for a specific identity. This "nativism" has been analyzed by W. E. Mülhmann, who characterizes it as "a process of collective action motivated by the desire to restore a group consciousness which has been compromised by the interference of culture. This is done by generating respect for the native culture."[14]

After acquiring political and then economic independence, the Third World demanded its cultural independence. At their Fourth Conference in 1973, the nonaligned countries spoke of "safeguarding their own personality, promoting in all fields their authenticity, which has been seriously alienated by colonialists."

The best way for such nations to recover their own personality and free themselves of cultural hegemony is to identify with a prestigious leader who serves as the Great National Symbol, the Great Allegory of National Identity. With his imposing presence, he is the best representative of the national culture in dealings with foreign countries. He is already what the nation will one day become.

Thus does Mobutu claim to represent the "authenticity" of Zaire. As he frequently says, "We do not want to be a copy of anything, but to be ourselves!"[15] He changed the country's name from the Congo to Zaire on October 29, 1971. He also changed his own Christian names from Joseph Désiré to Mobutu Sese Seko Kuku Ngwendu wa Zabanga. He changed his dress in favor of the *abacos* (an anagram standing for the French phrase, *à bas le costume européen,* or "down with European dress"), a high-collar tunic that replaces the "colonialist" shirt and tie. Mobutu also wears symbols of tribal authority such as a leopard-skin hat, and carries a sculptured ivory cane in the manner of Bantu chieftains. These symbolic changes have spread to the people of Zaire.

In July 1972, Chad began its "cultural revolution," including a return to authenticity which was dubbed "Chaditude," and an initiation rite called the *yondo*. President Tombalbaye (who was assassinated in 1973) changed his name to Ngarta (The True Chief) and imitated Mobutu in wearing the *abacos,* with matching silk neck scarf and pocket handkerchief, topped with a leopard-skin cap, the leopard symbolizing sexual potency.

EROTIC FUNCTION

It may well be that personalized power fulfills an erotic function whose intensity varies according to what sort of leader is in office. Such erotization of politics is negligible or nonexistent when the leader is a father figure or Mr. Everyman. But it is important to the charm leader and sometimes fundamental to the role of hero.

For the charm leader, politics is an exercise in seduction, almost an extension of Ovid's *Art of Loving*. For him, to govern is less to persuade than to seduce, using charm almost to the point of Don Juan.

"It's strange," Jean-Jacques Servan-Schreiber has noted, "but politicians are afflicted with the desire to be attractive to women. This can be a drawback because in extreme cases they tend to forget the real political issues and concentrate on being seductive."[16]

Theodore White noted that John Kennedy provoked a sort of excited reaction to his personality, and mentioned the definition of JFK given by a southern senator: He combines the best qualities of Elvis Presley and FDR in the minds of bobby soxers. And White says of Kennedy's fans that when he was still a candidate, and he passed by, teenage girls would hop and jump, crying "I saw him! I saw him!" As the days passed, the jumps seemed to become more rhythmical, making the girls look like jack-in-the-boxes who jumped up and down with sexy undulations.[17]

Jerry Brown also used his charm and provoked emotional reactions when running for governor of California in 1976. He appeared to exercise special magnetism on the feminine electorate. "For numerous women," *Time* stated, "his appeal is frankly sexual."[18] With piercing black eyes beneath thick brows and an angular face framed by long, graying sideburns, this 38-year-old bachelor liked to be seen with famous actresses like Natalie Wood or Liv Ullman. But this former seminary student also cultivated another image: that of an ascetic guru who slept on a mattress or on the floor of a simple house, renouncing the official governor's mansion, giving up the official Cadillac in favor of driving his old Plymouth to Zen centers in San Francisco or to religious retreats. He played these two images off against each other skillfully.

Another celebrity who used Hollywood starlets to accredit his image as a seducer was Henry Kissinger, who admitted that some women were attracted to him only because of his power. Power is a mighty aphrodisiac.[19]

Such erotization of politics even won Spiro Agnew's campaign for governor of Maryland. As his manager, Robert Goodman, put it, we had what we considered to be a really good-looking guy, and we mounted a sex campaign.[20]

In France as well, several leaders try to appeal especially to women voters. In Bordeaux, Jacques Chaban-Delmas organizes public meetings reserved for women only. Perhaps as a result of such attention, the weekly women's magazine *Elle* published a series of articles entitled "Gentlemen, We Find You Handsome," in which Chaban-Delmas figured largely.

During his presidential campaign in the spring of 1974, Giscard d'Estaing addressed France as if the country were a carnal — feminine — being, declaring that he wanted to "look deep into your eyes." That autumn the press did a number of articles about his private life, referring to several gamey affairs.[21] And on January 27, 1977, he went on TV for one hour to answer questions put by French women on women's rights.

This erotization of political campaigns recalls the erotization of advertising analysed by Violette Morin. The real, material qualities of goods offered for sale are replaced by "fluids" or suggestions intended to create a certain atmosphere around them. The erotic fluid has the advantage of appealing to everyone "because the libidinal tendencies it is based on do not depend on age, sex, or class."[22]

Today, this "aura of erotic fluid" extends from advertising billboards to political posters and televised campaign spots. Eroticized advertising gets a potential buyer's attention better. Similarly, erotized political propaganda is most effective in "selling" a candidate tinged with such "erotic fluid." But where political "sellers," not "buyers," are concerned, the appetite for power appears to correspond to deeper, more hidden, motives.

Participation in politics is often due to a desire for power. It is a way of proving one's virility by identifying sexual potency with political power. This is why politicians often seem bent on conquest and why they transform politics into an exercise in personal authority and domination similar to the macho vision of sexual relations.

According to Freud, the desire for power is often due to sublimation which represses instinctive impulses and deflects them from their original sexual ends. The individual then orients them toward "socially superior" ends such as professional or political ambitions. Freud defines sublimation as the replacement of the original objects of the libido by others which are not disapproved by the superego and society.[23]

Thus, for a government leader power can be a way of liberating the libido. But for those governed, he can at the same time become an object of desire, especially in charismatic, authoritarian systems, for charisma postulates the giving and abandoning of those who are subject to it. This is Wilhelm Reich's analysis: "the masses desired fascism." When a person with sexual difficulties and problems encounters a Fascist accustomed to preying on credulity and mysticism (that is, who uses sexual, libidinous methods), that person has an intense relationship with the Fascist. Abandoning himself to the führer and his ideology gives him a momentary release from his interior tension; it can transfer his conflict to another level where it can be resolved. "One does not have to be a psychologist to understand why the petit bourgeoisie, desperately frustrated sexually, why intellectually and sexually under-developed little shopgirls succumb to the flashy erotism of fascism, which gives both of them a sort of satisfaction, deformed though it may be."[24]

This might be called "a state of desire." Gilles Deleuze and Félix Guattari write that "the state is desire which is transferred from the despot's brain to the heart of his subjects. The most fantastic machine for repression is still desire, in the form of subjects *who* desire and the subjects *of* desire."[25]

This state of desire can take kinky forms, as if some delighted in being dominated and constrained by a super-powerful object such as a state that rules and punishes severely like an imperious master who both protects and threatens.

In this sort of state masochism, the passion for being dominated matches the desire to submit, amounting to what La Boétie calls "voluntary servitude." It is also what Stuart Mill calls "the prompt submission to tyranny"; what Hannah Arendt refers to as the instinct for submission — an ardent desire to be ruled and to obey a strong man.;[26] what Jean Paulhan dubs "the happiness of slavery."[27] Fascism is *The Story of O* on the scale of an entire society.

It would appear then that there is a sexual underpinning for fascism, that form of political sado-masochism based on violence. Rape and violence have the same basis, and Tchakhotine rightly refers to "the rape of the masses."

The film *Fascista* by Nico Naldini done in 1974 shows how the Italian masses gave themselves to Mussolini, the chest-thumping, booted Latin male. In it the erotic rapport between the Duce and the masses, voluptuously submissive to their political master, is perfectly clear.

In such a situation physical and verbal violence play an erotic role, helping to subjugate the masses to the master's will and fantasies. Collective ecstasy becomes a method of government. The dialogue between the masses and the leader on his rostrum crystallizes all sorts of desires, frustrations, and sexual dysfunctions.[28] The Duce "possesses" the crowd, which "submits" to this dominating, "phallocratic" power that exalts macho values.

German nazism also used the cult of the leader and of virility, along with calls to the instincts, an obsession with genetics, the negation of real sexuality, a sublimation of sexual energy converted into service for the state, calls for "assembly line" maternity, and so on.

Nazi government also included a macho aspect. Hitler declared that "the great majority of people have such a feminine mentality that their opinions and actions are determined much more by sensory impressions than by reflection."[29]

Other than such "sexist" observations on the "female" masses, it must be noted that all authoritarian regimes are based on a minimum of consent between subject and master, as in the Hegelian dialectic. All systems of this type are based on an abandonment due to fear and acceptance.

Bertolt Brecht observed that victims are rarely innocent. Their submission is often an obscure form of attachment that perverts and degrades them. Fascism never succeeds only because of the strength of its leaders. There must also be a nation willing to abandon itself to the doubtful pleasure of their domination.

In France, the most complete example of national masochism was to be found in Pétain, with the chief sacrificing himself for his people. "I make a gift of my person to France to lessen its misery," he said, along with calls for remorse, mortification and expiation. The marshal's frequent theme was "enough pleasure!"

In his first message to the nation, Pétain said, "we must learn our lesson from lost battles. Ever since our victory in World War I, the spirit of pleasure has prevailed over the spirit of sacrifice. We have been more interested in making demands than in serving the country. We stinted our effort, and today we have met with disaster."[30] And on June 25, 1940, he said, "You have suffered. You will suffer still more. Many of you will not return to your professions or your homes. Your lives will be hard . . . Our defeat is due to our abdications. The spirit of pleasure has destroyed what the spirit of sacrifice had built up."[31]

The castrating father was inviting the French to suffer, to reject the values of individual accomplishment, pleasure, and leisure, to renounce sensual delights. They must look more to moral order and the "repressive" values that contain sexual impulses: "Work, Family, Fatherland." To the "repressive" institutions that restrain sexuality: marriage, the authoritarian family, the Church, and so on.

The National Revolution was in fact a sexual counter-revolution. Pétain was the anti-Wilhelm Reich, plunging the masses into a sacrificial masochism, into an orgy of renunciation.

"Pleasure is finished!" wrote Gérard Miller. "But renouncing pleasure always leads to another sort of satisfaction."[32] For some, pleasure was to be found in this repression of sensuality, this suffering accepted. The Vichy regime would never have lasted without the masochistic passion for submission that millions of Frenchmen felt, happy as they were to be forced and constrained by a powerful state symbolizing sexual domination. The best introduction to Pétain is to read Sacher Masoch.

PERFORMANCES

Whatever the more or less obscure roots of power, the supreme chief is often performing for the public, exhibiting himself on the political stage. Here there is an interesting ambiguity in the French language, for in saying that a head of state assumes a function of *représentation*, we unconsciously use the term in both its politic-juridical and theatrical senses.

In the former sense, *représentation* means to replace someone, to act in his stead in exercising a right or authority. A member of the parliament "represents" his constituents, for example. But in the latter sense, *représentation* means peforming a stage play in public. From being a representative, the politician becomes an actor.

As it happens, a national representative is often doing both simultaneously. He acts in the name of the public while performing for the public. He exhibits himself to the people he represents. He mixes representative democracy and theater.

As a result, members of the public are not actors in politics, but spectators. They are invited only to admire and applaud those who represent them. They obtain a sort of political catharsis by contemplating others rather than taking part in the action themselves, by being voyeurs rather than participants. For them, government power is not more than a show, a spectacle that leaves them alienated. At the highest levels of the state, someone else is living their political lives for them.

The government show includes speeches and rallies, ceremonies and national holidays. The fervor of the masses is directed toward the national leader, the star and stage manager of government. But the climax of the show comes when political stars meet each other to externalize the personalization of power.

As Daniel Boorstin notes, celebrities help each other with their publicity. They gather together to mutually intensify their image, and they give the public all the details it wants about their relations.[33]

Show business stars often do this. An actress' fame increases when, for example, she becomes the wife or girlfriend of another star. Indeed, Elizabeth Taylor's fame is due less to her talent as an actress than to her string of marriages with well-known persons: Nick Hilton, Mike Todd, Eddie Fisher, and Richard Burton. And playwright Arthur Miller became a celebrity when he married Marilyn Monroe.

Celebrities live on celebrity in a state of symbiosis, and stars live with stars. A few examples include Fairbanks-Pickford, Gable-Lombard, Robert Taylor-Stanwyck, Sinatra-Gardner and Sinatra-Farrow, Olivier-Leigh, Montand-Signoret, and the like. But stars have other techniques besides marriage to stay famous. They have their festivals of stardom where each one basks in the reflected light of all the others, to the awe and bedazzlement of the press.

Political stars use the same techniques. They invite each other for visits or get together as members of a sort of political Actors Guild. They help each other to maintain their prestige. They congratulate each other. As King Hassan II said, on May 6, 1975, when he welcomed Giscard d'Estaing to Rabat: "You're a perfect pal." During his 1972 campaign, Richard Nixon used TV spots showing him with Brezhnev and Mao. Gerald Ford used the same tactics in 1976 to profit by the reflected fame of certain foreign leaders.

One of the latent functions of visits abroad is to promote the visiting politician's publicity in his own country. Often, presidential trips and summit meetings with all their decorum and pomp have no other goal or utility than precisely that. They are opportunities for co-production shows "on location" of the personalization of power. Just as some film sequences are done outside the studio, on location, some sequences of the political show are made outside the leader's home country.

Like movie stars, political stars also have their festivals, even if they are held under the auspices of the United Nations, the Organization of African Unity, the Common Market, OPEC, or the Conference of Nonaligned Nations.

But the government show's super-productions are the summit meetings between super-powers, like those held in Yalta, Potsdam, or Bermuda. Like the Paris Conference in 1960 between Eisenhower, Khrushchev, de Gaulle, and Macmillan. Like the Vienna Conference between Kennedy and Khrushchev. Or like the Rambouillet Conference between Ford, Giscard, Miki, Moro, Schmidt, and Wilson.

On these occasions, the political superstars meet with a flourish of trumpets — to take minor decisions. But each one takes home the very concrete advantage of increased prestige before his own public, having confirmed his status as a superstar by having been photographed side-by-side with other superstars.

DISTRACTION AND DIVERSION

Moreover, such meetings are the occasion for a spectacle, for play. They enable the state to exercise what some call its "play function."[34]

Leisure, play, and distractions become at one time or another a *homo ludens*, in Huizinga's phrase. One of the state's functions is, therefore, to organize society's play activities.

Machiavelli long ago advised the prince to "frolic and keep the people busy with holidays and games."[35] And the tyrants of Greek city-states between the 8th and 6th centuries B.C. used popular holidays for propaganda purposes. Pisistrates, for example, was a genius of political staging. In 556 B.C., he organized his entry to Athens under the protection of the goddess Athena, and had an actress playing that role welcome him in person.

In Rome the government show was even more developed. The republic had its holidays granted by the magistrates, with triumphal parades for victorious generals. The empire expanded this when the people demanded bread and circuses, keeping a large part of the population alive with free bread, olive oil, and wine. Without distractions, the idle were liable to form seditious groups. To counter this, the emperor gave the people holidays, as many as 175 in some years, with each trying to outdo his predecessor. Under Titus, the inauguration of the Colosseum was the occasion for one hundred days of uninterrupted merrymaking. By appearing at such ceremonies, the emperor made himself known, kept in contact with people, and tested his popularity, even if the spontaneous cheers did become organized into choirs under Nero. But these holidays were, above all, diversions to keep the idle public busy and divert its attention from real problems.

The French kings also knew how to use this technique, especially Louis XIV who turned his reign into a spectacle. He used the classic propaganda ploy of prestige, all his actions — sometimes including wars — were geared to impress the masses. Ceremonies, court etiquette, support for artists, the construction of Versailles — everything served to glorify him.

There exists a manuscript written in the king's hand entitled "How to Guide a Visit of the Domain of Versailles," which is a veritable handbook of psychological techniques for impressing foreign princes and captivating the French nobility. Offended in 1661 by Fouquet's lavishness, Louis XIV decided to use the same means to impress — ostentatious spending. This was his favorite way of symbolizing his power, of manifesting his status as king.

The ostentation of wealth became the ostentation of grandeur, and the king's emblem, a radiant sun, spread everywhere. Artists such as Le Vau or Mansart, Le Brun or Mignard, Girardon or Coysevox proclaimed the glory of Louis XIV with their works. Official historians and writers like Boileau and Racine celebrated his great feats, practically becoming public relations men of absolute monarchy.

As Louis le Grand, superstar of this supershow, put it: "The people are happy when attending a spectacle; this is the means by which we hold their mind and their heart." Here also the show served to divert attention from real problems. Obsessed by the memory of the Fronde revolt and anxious to prevent another one, the king domesticated the nobility by keeping it with him at Versailles, fascinating it with festivities and making it participate in the show. This costly spectacle made the nobility pay out enormous sums for such things as clothing, leaving it dependent on the king's generosity. To keep the nobility at court amused, Louis XIV made a spectacle of his life, insisting on a scrupulous observation of etiquette and surrounding the least of his acts with majestic ceremonial, down to and including getting up in the morning and going to bed at night.

Seventy-five years after the death of Louis XIV, the French Revolution enlarged considerably the dimensions of the government show, organizing mass demonstrations with grandiose staging. The national holiday on July 14, 1790 attracted 200,000 people to the Champs de Mars. There were Memorial Day on August 26, 1792, to honor those who died on August 10, Unity of the Republic Day and the solemn funeral for Marat in 1793, and the Feast of the Supreme Being on June 8, 1794, organized by the painter David, "grand master of holidays of the Republic."

Robespierre held the main role as president of the Convention. While choirs intoned a specially composed hymn entitled "Father of the Universe, Supreme Intelligence," he lighted the flame before a statue of Atheism. Then, marching at the head of the column of members of the Convention, with each member carrying a boquet of flowers and ears of wheat, he proceeded from the Tuileries Gardens to the Champs de Mars, where a symbolic hillock topped with the Tree of Freedom had been erected.

The objective of these vast liturgical assemblies? To strike the public imagination, mobilize it and involve it in a collective ritual. Later, mass demonstrations in Red Square or Tien An-men Square would be held for the same reason. Participation in such rituals has become an act of allegiance to official beliefs.

Other regimes, like fascism or nazism, aim not only at raising the consciousness of the people, but at creating a "mass psychology" by using gigantic demonstrations, whether in Rome or in the stadium at Nuremberg.

Here, following Durkheim's theory, the demonstration has the double aspect of ceremony-spectacle and diversion. Diversion also in the sense of diverting attention away from true problems and realities. The public lives in a surrealistic atmosphere of festivals and games, like plebians during the Roman empire.

Other political systems also mix show business and politics in a minor way. American elections are the occasion for confetti, parades, and majorettes, and each national political convention has a show business style orchestra. At the Democratic National Convention in

1976, Peter Duchin's orchestra, perched on the bleachers behind the official rostrum, played the traditional hymn, "Happy Days Are Here Again." At the Republican National Convention, Manny Harmon's orchestra, presented by former actor and senator George Murphy, played "God Bless America." Mrs. Betty Ford, presented to the public by Cary Grant, even danced the bump with Tony Orlando.

For that matter, political rallies are often held in places generally reserved for shows or sports events like Madison Square Garden in New York, where the Democratic Convention was held, or the Walnut Street Theater in Philadelphia, where the first Ford-Carter debate was held.

So it can be seen that politics does have its play function. Indeed, we often speak of the "political game," as if politics also constituted entertainment, amusement, recreation.

And, as with a show, we speak of the "public" to designate the people. Some refer to what they consider to be the public's taste for theatricalization, arguing that politics must use star system techniques to save it from the public's lack of interest, to adapt it to "mass culture."

From the moment when the television viewer can choose between his president, a film, and a variety show, the president has to become an entertainer to compete effectively with show business professionals and keep his popularity rating.[36] In short, to compete with stars, political stars have to use their methods and personalize their "performances."

Politics is not only entertainment for the public. It can also be entertaining for the leader — a pleasant game and pastime. In his *Theory of the Leisure Class*[37] Veblen lists four noble activities: politics, the martial arts, the ministry, and sport or hunting. Only the "leisure class" has the necessary time and money to engage in them, while the rest of society is absorbed in more humdrum tasks.

In a wealthy patrician family such as the Rockefellers, the Kennedys, or the Giscards politics can become one of Veblen's "leisure activities," an agreeable pastime or hobby. It is as if it were less a question of attaining one's ideals or carrying out a project than of finding one's personal happiness in public life, all the while having fun and thoroughly enjoying oneself.

"These are games for princes," La Fontaine would have said of these people who play the "political game" for personal pleasure. And

Pascal observed long ago that government is a permanent diversion that protects against boredom and thoughts of death:

> It is a source of happiness for persons of high state to have a number of people around to divert them, and to have the power to maintain that sort of life . . . Take guard against this. For to be a superintendent, chancellor, or first president is to be in a situation in which a great many people come from all sides starting early in the morning, leaving not even one hour of the day when they can think about themselves.

Actually, the leader is the main spectator at his own show. He is the one who enjoys it most, recalling Bergson's observation, "theater is a game that imitates life." But this "amused king" also diverts his public.

THE LIGHTING UNDERSTUDY

In its root sense, *to divert* means to turn aside. Applied to an individual, it means his attention is distracted from the essential problems that he should be concerned with. It is precisely in this sense that Pascal uses the word *divertissement*.

A *divertissement* is something that turns man aside from the discovery of his own nothingness. It amuses us and it abuses us. It fools us. A political *divertissement* gets the public's attention and concentrates it on the deeds and postures of the leader. Personalization obscures real problems and those who hold real power, such as industrial and financial circles, the technocracy, the bureaucracy, and so on, that work in the leader's shadow.

He thus comes to resemble the lighting understudy, the actor who replaces the star while the lights are being adjusted on a film set. Although he has all the lights focused on him for a while, he is never more than a stage prop. Other forces behind the scenes are the ones that count.

Was France's politics after 1958 really run by de Gaulle, the political star holding stage center with all the lights focused on him?. Or was it really economic action by large industrial and financial groups, or even actions taken by the bureaucracy and technocracy that counted the most?

And in a Socialist country or Third World country, is the prestigious behavior of its leader, going from one rostrum to another, from one international conference to another, what really counts, or is it not rather discreet actions taken by the bureacracy, exercising real power while the leader is off representing the country?

Who holds real power? Is it the supreme star constantly under the spotlights? Or is it not rather the dominant class — or ''new class''[38] — which camouflages its hold on power thanks to all the lights being on the chief understudy and blinding the public, which is kept unable to tell who actually is making the decisions?

It does not matter whether the dominant class participates personally in the institutionalized workings of the state.[39] Often its members prefer not to. They prefer to let their auxiliaries — political actors who put on the show that dazzles the public — do that. They find the best way to turn attention away from the realities of the situation, to mask the true class nature of state power.

Far from being an active force in public life, star system government becomes no more than a facade. Personalized power highlights secondary matters and dissimulates the essentials. It focuses the spotlights on the understudy, the better to divert and distract the public so it can be dominated by this artificial and illusory fascination. Behind the spotlights is the hidden face of state power.

This occultation function of personalization, like the preceding ones, leads to dysfunctions and obstacles to good government and the proper use of the political system that are the negative consequenes of personalized authority.

The late Chairman Mao reviewing a National Day Parade.

Former Ugandan President For Life, Idi Amin Dada, at the opening session of the Organization of African Unity in Libreville (1977).

Star System Government:
Government of Illusion

*"Sire, it is not everything to be
king of France."*
— RONSARD

As we have seen, the personalization of power has not only its latent or manifest functions. It also has its dysfunctions, its disadvantages, its risks for the political system to which it may render a disservice by obstructing its efficient functioning.

It remains to measure the costs of personalization, or what a Gaullist cabinet minister used to refer to as "the overhead costs of having a great man."

ANTI-REASON

Propaganda traditionally used to be a question of ideas and opinions. It spread doctrines and political platforms, appealing to the citizen's judgment and reason.

Today, the persuasion industry spreads images more than ideas. It reduces the struggle between conflicting ideas to one of rivalry between persons. It substitutes a sort of dramatized play, complete with star actors, for the difficult confrontation of arguments and theses.

Personalized power systematically simplifies everything. It scales down the debate on public affairs to elementary, even caricatured, forms that can be understood with no effort. It exploits the public's distaste for reflection and juggling abstract concepts and the examination of purely logical arguments.

As Gerald Rafshoon, Carter's adviser, puts it: "We realized that the issues were less important in the eyes of the voters than the candidate's personality, authority and competence . . . The issues are too complicated for people. What they wanted was a leader they could have confidence in.''[1]

Star system government seeks to seduce rather than to convince, to charm more than to persuade by logic. It invites voters to choose a man rather than a policy, imagery rather than ideology. It simplifies the public debate to the extreme. It removes or covers over all its difficulties and complexities. It takes politics down to the level of the comic strip, not to say a boxing or wrestling match.

Often it means deprogramation. The presentation and packaging of the political "product" is all, its content nothing. Form supplants substance, and the leader's personality and style is more important than his ideas or projects.

In this regard, Jimmy Carter's precampaign in 1976 was a model of the kind. "Jimmy Who?" everyone asked in the beginning, when he was an unknown. "Jimmy What?" they asked later, trying to understand what he stood for. Carter did not stand *for* a political program; all that counted was his personality. He "infantilized" the public. "The people are not going to choose their president on the basis of ideology," he said.[2] And as a matter of fact, he "sold" not his ideas or doctrine, but his charm and attractive profile. His message was simple: "Trust me." As for the rest, his platform was no more than an assemblage of nebulous generalities or pious notions in the form of a sermon.

Vague ideas and platitudes — these are the basic tools of the catch-all candidate concerned with being acceptable to everyone without offending anyone, quick to go from left to right, depending on circumstance and audiences. The Democratic National Convention nominated Carter without anyone's really being able to say what his ideas and projects were, or even if he had any.*

Jerry Brown played the same game during his campaign for the nomination. He "sold" his personality instead of a rigorous, well-constructed program. His motto was, "In this profession, being a little vague is useful."[3] *Time* said of this mediagenic candidate, who

---

* On the other hand, the platform adopted by the Democratic Convention was precise on the issues and presented real differences with the Republican platform. The choice between the two candidates was not the choice "between Coca-Cola and Pepsi-Cola" as it was abusively described by an American journalist.

remained so blurred in his positions on the issues, that he was a political Rorschach test — people would see in him what they want to see.[4]

During the legislative elections of 1976 in West Germany, the two main parties declined to present distinct platforms or to make a real effort at delineating their ideas. They preferred to concentrate their propaganda on the personalities of Schmidt and Kohl. It was an ultra-personalized, almost depoliticized campaign, run more by advertising agencies than by the parties themselves, in the American style.

France has also gone in for deprogramation. Gaullism preached empiricism and pragmatism, treating all references to an ideology or a coherent program with suspicion. Why "program" action? The leader should count only on himself and his intuition to decide what is best, depending on circumstances.

In such a case, an election can only be an act of faith in the leader, with the voter signing a blank check. Far from deciding on the options, he abdicates his political responsibility to the leader, who decides for him. This was implicit in the following dialogue on a radio program during the 1965 presidential campaign:

> Pierrre Mendès France: If you vote for Mitterrand, you know what he represents . . . He has declared his position on a certain number of issues and has said what he would do if elected . . . On the other hand you have no idea what policies you are choosing when you vote for de Gaulle.
>
> Michel Debré: For France.
>
> PMF: Is it for or against better relations with China?
>
> MD: It's for France, that's what it's for.
>
> PMF: Is it for or against better relations with West Germany?
>
> MD: It's a vote for France.
>
> PMF: No one knows. It is not enough to say that it is a vote for France. I would like to be able to decide my vote on the basis of clearly defined policies that I can understand. Only then will I consider that the French people have been consulted.[5]

During the same election, George Pompidou, then premier, declared: "It is not up to the French to choose their future. They have to choose the person to whom they will entrust that future during a certain number of years.''[6]

When it seeks popular support, heroic authority appeals more to sentiment than to reason, to hypnosis rather than to alerting citizens, by manipulating their infantile needs for dependence.

When Georges Pompidou was himself candidate for the presidency in 1969, he also came out squarely for very general ''objectives,'' saying ''the word *platform* does not belong to the Gaullist vocabulary . . . You know, I don't like the word *platform*.''[7]

Actually, the Gaullist majority always had a great deal of trouble to construct a platform. It went from the Provins platform, which was hurriedly thrown together in 1973, to the idea of an ''Advanced Liberal Society'' slowly elaborated by Giscard d'Estaing.[8] This is typical of the right in most countries.

Everywhere, the right limits its ambition to managing society as it is, occasionally going so far as to reform some slight detail. It is therefore normal that it is not very good at doctrinal precision or ideological invention. Its platform often amounts only to a sort of ''Open Letter to the Happy Few.'' The right usually attempts to focus the public debate on personalities rather than policies, as it did in France in 1974.

Politics thus tends increasingly to lessened individual participation, less emphasis on platforms, and what we might call anti-reason. Emotions, impulses, and intuitions are its basis, for personalized politics is not composed of cognitive elements but affective ones. It promotes a process of ''cultural de-secularization.'' Emotions are more important than reason, and rational judgment takes second place to feelings of attraction or antipathy.

Instead of reacting to carefully examined arguments on the issues, instead of choosing on the basis of carefully compared ideas and platforms, citizens vote for a skillfully composed personality. They decide as a function of a candidate's charisma, charm, or good looks — at least as they are staged by their political advisers.

Joseph Napolitan admits: ''Television is perhaps the most emotional of the media, and I see nothing wrong with using emotions. Most people vote with their heart rather than with their head. Elections are won or lost with emotion, not with logic.''[9]

Thus does personalized politics trade in impressions rather than information, emotions more than convictions. This is why it is "anti-reason," blurring the public's judgment and substituting personalities for platforms.

ANTI-REALITY

Not only is personalized politics anti-reason, it is also anti-reality. For it tends to create an artificial universe out of touch with reality. And this is serious.

What is the state, after all? Setting aside myths and mysteries, political science gives a prosaic, concrete answer: the state is only an instrument for converting social needs into political demands. It must remain alert to the people's needs and feelings. It must be aware of trends and adapt to realities. It must inform and be informed.

Several analysts, drawing their inspiration from cybernetics, consider the political system to be a communications system. Enclosed in its own environment, it sends and receives a constant stream of "messages." A continuous flux of information circulates from the government to society and from society to the government. The flow goes through various communication networks which act as the nerves of government.[10]

In this way the political system receives essential information, including indications of its own situation, which it can use to modify itself. This amounts to feedback, with the system reacting and adapting itself to information it receives. Thanks to such "warning signals," it can make the necessary "trajectory corrections" to respond better to the needs of society.

The destiny of a regime, therefore, depends on the diversity and reliability of the information circuits it can use. In representative democracies, these are formed by houses of congress, political parties and local government. But sometimes these circuits can be disconnected. This is often the case in France under the Fifth Republic, which is run on what we might call "the solitude principle."

As Montesquieu noted, each regime is based on a principle that expresses its real nature. For the Fifth Republic this principle is solitude. It forms the heart of Gaullist doctrine, which considers parties to be a divisive and weakening factor for a state. Since parliament is their citadel, the president has to keep as far as possible from it in order to govern from on high, "powerful and solitary" as de Vigny's Moses.

It is a noble ambition. It omits only one important detail: these detested structures are also the indispensable means of communication to and from the government. Without them, it is deaf and blind.

With its defiant attitude toward the representative assemblies and the parties that support them, the Elysée Palace is condemned to solitude. The only other way it can communicate with the country is through the administrative technostructure, which is naturally subservient and transmits only the information it chooses to. The greatest danger for such a government is this self-information coming only from its own services. If the man at the top contents himself with one source of information, he becomes a prisoner.

The technobureaucracy reigns at all levels: in the cabinet, the government agencies, the prefectures. With its strategic position it can, if it likes, cut the other communication circuits and block or filter information. Then it can transmit to government only the most reassuring messages, the ones it wants to hear.

Use of this selective memory, to the exclusion of other sources of information, leaves the government out of touch with the country, functioning in a closed circuit. Without real communication with society, it cannot satisfy its needs.

This "solitude principle" is made even worse by what Norbert Elias, in a different context, calls "the court society." In the "castle" around the president, advisers form a closed society like a medieval court with its flattering barons and petty nobility. It is a universe where deference and reverence shield the chief from society at large.

In the United States such situations rarely arise. "We must dip into public opinion as into a bath," said Lincoln.[11] Nevertheless, Richard Nixon kept as far as possible from the public, the press,[12] the Congress, and the parties, including his own. He became mysterious and inaccessible, meditating his great projects far from the outside world. He stayed in San Clemente or at a Camp David transformed into a fortress behind a triple fence of barbed wire — or at the White House, where the guards wore uniforms worthy of Buckingham Palace.

How did his own assistants describe it? John Dean said that the White House is a world apart.[13] Dwight Chapin said that they live there practically on an island.[14] And Tom Charles Houston observed that anyone who has been to the White House can only have the impression that it is in a state of siege.[15]

How can we explain this monarchical style of government which led Nixon to concentrate his power in solitude? Arthur Schlesinger theorized: Nixon, they say, admired no modern statesman as much as de Gaulle . . . After his reelection he began what might be considered an attempt to institute an almost Gaullist regime in the United States.[16]

Moreover, this solitary figure surrounded himself with shadowy assistants who established a screen between him and the outside world. Direct access to the president became very difficult. Communication with him was possible only through one of his advisers, who jealously mounted the guard around him. This became known as "the Prussian guard," since his chief assistants were of German origin. There were Haldeman, the watchdog, and Ehrlichman, the "Kissinger of internal affairs." Both pulled an iron curtain between Nixon and the outside.

His advisers also mixed government with advertising methods, several of them having come from that background. Haldeman, who had been Nixon's campaign director in 1968, and Ziegler, the press secretary, had both been at the J. Walter Thompson agency. That gave them a tendency to manipulate public opinion to "sell" the president's policies, even if it did somewhat deform the facts or their presentation.

But this sort of disinformation can boomerang against its originators. Over the long term, those who manipulate opinion end up being intoxicated by it themselves. This process of "internal self-suggestion" was described by Daniel Ellsberg. In the end, the tricksters start believing their own fables and become their own victims.

It has been observed that the president of the United States can become the victim of total intoxication[17] by constructing an artificial universe free from criticism and bad news — he invents a parallel reality that replaces factual reality, and ends up believing this official version of things. He is hoisted by his own petard due to this self-intoxication which affects both the public and himself.

Caught in his own trap, the solitary leader can no longer distinguish the true from the false, the real from the imaginary. He moves in a parallel universe where everything is optical illusion and false perspective. Jeb Stuart Magruder said of the White House that you live in an unreal world when you work there.[18]

Nixon's last days in that White House were those of a solitary man lost in his fantasies and unable to keep up appearances.[19] They illustrate what might be called "state autism"; a refusal of all contact with the outside world turns the leader in on himself. He lives in illusion, a fiction, and loses his sense of what is real.

The Watergate scandal and the president's resignation marked America's turning against manipulation and lies and a whole system of unreality. But such propagation of "official truth" is naturally easier in authoritarian systems than in liberal regimes, where checks and balances including the congress, the parties, an independent press, and so on, finally bring a leader back to reality.

Stalinism showed how official, bureaucratic truth is created. Mao also wrote: "Every party or state leader, when he puts himself above the party and the masses instead of remaining among them, ceases to have a complete and penetrating view of affairs of state. In such conditions even as eminent a statesman as Stalin is inevitably led to make erroneous decisions that do not conform to reality on important matters."[20]

Closed off in the Kremlin, covered with honors, Stalin considered himself omniscient and infallible. He even made judgments in the arts and sciences. "Truth," notes Roy Medvedev, "was not what corresponded to the facts as revealed by empirical research, but what had been declared true by Comrade Stalin. To prove that a given proposition was true, we had to support it with quotations drawn from the 'classics of Marxism-Leninism' and especially from the works of Stalin, which had recently been christened as classics. When one met with facts that did not coincide with theory, we hid them, deformed them, or simply ignored them."[21]

Medvedev was referring to the social sciences, but the same was true of the natural sciences, as Lyssenko's dominant position from 1934 to 1964 shows. And bureaucratic truth still prevails. In 1976 the great biologist Zhores Medvedev was interned in a pyschiatric ward after publishing *The Greatness and Fall of Lyssenko*, which criticized the ideological straitjacket of Lyssenko's erroneous theories on genetic inheritance of acquired characteristics.[22]

This sort of isolation and self-intoxication leads to wrong and ineffective decisions in the most diverse fields. Khrushchev's report denounced Stalin's military mistakes, whereas before he had been the "great captain, the invincible military chief, a strategist without peer in history.'' In 1942, near Kharkov, the enemy was threatening to wipe out large Soviet troop concentrations. Krushchev phoned Marshal Vassilevsky, Stalin's close assistant, to request an urgent change of operational plans.

"Take a map and show Comrade Stalin the situation." It should be noted that Stalin always drew up his battle plans using a globe. There was movement in the room.

"Yes, Comrades, it was with a globe that he decided where the front line would be. So I told Comrade Vassilevsky, 'Show him the situation on a map.'"

One day after the war, Anastas Mikoyan said that Khrushchev had been right, and that he regretted not having taken his suggestion. Khrushchev reported:

"You should have seen how mad Stalin was. How could anyone suppose that Stalin had not been right! Was he not, after all, a 'genius,' and weren't geniuses always right? Everyone can make a mistake, but Stalin thought that he was always right. He never admitted having committed an error, large or small."[23]

Today, several Third World leaders yield to the same self-satisfaction, cut off from reality and living in a closed world surrounded by devoted courtiers.

Nothing — neither a true parliament nor multiple parties nor a free press — indicates his errors to the supreme leader who is reputed to be infallible. Nobody holds free and public debates or draws attention to problems and issues.

Result: a mediocre, sclerotic management of public affairs, which inevitably gets bogged down for lack of verification and structures for a dialogue between government and citizens. Without real information on real problems and needs, a government that believes itself infallible and refuses to be enlightened by freely expressed criticism necessarily accumulates faults and errors. The ransom of personal power is therefore often failure, as well as obsessive propaganda that ceaselessly cries the leader's "triumph" until he himself is dazed.

THE MADNESS OF POWER

Lord Acton said "power tends to corrupt and absolute power corrupts absolutely." Use of unlimited power can threaten a man's psychic balance. To be sure, Caligula, who named his horse consul, belongs to antiquity. But recent times also provide examples of mental problems of those in power.

The first form they take is a persecution complex. In such cases a leader can believe he is the object of permanent plotting the way Macbeth was threatened by his victims in his dilirium.

The Khrushchev Report describes Stalin as neurotically suspicious, a man who would stare at the person with him and say "why do you have a sneaky look today?" From 1936 to 1938, Stalin fabricated imaginary plots, like the one he accused Marshal Toukhatchevski of.

After the war he "became still more capricious, irritable, and brutal; in particular, his suspicions grew and his persecution complex reached incredible proportions. In his eyes, many loyal Communists became enemies."[24]

In 1952–1953, a few months before his death, Stalin invented the "white smock plot," which he claimed had been hatched by Jewish doctors to kill him. To Politburo members who expressed surprise at how little evidence he had, Stalin replied "you are as blind as newborn kittens. What would happen without me? The country would perish because you don't know how to recognize enemies."[25]

Today, several African leaders also track down conspiracies which are often imaginary. In February 1975 in Chad, there was the "black sheep plot." The accused were said to have buried a black sheep alive, symbolizing President Tombalbaye, while three marabouts chanted incantations to bring about his fall.[26] The verdict: seven years in prison for the two men accused.[27]

Another, all too frequent trap is megalomania, which follows absolute power like its shadow. The supreme leader thinks only of his glory. He lives in the illusion of his own majesty to the point of succumbing to delusions of grandeur.

How could he resist the constant hommage paid him by flatterers and the echo of his own propaganda? How escape giddiness or hallucination when the supreme leader sees, day after day, the media present him as the builder or savior of the nation, when the least of his actions is celebrated as a triumph? Also, this dreamer lives in the company of other dreamers as he goes from one official trip to another: other chiefs of state, his peers, who are hallucinated by their own personality cults. They also live detached from reality.

Extending the limits of the hero's role, some go as far as quasi-deification, like Nkrumah. Others give in to Nero-like hubris, like that black Ubu of Uganda, Marshal Idi Amin Dada.

This six-foot-six, 265-pound colossus was, formerly, a sergeant in a Scottish unit of the King's African Rifles, the famous colonial regiment. This is doubtless why he proclaimed himself "the uncrowned King of Scotland" at the end of 1976. He is also a former middleweight boxing champion, whose ability to transform the outrageous into publicity for himself is reminiscent of Muhammad Ali.

This Moslem, welcomed to Tripoli by Colonel Qaddafi who promised him all necessary help to get along without Israeli assistance, became a fanatical anti-Zionist. In a telegram to Kurt Waldheim, UN Secretary General, he expressed his regret that Hitler had not exterminated more than six million Jews. He said later he planned to commission a statue of Hitler.

Marshal Amin has sent many telegrams to the great of this world as dialogues with them as equals. He proposed his services to Queen Elizabeth to help get Great Britain out of its economic crisis. He demanded an accounting from Richard Nixon on Watergate. He advised Jimmy Carter on how to form his cabinet, and so on.

In June-July 1975, he inaugurated the idea of taking a state hostage. He imprisoned Denis Hills, a British professor of English literature at the University of Kampala, for having called him a "village tyrant" in the manuscript of his book, *The White Pumpkin*. Then began a long effort at extortion. Hills would be executed if Great Britain did not give in to various demands, including stopping "campaigns of disparagement" in the press. Concerned above all about his image, Amin admitted his objective: to force "the British and especially the press to speak better of him."[28]

London sent two of Sergeant Amin's officers to Kampala bearing a message from Queen Elizabeth asking for mercy. But in vain. The new demand: Hills would be executed unless James Callaghan, then Secretary of the Foreign Office, came to Kampala. Finally Amin obtained satisfaction and let his prisoner go. He had mobilized the international press and public opinion for several weeks, and concentrated the world's attention on Uganda and its president by using means that were odious and grotesque.

A few months later, on January 25, 1976, there was a big military parade in Kampala to celebrate the fifth anniversary of Marshal Amin's ascension to power. On the official rostrum beside him were two other champions of modesty: General Mobutu and the future Emperor Bokassa I.

July 1976. A reception was given to mark the opening of the annual Organization of African Unity summit meeting, which was held in Kampala and at which Marshal Amin presided. He arrived sitting on a palanquin borne by four British businessmen and flanked by a Swede carrying an umbrella. A few days later, London broke off diplomatic relations with Kampala. Amin parried by declaring that any British subject desiring to be received by him would have to kneel before speaking.

Such extravagances would amount only to clowning if they were not accompanied by the worst sort of violence. In five years, from 1971 to 1976, Amin's regime has doubtless cost the lives of 50,000 Ugandans and perhaps as many as 200,000. Entire villages have reportedly been machine-gunned, and thousands of bodies thrown to the crocodiles in the Nile.[29]

On a more benign level there exists an ultra-possessive passion of power. Convinced that he is indispensable to the happiness of his people, the supreme leader brutally represses all those who do not agree.

This passion for personal power transforms certain democracies into hereditary quasi-dictatorships, as in Indira Gandhi's India. Not only did she declare and maintain a state of emergency in the country and modify the constitution to hang on to power as long as possible; she also prepared her son Sanjay to succeed her. Until then, Sanjay had been known mainly for his playboy habits, for this marriage to a cover girl, and for the Maruti, a small car he tried, unsuccessfully, to launch on the Indian market. But Sanjay had one great quality: he is Mrs. Gandhi's son. And this ''heir to the throne'' would be the third member of the Nehru family to become prime minister. Dynastic legitimacy would replace more and more democratic legitimacy.

Similarly, President Kim Il Sung of North Korea has his son Kim Jung II as presumptive heir. In a more minor key, Leonid Brezhnev saw his son Juri promoted to vice-minister for foreign trade in December 1976, a few days before Brezhnev's 70th birthday was celebrated with great pomp.[30] In January 1977, Mrs. Elena Ceausescu, wife of the secretary general, Nicolas Ceausescu, became a member of the

Communist party's politburo and thus the number two official in the government.[31]

THE VIOLENCE OF POWER

There is worse. For personal power is often imposed through state violence. Anxious to maintain his primacy or even his cult, the supreme leader imprisons or physically eliminates all competitors and opposition.

The hidden and bloody face of star system government is often that: kangaroo courts, jails, hangmen, execution squads, and gallows. In the corridors of show business power, people are killed and tortured to eliminate any other actors and keep them from upstaging number one.

Mussolini had Matteoti assassinated. Hitler got rid of Roehm, the first in a long series of victims. Franco's regime was based on a million deaths in the Civil War. Just before he died, five anti-Franco militants were executed on September 27, 1975. Thus does state terrorism attempt to paralyze its opposition through fear; thus does personal power become a permanent horror film.

Stalin worked hard to eliminate his equals or rivals, to abolish the past so that no one would remember an era when there were several leaders sharing power. The trials came one after the other: 16 persons, including Kamenev and Zinoviev, in August 1936; 17 others, including Piatakov and Radek, in January 1937; Marshal Toukhatchevski and several Red Army generals in June 1937; 21 more, including Bukharine, Iagoda, and Rykov in March 1938. Finally on August 20, 1940, Leon Trotsky was assassinated in Mexico.

The ranks of possible leaders were decimated by such elimination. The Khrushchev Report confirmed that out of 139 Central Committee members elected at the 18th Congress, 98 — or 70 percent — had been arrested and shot, most in 1937-1938. As Stalin's successor said: "Whoever opposed his conception or tried to explain his viewpoint and the correctness of his position was destined to be removed from the collective leadership and, consequently, to moral and physical annihilation."

Today, state violence dominates the Third World. President Sékou Touré lives in constant fear of a plot, admitting that "the Guinean revolution was born in the framework of a permanent conspiracy."[32] He claims he has successively repressed plots by "teachers" in 1961, "tradesmen" in 1965, "soldiers" in 1969, an attempted landing by Guinean exiles in 1970, and a coup d'état attempted by two cabinet members in 1976.

Real or not, these conspiracies give a pretext for bloody purges that have struck at the Guinean political class for 20 years. Nearly all Touré's rivals from the 1950s, like most of his former comrades in the battle for independence (Magassouba Moriba, Keita Fodeba) have disappeared one after the other. Guinea has been emptied of its elite and one-quarter of its inhabitants, who have become refugees in neighboring countries.[33]

In the Sudan, General Gaafar Nimeiri also reigns through repressive terror. In July 1971, 20 members of, or sympathizers with, the Communist party were executed. In September 1975, 16 persons paid with their lives for the failure of an uprising. On July 2, 1976, a new conspiracy was discovered. By Nimeiri's own admission, 700 persons were killed "in combat" between July 2 and 5. On August 4 — while 200 others were still waiting to be "judged" — 81 civilians and soldiers were executed in Khartoum after speedy trials before special courts sitting in closed session.[34]

All these attempted coups d'état constitute the exercise of counter-violence against state violence. They are the very ransom of personal power. Every dictator, hanging on to power as long as possible, forces his adversaries to try extreme solutions in the absence of any possibility of replacing him through democratic means. The only solution to get rid of this absolute and violent power is to oppose it with counter-violence. That is why there are periodic coups d'état in such countries.

In those countries where the mechanisms of liberal democracy are unknown, violence is often the only means of effecting a change of president or of government. The changes that could be obtained under France's Fourth Republic with a crisis in the National Assembly require a coup d'état in Bangladesh. It was enough to vote against Monsieur Queuille, but citizens have to take up arms to overturn Mujibur Rahman.

That explains the frequency of coups d'état in the Third World. During the period 1963 to 1975, there were 15 in Latin America and 28 in black Africa. Often they resulted in the death of the chief of state, as in Nigeria, where three of the four presidents over a ten-year period died violent deaths: Abukabar Tafewa Balewa in January 1966, General Ironsi in July 1966, and General Mohammed in February 1976.

In 1975 alone, there were four chiefs of state assassinated: President Ratsimandrava of Madagascar in February, King Faisal of Saudi Arabia in March, President Tombalbaye of Chad in April, and Sheik Mujibur Rahman, president of Bangladesh, in August.

But even in liberal countries star system government can provoke murderous reactions. By mobilizing passions, it precipitates that paroxism of refusal that is an assassination. The more the leader plays the star, the more he risks this rejection by those who cannot stand to see his show go on.

Moreover, the assassin's gesture insures that he will become a star in his own right, like Lee Harvey Oswald or Sirhan Sirhan.

The target is most often a charm leader or hero, the superstars of the political supershow. Lincoln, Roosevelt, de Gaulle, the Kennedy brothers were all targets. But even the common man leader can excite the murder impulse, as Gerald Ford did when he escaped two assassination attempts in 1975 by Lynette Fromm and Sara Jane Moore.[35]

Several political murders, like that of King Faisal by his nephew, illustrate the Oedipus myth and the slaying of the father. The all-powerful leader symbolizes the father who keeps the son from realizing his dreams. But leaders who are struck down or preserved by violence are often only heads of illusory governments.

STATE NARCISSISM

Such governments are illusory, first of all, because the supreme leader confuses words and deeds. He is a bringer of verbiage and dreams, and he becomes completely absorbed in this function as he makes the rounds of world capitals and international conferences. So busy is he with this largely oratorical work that he leaves the exercise of real power to his assistants.

Always putting on his road show, this official state puppet has neither the time nor the desire to run the government; he is much more interested in seeking public adulation or admiring his own image. He has been caught in the trap of his own propaganda, and ends up believing in the false picture he holds up for the masses.

In an extreme case, he does nothing. He *is* nothing but his own fascinated spectator, lost in permanent contemplation of his own image. In his way, the supreme leader becomes Narcissus.[36]

In the well-known myth, Narcissus disdained the love of the nymph Echo, who died of despair and continues to make the forests ring with her cries. The gods punished Narcissus by condemning him to fall in love with his own image. He preferred looking at himself in the waters of a spring, was incapable of leaving it, and died there of langour. His name has been given to the flower that grows near springs and whose bulbs are considered to have sedative powers. The word *narcotics* is linked to his name through their common Greek root, *narké*, which connotes langour, sleepiness, and inactivity.

In love with himself, bewitched by his own reflection as seen everywhere on posters and TV screens, the Narcissus-leader spends all his energies admiring his own image. Caught in the trap of his own reflection, he spends all his time in self-contemplation and self-satisfaction, neglecting to act. And the government becomes his mirror, while he leaves the workings of it to others. This dreamy prince comes to do only one thing: providing a spectacle instead of effective decisions based on facts. Sometimes, this spectacle goes on after his death. He continues to be an opiate to help his people forget their travail.

May 1975. The Duvalier family inaugurated a grandiose mausoleum in Port-au-Prince dedicated to the memory of Papa Doc. It cost over $200 million, nearly 2 percent of the national budget. This, while the Haitian government was announcing that there was famine in the northwest of the country.[37]

Thus do dead leaders continue to govern the living, like eternal pharaohs. Or like Lenin and Mao.

Even while alive the supreme leader is sometimes a phantom, an ectoplasm, a government zombi. He is that "lighting understudy" on which the media focus their bright lights, while true power is being exercised elsewhere, in his shadow.

The media concentrate on the nominal head of government, building him up and attributing to him many decisions that in fact are not his. For often, under the cover of this pseudo-king, the essential decisions are being made by teams of technobureaucrats or economic and financial groups.

Occasionally the supreme political actor deliberately attracts public attention to his antics in order to keep it away from the real power in the country. In such cases, the apparent power covers for the real power.

THE SIMULACRUM OF POWER

Show business government is often only a simulacrum. And the vaunted prestige of *The Sword's Edge* is the main instrument of this political mystification.

The word *prestige* comes from the Latin, *praestigium*, meaning artifice and illusion, and is generally used in the plural, *praestigia*, to designate slight-of-hand, phantasmagoria, and juggling. *Praestigium* therefore amounts to trickiness and imposture. And the *vir praestigiosus* is the man who creates illusions, a charlatan. The adjective prestigious means tricky, fraudulent, or illusory.

Theophile Gautier spoke of "all the prestiges necessitated by a complicated staging." But by 1750, the sense of the word was modified to mean striking the imagination, inspiring admiration by influence and worth.

But the prestigious leader remains the prestidigitator who blinds or dazzles with his tricks. And politics based on prestige is really a politics of illusion, an imposture.

Fundamentally, government by prestige is based on illusion, on the error of perception caused by false appearances. Fundamentally, it substitutes seeming for being, in order to construct a world of tinsel and appearances untroubled by objective reality. It is a world of parabolic mirrors which reflect a deformed, enlarged image of the chief.

As Feuerbach said, ''our age prefers the image to the thing, the copy to the original, representation to reality, appearance to being. What is sacred to it is only illusion.[38]

It is a whole world made of mirages and reveries, appearances and dreams. It is composed by leaders who slip from the image to the imaginary, who restructure reality with poetic license, who build a universe of stage settings, well apart from real life.

Beneath the greasepaint and posturing, beneath the words and phrases, politics becomes a falsification of life and an inversion of the real. It is based on swagger and bluff, and evokes a series of mirrors that reflect to the infinite: as in ''Las Meninas'' by Velásquez as described by Michel Foucault; as in Corneille's L'Illusion Comique, that play about a play. It remains for us, like Alice, to go through the mirror, to go beyond the reflection, and to discover the reality of things.

For the idol is often only a hollow statue empty of any real content. Or a ''celebrity'' fabricated from nothing. Boorstin has observed that famous men are not necessarily great men.[39] Before, fame was acquired slowly, through high deeds. Today, with the mass media, renown can be fabricated and admiration created for ersatz, synthetic products thrown together hastily.

We need only recall how extremely fast Gerald Ford or Jimmy Carter acquired immense fame to understand to what extent an artificial, improvised ''star'' can replace an authentic ''hero.''

The hero, whether Washington, Bonaparte, or Lincoln, was known for his real exploits. The star becomes famous through his brand image. The hero was self-made; the media and public relations experts made the star. The hero was a great man; the star is a great name.

His only claim to fame is that he is well known. He has no other notoriety than his very notoriety. This is not a tautology, but an objective observation. The media specialists and campaign managers fabricate and impose celebrities. Once launched, they appear and reappear in the media, not because of their real qualities or performances, but because of their artificially created fame.

Celebrity is a ''human pseudo-event.''[40] Just as pseudo-events put spontaneous, real events in the shade, so do celebrities upstage true heros. They are better adapted to the needs of the media than real, unknown heroes such as scientists, for example.

In any case, the star system always prefers form to substance and personality to deeds. The star is more important than the film, which is only a vehicle for his or her fame. The public goes to see Brando or Newman more than a particular film.

Even in literature the author often becomes more important than his work. The literary scene is dominated by stars such as Truman Capote, Norman Mailer, and so on. Best-sellers are often not so much literary works as signatures, known almost exclusively due to their author's fame. One French publisher has even named a series "Best-Sellers," and its works are all designated beforehand and promoted to be just that.

THE CITIZEN SPECTATOR

In the case of celebrities, illusion replaces reality, especially in public life transformed into a showcase of images. The image replaces the original and eclipses the facts.

Illusion can be defined as an image mixed with reality. And the public is inundated with illusion, mirages, and tricks. It lives in a world of artifice and falsehood, where everyone ends up believing in the reality of his own publicity and his own image.

Self-intoxication and self-disinformation take their toll. Benumbed, the public contemplates an unreal world in which facts are confused with speeches, real life with imaginary life. Politics is a permanent blur; vaguely bewitched, vaguely half asleep, the spectator becomes a dreamer who prefers fantasies to prosaic, painful reality.

It is urgent that we wake up and again make distinctions between dreams and things, between illusions and facts. Each of us must break out of his own state of enchantment and get used to receiving messages that come to use from the real world outside, without being counterfeited by those past masters of dreams who are the political stars and their media consultants.

The first imperative is to strip the mask from illusion, to lay bare the artificial, to rediscover reality. We must recreate a public life that does not transform citizens into dupes and spectators dizzied by the flow of images with no relation to the real.

For government has become a show. With the mass media, the government show has replaced the exercise of power, much as "sports shows" or "sex shows" have replaced practicing those activities. As we have seen, the person who watches a televised political debate is not engaged in politics any more than a spectator at a football game plays football or the spectator at a pornographic film makes love.

In politics, as in everything else, we are becoming voyeurs. The citizen takes pleasure in simply watching political leaders perform before his eyes. He no longer derives satisfaction from action, but from passive contemplation. Lacking time to get the most out of people or things, each of us pays others to have relationships for us. We pay actors to live and love for us. And through our taxes, we pay politicians to act and govern in place of ourselves.

Selling the spectacle of relations that others have in our place has become big business. The success of campaign management firms, for example, is really the success of political show business. Impresarios and political managers, actors and politicians fulfill the same social function: giving a show to those who don't have the time to live their own lives.

Today's isolated man turns to shows for his life. His social relations are reduced to the theater or to the solitary voyeurism of television. He lives only via those few individuals whom he watches live. All this represents the impoverishment or the negation of real life. And such spectacles become, in professional terms, "the expression of the separation and remoteness between man and man."

This use of spectacle decomposes the mass of citizens into a public of millions of disassociated atoms without rapport, without true relationships. On the stage, the political actor also feels this same isolation. Always doing his act, he is without any direct and authentic rapport with his spectators. Even when he is surrounded by a mob of admirers he feels alone and abandoned. He is known to millions of fans, but unknown as a man.

This paradox of "crowded solitude" preys on political stars as much as on the idols of show business. Never allowed to be himself, always exposed to public view, the political actor also lives in isolation.

In any case, for the citizen spectator this show is always frustrating and alienating. Always invited to admire and to obey, he regresses from a "participation culture" to a "spectacle culture," if not a "submission culture."

ALIENATION

There is less and less true participation. Citizen-spectators take part in politics the way they take part in the Olympic Games: from their armchair. They let politicians live their political lives for them, casting a distracted eye over them from time to time.

Brecht wrote that one must be either a political subject or a political object; there is no other choice.[41] The citizen-spectator is a manipulated object without autonomy, thanks to turning over his right to participate to others. In the end, the citizen-spectator, this worshipper of false idols, ceases to belong. He sinks into alienation, becoming a stranger to himself and to his true nature. As Feuerbach describes it, he projects and admires in an exterior idol everything he himself has cut out of his life.

This alienation constitutes an abolition, or a lasting limitation, of his personality. It can provoke a feeling of uneasiness, assuming the citizen is aware of this insidious alienation, which is often difficult to perceive.

In many countries of the Third World, the "sovereign" people count for nothing. They are marginal or absent from the political game, which is limited to a small circle. The people are called on only to ratify and applaud through plebiscites. This explains why African elections always produce a massive vote for the single or dominant party and its leaders, especially in presidential elections. In 1970, Hamani Diori and Houphouet-Boigny each won 99.9 percent of votes cast in their respective countries.[42] These results are obtained in election after election. On August 8, 1976, Ould Daddah was triumphantly reelected president of Mauritania, the voters again confirming their choices made in 1961, 1966, and 1971.

In such countries the competition is not terribly great, the elections usually concerning only a single candidate. This avoids surprises. The opposition, when one is tolerated, is practically forbidden to use the information media, which are mobilized for the supreme leader.

In any case, pluralism is not a trait of these ultra-personalized regimes, which prefer to practice a strong concentration of powers, sometimes to the point of caricature.

In April 1976, Marshal Bokassa, then a simple president for life in the Central African Republic, made an important cabinet shuffle. Of the 23 ministers, the chief of state — already head of the government, minister of justice, minister of defense, minister of veterans, minister of public administration, and minister of social security — took on three more cabinet jobs: commerce and industry, postmaster, and information.[43]

Such alienation is not limited to developing nations. Under less caricatured and less violent forms, it also concerns developed countries — France, for one.

Abdication of the people's sovereignty in favor of a supposedly infallible and omniscient "guide" was a characteristic of the Gaullist principate. A series of referendums and plebiscites confirmed this. Were the citizens of France voting for a political line that would hold for the future? No. They were invited to ratify the past and applaud their chief, to vote on a man more than on a political program. The nation was encouraged to believe that everything would be taken care of by a providential man, without its having to choose its own future. It was asked to transfer its sovereignty to a "guide" who would decide for the country on all questions.

Some called this abdication a "direct democracy" on the pretext that it was based on a direct dialogue between the people and their master. But how can something be called a dialogue when it amounts to unilateral communication in which the supreme leader — when and how he wants, on the subjects he chooses — invites the people to reply with monosyllables?

This parody of communication is founded on contempt for the masses, who are offcially flattered and secretly disdained. They are treated like helots who are unable to understand the real problems of diplomacy, economics, and the like, and are considered to be indifferent to the general well-being. Thus they were not seriously informed and consulted, but pacified with vague remarks.

Analysing the relationship between statesmen and public opinion, de Gaulle wrote in *The Sword's Edge* that the public was grateful to statesmen "less for being useful than for being pleasing . . . So the politician does his best to seduce it [public opinion], dissimulating and saying only what is useful." In short, a politician cannot "act without feigning."

From this viewpoint, politics becomes the art of disembling and pretending. It becomes a travesty instead of being informative on the real issues. This keeps the people from getting involved in the important decisions, which are reserved for the leader. Politics thus becomes what Paul Valsery feared it was: "the art of keeping people from managing the matters that concern them." But there can be no true democracy except when the people are kept abreast of the issues and able to make real decisions.

In France, the seven-year duration of the presidential term consolidates the public's alienation. A real chief executive cannot be elected for such a long period: it is better suited to regimes in which the chief of state plays the role of arbiter and has a ceremonial status. For any other role it is dysfunctional.

The seven-year term leads to frustration by shunting the people aside. The minimum one can ask of a true democracy is that the people decide on the major options. At sufficiently close intervals such as every four or five years, universal suffrage chooses those who will govern and the options that they will have to follow. But electing a president for seven years on the basis of a seven-year program is not so much politics as a guessing game.

The electorate is no longer master of its destiny. It turns this over, every seven years, to an inspired mandatory. The presidential election comes to resemble the royal consecration in the cathedral of Rheims. It crowns an elected monarch who will run the country at his discretion.

Occasionally certain presidents in office have a case of scruples and submit — at last — a detailed program to the people. Thus Giscard d'Estaing published his book, *Democratie Française* on October 11, 1976 — nearly 900 days after entering the Elysée Palace — to explain his ideas on government. This marked a new conception of democracy: the public votes first and later, much later, it learns the candidate's platform. Doubtless this represents progress toward government by the people.

THE SHOW'S COST

This spectacle of personalized power does not result only in alienation. It also is costly. It is difficult to estimate exactly the cost in authoritarian regimes, although they are the ones that spend the most to glorify their leaders. But in liberal systems the cost can be evaluated with an accuracy that varies according to local legislation and political mores.

In the United States, the cost is on the scale of the country's geographical, demographic, and economic size. Through 1976 it increased steadily. A presidential election cost $140 million in 1952, $200 million in 1964, and $300 million in 1968.[44] On the Republican side alone, the cost of reelecting Richard Nixon in 1972 was $60 million. The Democrats had only $27 million for George McGovern.[45]

Even state-level campaigns have become extremely costly. In 1965 Napolitan estimated that a senatorial or gubernatorial campaign cost at least $1 million in the ten largest states.[46] In 1972 his estimation went up to $1.5 for a senator's seat.[47]

And these figures are only averages. They run higher with wealthier candidates. In 1966 Milton Shapp, advised by Napolitan in the Pennsylvania gubernatorial race, spent $2.5 million.[48] In 1970 Nelson Rockefeller is said to have spent $7 million to $10 million to win his fourth term as governor of New York.[49]

More than anything else, radio and TV costs are the biggest item in an election budget. This is as true for a gubernatorial candidate — in 1966 Rockefeller spent $6 million, of which one-third went for radio and TV time — as for a candidate for the White House.[50]

In 1968 Nixon's radio-TV campaign cost $12.1 million and Humphrey's $5.9 million. These official figures, given in September 1969 by the Federal Communications Commission, concern only time purchased. They must be increased by 25 to 50 percent to take into account costs of producing various broadcasts, films, and spots.[51]

In the last days of the 1976 campaign, Carter spent $2 million and Ford $10 million to $12 million for virtual audio-visual bombardments.[52]

Besides radio and TV costs, other costs run up. There are rentals of halls and private planes, fees of campaign managers and consultants, polls, analysis of the electorate, simulations, and all the rest.

Electoral costs are going up in Europe, too.[53] This is clear in France, with the presidential elections of 1965, 1969, and 1974. In 1965, François Mitterrand's campaign cost between $160,000 and $200,000. Separate campaigns run in his name by the Socialist party and Communist party must be added to that. Jean Lecanuet's campaign must have been even more costly. Mitterrand estimated that de Gaulle's posters alone cost $2 million and his other campaign material $600,000.[54]

In 1969 Michel Rocard, the PSU candidate, estimated his costs at a modest $60,000. An independent candidate, Ducatel, figures his at $70,000. Communist candidate Duclos announced expenditures of around $600,000.[55] Poher's were about the same. But Georges Pompidou's must have cost much more, considering his much greater use of posters.[56]

In 1974 Giscard d'Estaing's costs were estimated at around $3 million, most of it going for posters.[57] Mitterrand's was about half, or $1.4 million.[58] The figures were even more unbalanced if we accept Mitterrand's estimate of up to $12 million for Giscard.[59]

So campaign costs in France are comparable with those in the U.S. if we weigh them with the demographic and geographic differences.

In the U.S. an average presidential campaign costs around $30 million. That was the cost of McGovern's in 1972. It is also the ceiling fixed by law on May 11, 1976 on a candidate's expenditures.

Without considering the smaller geographic scale of France which means lessened travel costs, the French electorate of 30 million is only one-fifth of the American, with 150 million voters. We should therefore divide $30 million by five, which gives $6 million, to find the cost of a French campaign if it respected American norms.

Moreover in France, unlike the United States, use of state-run TV is free, whereas in 1976 both candidates for the White House devoted about half of their budgets to buying air time. Thus a French campaign should cost not $6 million but half of that, or $3 million.

This is precisely the figure proposed for Giscard d'Estaing's campaign; thus considering the French population and TV costs, his was as expensive as Ford's or Carter's. But if we accept Mitterrand's estimate of $10 million to $12 million, Giscard's campaign would have cost nearly four times as much as an American campaign.

Such election costs have an initial disadvantage. They create a difference in campaign means between candidates, depending on their resources. This is especially true between the left and the right, which is always better off thanks to support from industrial and financial circles.

In the United States the Republicans, favored by business, are better able than the Democrats to buy the expensive services of campaign management firms and other costly items.

In 1972 as in 1968, Democrats and Republicans had unequal resources. According to Hubert Humphrey and his chief manager,

Lawrence O'Brien, the Democrats would have won in 1968 if they had had sufficient funds earlier. Of the $5 million to $6 million contributed, most came in during the last week. That was too late, for example, to buy TV time in the key state of California. With $10 million, O'Brien says "we would have clobbered Nixon."[60] There is not much difference between saying that and thinking that the presidency can be bought.

Even within the same party, the difference in resources can exercise a strong influence on candidates in the primaries.

When he was up against the Kennedy clan in 1960, Humphrey described himself as the corner grocer against a supermarket.[61] As 1972 approached, Edmund Muskie noted, in an obvious reference to Edward Kennedy, that he was glad to discover that a poor boy could become president of this country if somewhere along the way he found $20 million to pay his campaign expenses.[62]

On the Republican side, Nelson Rockefeller, thanks to his family fortune, freely financed his campaigns for the position of governor of New York. The first in 1958 reportedly cost him $1.8 million, including expenditures by the Republican Senator from New York, Kenneth Keating. The second in 1962 cost $2.2 million, including the expenses of Republican Senator Jacob Javits. In 1966 Rockefeller and his Republican colleagues in New York spent $5.2 million.[63] To win his fourth term in 1970, Rockefeller reportedly spent between $7 million and $10 million, compared to $2 million by his Democratic rival, Arthur Goldberg.[64]

Cases like the Kennedy brothers, the Rockefeller brothers, Bentsen, Scranton, or Shapp prove that well-off candidates use their family fortunes to advance their political careers. Commenting on the 1970 Senate race, Ralph Nader observed that out of the 15 main candidates from the seven biggest states, 11 were millionaires. The four who were not, lost.[65] Such distortions are serious, and they do not exist only in the United States. Far from it.

An election is not entirely free when pressure is exerted on the voters, when certain candidates can afford large-scale use of sophisticated and ruinous campaign techniques such as polls, marketing research, posters, and so on. Such a candidate automatically has a dominant position if not a monopoly on the electoral market, and alters the citizens' free choice. Certain candidates spend so much that they virtually buy their seat in Congress, a practice that recalls France's *Ancien Régime* with its government jobs for sale.

Moreover — and this is the second disadvantage — this sort of heavy campaign spending requires financial help that is not always disinterested. Too many candidates ask financial circles for assistance, and these businessmen then consider their contributions as an insurance policy or investment, counting on the newly elected congressman to remember them. For the government has it in its power to accord all sorts of favors to business, including subsidies, tax breaks, pressure on over-zealous officials, advantageous contracts, laws and regulations that boost profits, protectionism, a foreign policy adapted to the needs of exporters, and the like. These abuses and pressures are a pollution of democracy, and they occur in many countries.

March 1971. The U.S. Department of Agriculture declared that the milk price support would not be increased. Thirteen days later, it announced an increase of 6 percent. In the meantime there had been a White House conference of milk industry leaders where it had been decided to spend an estimated $225,000 on Nixon's election campaign. (That figure was given by Ralph Nader, *Newsweek* estimated it at $300,000, and *Time* $322,000.)[66]

February 1972. The press revealed that ITT had reportedly promised to spend $400,000 on Nixon's campaign, provided that the Department of Justice suspended its antitrust action against the company. The attorney general at the time was John Mitchell, who had been Nixon's campaign director in 1968 and 1972.

Such collusion, corruption, and pressure related to campaign funds is occasionally revealed by congressional investigating committees such as those on Watergate or on multinational companies like Lockheed Aircraft.

December 1974. Prime minister Kakuti Tanaka, victim of a "Japanese Watergate," resigned in the wake of press disclosures about his immense fortune. In January 1977 he was tried for having received $1.6 million from Lockheed.

This is how democracy is corrupted, and certain economic financial powers are willing to foot the bill. The risk is that politicians will be tranformed into a theater group supported by the dominant class. Their job then is simply to put on a show to amuse and abuse the public, to deflect its attention from what is going on behind the scenes, where the wealthy become ever more prosperous and organized.

Governor Jerry Brown campaigning at the University of Southern California (1974).

The Last Performance

"Politics is everyone's business."
— PIERRE MENDÉS FRANCE

The political stage everywhere is monopolized by a political actor who transforms citizens into spectators and party militants into extras, while he gives his one-man show. How can we any longer tolerate this distressing distortion of democracy? How can we hesitate to do whatever we can to make his last performance? But what, exactly, can be done?

DEMYTHOLOGIZE

The first thing to do in order to abolish the government show is to demythologize the state. For to get the government out of show business, it must be stripped of makeup, myth, and its prestigious, mysterious aura.

At bottom, there have always been — in France more than elsewhere — two conceptions of government: power government and republican government.

The former conception, of monarchial origin, derives from the Roman Empire. After the feudal regimes of the Middle Ages, it was articulated by Machiavelli in *The Prince*, in which he was the first to use the term *state* in its modern sense. This sense of the term was illustrated in France by Richelieu, Louis XIV, and Napoleon.

For them, the state was synonymous with sovereignty and authority. It was the supreme power which dominated, ruled, and mastered. In it and by it the nation was realized. Outside the state there was no salvation; it commanded respect and obedience.

The corollary of this was that authority came from on high. Power was a fascinating and mysterious game, and politics was too complex for ordinary mortals. It was best for them to leave it all to princes and heads of state skilled in its exercise, and everything would be well.

This is exactly what de Gaulle said in *The Sword's Edge*: "Both armies and peoples have everything they need when they have excellent leaders."

On the other hand, there is another conception, less military and regal. It was the one that inspired the American War of Independence and the French Revolution. It has also inspired all France's republican governments except the Fifth Republic.

The state, it holds, is not a metaphysical entity but only the nation's juridical form. Far from being transcendent, it simply organizes services required by the community and is therefore only an instrument to be used by the citizens. In the full etymological sense of the word, the republic is "the public thing." Politics in a republic is everyone's business.

This duality of conception has marked both the law and political science. It has divided jurists into two schools of thought. For one, the state is defined above all by the exercise of public power. It is the incarnation of sovereignty, proceeding essentially by unilateral decisions that are imposed on the public. For the other, the sovereign state is only a harmful myth. The state is nothing more than a network of public services instituted to meet the concrete needs of the population, such as security, justice, and well-being.

This salutary realism is gaining ground today in political science. To be sure, some still consider political science to be the study of the state seen as the perfect society and supreme reality. But for many others it is simply the study of government, wherever it is to be found. In this sense, an organizational approach places it among other social organizations. It reduces the fetishism of government by describing analogous arrangements of authority, even on a small scale such as in business or private associations.

Systematic, functional analyses have demythologized government. Before, it had "powers"; today, it exercises its "functions." The political system becomes one part of the social system, a simple, even vulgar machine used to convert social needs into political decisions.[1] This process of transmutation implies that the government is to be informed of social needs by individuals and groups. It therefore requires their autonomy and initiative. It is precisely this that distinguishes republican government from power government.

These two sorts of government rest on two different principles. The principle of republican government is liberty. It cannot know and satisfy the public's needs unless it lets everyone express himself freely. It was no accident that the French Revolution began with a Declaration of the Rights of Man and of the citizen. It was no accident that the Third Republic began by legislating public rights. It instituted or increased local rights in the departments and communes in 1871 and 1884, the right of association in 1881, the freedom of the press in 1881, labor rights in 1884, and so on.

The idea is simple and powerful. The government is legitimate only if it satisfies collective needs. And it cannot know them except by facilitating their free expression through various channels. It is the citizens' freedom that gives the government its strength.

The power government inverses this order. It considers that only a strong government can promote the liberty and prosperity of the citizens. Its chief principle is authority.

Eager to regulate everything, the power government absorbs and centralizes more and more activities. Supported by a technobureaucratic apparatus, it directs, commands, orders without really listening or informing. In its arrogance of power it keeps its distance from the parliament and intermediary bodies and mistrusts community-level associations. The power government keeps the nation in tutelage, making its citizens happy without their advice, if not actually against it.

Actually the power government naturally follows its monarchical inclinations. Constantly increasing its range of regulation, it becomes more and more difficult to manage, which then requires stronger centralization. Finally the entire government is concentrated in the person of the head of government. De Gaulle was only describing the usual state of things in a power government when he declared in his press conference of January 31, 1964: "It must of course be understood that the indivisible authority of the government is entrusted entirely to the president."

In such a case, citizens must watch passively as authority is exercised, without attempting to influence it. Everything is done without them, thanks to the machinery of the government show, the final stage of power government, which asks only admiration from its bedazzled subjects.

RELEARNING DISRESPECT

Organized society of course cannot exist without government authority. But it must not be the object of reverence, complaisance, or deference. We need to relearn disrespect and insolence, and to stop idolizing those who run the government. As the french writer Alain advised, "Do not acclaim; acclamation always influences the heart."

We must distinguish between obedience, which is necessary to effective government, and unnecessary, nefarious submission. Alain preferred resistance to submission: "Resistance and obedience are the two virtues of the citizen. Through obedience he insures order; through resistance he insures liberty." For "to obey is not the same as to respect."[2] To stop being a spectator and to become a citizen again, the individual must stop adulating the government. He must learn a certain insolence toward this Leviathan puffed up with pride and bombast.

In a democracy, the government is not the superior but the servant of the citizens. It is up to them to remember that it is theirs, that the elected representatives are theirs. They hold their positions through the citizens and for them. It is up to them, then, to check on government by recalling a basic truth: they are the government.

In antiquity government power was considered not a privilege but a duty. It was accepted out of a sense of civic obligation, almost against one's will. We must return to that democratic simplicity that demythologizes and banalizes government, making it the common task of all. We must do away with the mystery and spectacle of government.

As a good "citizen of Geneva," Rousseau wrote in *The Social Contract*: "Straight and simple men are difficult to fool because of their simplicity: lures and fancy pretexts do not impress them. . . . When we see in the happiest country in the world groups of peasants conducting the affairs of state beneath an oak tree and always conducting themselves properly, how can we help feeling scorn for the refinements of other nations which make themselves famous and miserable with so much art and mystery?"[3]

In truth, politics is everyone's business. It must cease to be monopolized by the technocrats who run government and who remain far from real life, isolated in the artificial paradise of great public buildings. It must no longer be left to political professionals, to bureaucrats who run things from the National Assembly, that "house without windows.'' Politics must not remain the inner sanctum of those two castes who serve as the stagehands of the government show.

INFORMING

How can a people become responsible citizens instead of spectators? How, if not through education? To be sure, liberty cannot be taught, but education prepares the way for it. And liberty can prosper only when a people has acquired the right habits.

Education can teach how to work against the government show by producing aware, responsible individuals who know how to exercise their critical faculties and their freedom of choice; who know how to resist lies, myths, and propaganda; who know how to react as autonomous citizens and not as automatons.

We often smile in France at the notion of the Third Republic schoolteacher, that ''hussar of the republic.'' But it was indeed such public education in civics that tranformed a mass of subjects into citizens. It gave full meaning to the exercise of universal suffrage.

Owing to a lack of proper education, universal suffrage in France was no more than myth in 1848. The electorat willingly voted in a plebiscite for Lous-Napoleon Bonaparte, preferring to vote for a name, a man, rather than for a program that most citizens were unable to understand.

Today, in this last quarter of the 20th century, there must be a new teaching effort to produce a new advance in democracy. Problems are more and more comlex and technical in advanced industrial societies. Without sufficient information on them, universal suffrage again risks becoming a myth or an appearance. It risks being only a plebiscite in favor of the masters of the government show, while real power of choice is exercised elsewhere in the shadows by large economic groups or by the technobureaucratic apparatus with its special knowledge.

To prevent this risk, teaching of public affairs must be emphasized in high schools and universities. Traditional civics instruction must be enlarged to give each individual more than simply the rudiments of economics, law, sociology, and political science. In this way each individual would become an alert citizen able to vote on the complex issues of the day. He would no longer turn over all decision-making power to so-called specialists of public affairs or to the princes of politics who play the oracle or inspired magus.

Other than the educational system, the informational system of press, radio and television must have a central place in the combat against the government show. Today it often transforms information into a spectacle or a comic strip. Tomorrow, it could dispense with this infantile regression and inform the public on important issues, creating a "right to know."[4]

This is a right that should have a high priority on the list of rights of man and of the citizen. Without it, democracy is not possible. Without it, the fundamental decisions are beyond the electorate, which must leave them to the minority who monopolize access to the files. That creates a "knowledge elite" who controls the government show and which includes the leaders of the economic establishment and the technocracy.

This technostructure accumulates knowledge the way others accumulate capital. They turn this knowledge into power to shape society the way they want it. They also form a new caste that dispenses information as if it were alms: parsimoniously, condescendingly.

Today information is too often given out as if it were a special favor. Occasionally it is simply embargoed. This is what must be changed by establishing the right of all to all information.

Everything must be done — in the media and in the educational system — to enlighten citizens on the real issues of our time so that they may decide for themselves, by themselves. Today's decisions represent choices in the sort of civilizations we want. They must be widely and openly debated. They are too important to be made in secret by a handful of cabinet officials.

Democracy must be a glass house. It can never be a closed club reserved to a few administrative and economic experts who happen to have the necessary information; that, leads to a new aristocracy.

We must abolish the politics which Paul Valéry defined as "the art of keeping people from managing the matters that concern them." We must make politics everyone's business.

FREEING TIME FOR PUBLIC LIFE

Democracy cannot amount to a minute of liberty every five to seven years. It cannot be only the ephemeral gesture of the voter who slips a ballot in a box and then nothing until the next election, a passive witness to politics practiced by others, often for lack of time.

Today society metes out barely enough time to live and to be oneself. Today's hypertense society devours human time. The ideal, of course, would be another society in which everyone could find time to fulfill all his potential, without being limited to a single role such as worker, housewife, or professional politician; in which everyone could find time to engage in professional life, family life, and public life, rather than being restricted to one of these functions. In short, rather than being only one-third of oneself.

This presupposes a rupture with the traditional division of labor, which encloses each person in one stereotyped role and only one. It involves a different division of time between work time — which needs to be reduced — time for private life — for friendship, love, and family life — and time for public life.

In this way each person, if he or she wishes, would have the time to be active in political parties or private associations in the general interest, or even to exercise local or national elective functions. That person could do this instead of being, as today, a passive spectator watching political actors, instead of being Veblen's "leisure class," that wealthy minority which almost alone has the means to participate in that "leisure activity" that is politics.

DIFFUSION OF GOVERNMENT POWER

As a result, government would be all the less of a show, since it would be more widely spread and ordinary. It would be scattered around, dismembered, with multiple and effective "counter-powers" providing checks and balances on the centralized government.[5]

What is imperative is to counter the excesses of government power, to interrupt the process of further concentration of power by a redistribution of power.

Counter-powers reduce the concentration of power in the hands of government by decentralizing authority. They raise obstacles to the continuing expansion of central authority with its obsessive spectacle.

This means decentralization, including more power to the citizen to ensure real participation in all decisions. In France, the notion of local power must be adopted so that citizens can have more control over their own lives and future.[6] The regions must become self-governing with their own elected assemblies and executives instead of being ruled from Paris by prefects.

This redistribution of power at different levels would deflate the government show and limit some of its more outrageous excesses. As one source of government power among others, the central state would lose some of its arrogance. For its prestige would no longer be the same in the eyes of the public.

Moreover, this redistribution would increase democratic control over and effectivenss of elected representatives, providing that it is accompanied by a limit on the number of positions that may be held simultaneously. It would be forbidden, for example, to hold both local and national elected offices.

LIMITING AND FINANCING CAMPAIGN EXPENSES

To end the government show it is also necessary to reduce and modify its resources. This would prevent the risks of abuse, pressure, and corruption that are the pollution of democracy. In general, three types of measures can be mentioned: publishing campaign expenditures, limiting them, and state financing of them.[7]

Voters should be able to cast their ballots in full knowledge of who is financing whom. In West Germany, a law passed on July 24, 1967, and modified on July 22, 1969, obliges each party to present a detailed accounting of its financial resources. In the United Kingdom each party publishes its annual budget since the Companies Act of 1967 obliges companies to declare their political contributions.

Campaign expenditures could also be limited to prevent costly or sumptuous ones. This is also the English solution, with the Representation of the Peoples Acts of 1949 and 1969. These laws do not limit party expenditures on the national level, but local candidates cannot spend over £1075, plus a fixed amount that varies according to the number of voters and to whether it is a rural or an urban district.

But the most equitable solution is state financing of campaign expenses, as in West Germany. Total state expenditures there are calculated on the basis of 2.50 marks per registered voter. They are distributed among the parties as a function of votes received in legislative elections. In France, this would amount to about $1 per voter, which is not much to pay to separate politics and business. What better use of public monies than to subsidize democracy?

Several countries have come to this conclusion. Sweden began giving indirect aid to party youth organizations and newspapers, and in 1966 started direct financing of parties. Italy's law of May 2, 1974, provides for state contributions to cover party campaign expenditures.

In the United States, following Watergate and the Vesco affair, the congress adopted the Federal Election Campaign Act on October 15, 1974. The law was partially invalidated by the Supreme Court on January 30, 1976, but a revised version was promulgated on May 11, 1976, and called the Federal Election Campaign Act Amendments of 1976.

This legislation provides the possibility of financing, through public funds, of presidential campaigns. From primary elections a candidate who raises private contributions reaching $100,000 (with at least $5,000 from each of 20 states) can have public funds up to $4.5 million. The major parties can obtain optional public financing for their national conventions. For the actual presidential campaign, the two parties' candidates can, if they wish, be totally financed from public funds if they refuse all private contributions.

The law also limits contributions and expenditures. Individual contributions are limited to $1,000 per election. Candidates' contributions from their personal or family fortunes are limited to $50,000 if they accept public financing; otherwise they are unlimited.

The rule for expenditures is to limit them for every candidate taking public funds. The limits are $10 million for primaries, $2 million for the national convention, and $20 million for the national campaign. In addition, each party can spend two cents per voter, amounting to around $3.3 million.

This legislation constitutes an enormous step. Limiting expenditures gave greater dignity to the 1976 campaign, with less ballyhoo and overstatement; it usefully cooled the campaign climate.

Still, the law has two loopholes. It is valid only for election to the White House, and if the candidate refuses public financing there is no limit on his expenditures or the amount of his private funds he can employ. And in any case, "indirect expenditures" are not limited.

In 1976 both Ford and Carter chose public financing. In the future, all candidates except the very richest will certainly imitate them. That year the general ceiling on authorized expenditures for the primaries was $13.1 per candidate (including a 20 percent increase for fund-raising expenses). Ford and Carter each received $21.8 million for the actual campaign. Following their nominations, they could receive no outside contributions except a maximum of $3.3 million paid by their parties' election committees. The expenditures in 1976 were thus considerably less than those in previous presidential elections.

Compared to that, the situation in France is triply negative, having neither publication of party financing, nor ceilings, nor sufficient public financing of campaign expenditures. This, despite Premier Pierre Messmer's position in October 1972 favoring publication of resources. Despite also the proposition by Michel Poniatowski in September 1972 for public financing and ceilings. And despite Giscard d'Estaing's suggestion during the presidential campaign of 1974 that the state finance campaign expenses. Since the time Giscard became president nothing has been done to carry through his suggestion. All that exists in France today is very insufficient public financing for printing ballots, posters, and circulars as well as the costs of putting up posters for National Assembly candidates who receive at least 5 percent of the vote. Besides that, presidential candidates received a lump sum of $20,000.

As long as true public financing has not been instituted, as long as there are no ceilings on expenditures, it will be impossible to obtain either real equalilty in France among candidates or the abolition of the government show.

DEMAND A PLATFORM

The public today is drugged by the political show industry, including giant billboard portraits, TV close-ups, advertising mirages. How long will this world of illusion, hallucination, and dreams supplant reality?

Candidates must stop perverting democracy by presenting an image instead of a platform, by incarnating persona rather than projects. We must do away with this state-run circus, this vulgar vanity fair that leaves us alienated.

The minimum democracy to be accepted is one that lets the electorate make the important decisions. This must be done at sufficiently close intervals so that the voter can himself choose directly and immediately the main options that his government will follow during the legislative and presidential terms. This is not just deciding who will govern. The real question is, who will govern to do what?

If it is not presented with platforms, suffrage is reduced to expressing allegiance or hostility to a person. We must put a stop to this carnival of images and profiles, this decadent exhibition. This kaleidoscope of personalities is not democracy. It is the opposite of it. Voters must be permitted to express themselves directly on a given policy, with full knowledge of the issues.

Democracy means sovereignty of the people. It means the possibility for them to choose their own political destiny by voting on platforms, propositions, and options instead of voting only for a man who, once elected, remains free to act as he sees fit.

The first duty of candidates is to define their policies and platforms, to explain to the country the issues and alternatives it must decide with its vote. The objective is to have a contract with public opinion on clear and precise options without any ambiguity, equivocation, demagoguery, or illusion. Each voter must be able to express himself on the collective destiny. Then, the elected representative must maintain a frank and frequent dialogue with his electors. He must confer with them as often as possible in order to create the permanent democracy that will replace the government show.

Without this minimum of moral substance, democracy is only a vain exhibition instead of being the common good. For it must be remembered that "politics is everyone's business." It must not become the monopoly of a few superstars.

THE POLITICAL COUNTER-CULTURE

Democracy is above all a moral code. The government show ceaselessly transgresses that code. So to change public life this permanent exhibition must be opposed by a counter-politics or a political counter-culture.

A counter-culture is the opposite of the dominant culture, in the sense of civilization or simply life-style. In politics, it amounts to a new way of being, of thinking, and of acting politically. This counter-politics could be founded on three decisive counter-values: sincerity, simplicity, and solidarity.

Sincerity, because politics today is too often a flight from truth and reality. This is particularly clear during electoral campaigns with their promises and optimistic forecasts which leave the real problems, dangers, and crises in the shadows.

The root cause of this, consciously or not, is contempt for the electorate. In the eyes of some leaders, the voter is unable to understand what is really at stake. This helot cannot comprehend economics, diplomacy, and the like, so it would be vain to try to explain the real problems and dangers to him. Since every society hates a Cassandra, that could also be dangerous for the candidate.

So it is better to make promises, even demagogic ones, leaving the issues aside. This way, leaders exercise a euphoric function, administering tranquilizers to the body politic.

On the contrary, elections must serve to enlighten and inform the electorate on exactly what is at stake. They must be the occasion to fulfill an informational function instead of a tranquilizing one. That is what voters really want: to be treated like adults, not like children from whom the truth is hidden. They want to decide themselves on their future without being manipulated or intoxicated.

Besides this desire for sincerity and clarity, there is also a profound desire for simplicity. Politics has become a talk show, but true political discussion has been degraded. It has become a language game more than a means of communication. It is a language with two dialects, techno-speak and ideo-speak.

Techno-speak is of course technocratic jargon, the one used by many cabinet officials when they speak in affected, cabalistic terms. This technocratic dialect borrows its vocabulary from economics: *stagflation, turnaround, negative growth, stop and go, cash flow*, and so on. There are also the mysterious initials such as GNP, SDR, MIRV, OPEC, and the rest. The function of this language is not to inform the public, but to impress it and dazzle it, to escape from its control. Who would dare challenge an expert capable of using such erudite language?

This state jargon thus serves to legitimize and justify the power of the new mandarins. It recalls Molière's doctors abusing Latin. It is a cheap and easy way of giving an illusion of competence and of avoiding criticism by setting up a smokescreen. This abstract, esoteric, cryptic jargon creates a deliberate rupture of communication between the government and the governed, which no longer speak the same language.

The second dialect is ideo-speak. This is the language of political ideologues and theoreticians. They have their litanies and incantatory formulas inherited from ancient doctrines, complete with their terminologies and phraseologies. It all makes the initiated feel secure and outsiders feel even more outside.

These two dialects produce the same result: a lack of real communication, a language gap between leaders and led. Political language becomes an exchange of coded signals, where signs count for more than the ideas expressed. The linguistic forms take on their own existence, with the signifier becoming more important than the significance.

With language ceasing to be a means of communication between government and the people, one is reminded of Talleyrand's remark: "Speech was given to man that he may hide his thoughts." This is true at least for the average citizen who is not expert in semantics or lexicological analysis and who is therefore unable to decode today's political jargon, which in any case is too artificial to deal with the reality of today's problems.

We must find another political language. One that is simple, clear, and direct. One that is accessible to all, even if less "spectacular" — a language that clarifies issues and choices to enable each voter to make his or her own decisions democratically.

The third counter-value is solidarity. It is more necessary than ever to react forcefully against the spirit of personal ambition that pollutes public life. It is necessary to discover once again the sense of community and brotherhood.

Politics is not only a game for young Turks. Careerism is ridiculous in politics, along with honors, power, and glory. To take part in politics simply out of a desire to be elected and satisfy a personal ambition is derisory.

What counts is the ambition to accomplish something in the name of public service; to improve the commonweal and make life better. There is no more place for Rastignac in 1978. There must be an end to egopolitics with its egocentrism and vanity. Politics can be something else. It can be, literally, a public service.

Neither is there any place for Narcissus in our day. And politics will never become service oriented if it does not cease to be show business, an affected diversion spreading illusion and dreams.

Will the public long continue to accept this permanent festival, this show that diminishes our lives? Will it long tolerate these political stars, these avid and capricious idols who argue over the lead role in the absence of any ideas, projects, or platforms? Will it continue to stand for all these media consultants, these campaign managers who drug public opinion in order to sell their products?

When everything is degraded and perverted, when all is corruption, the decisive virtue is sometimes simply to say no. That is what the public is beginning to do, in France and elsewhere.

Listen to the deep, subterranean murmur. Listen to the indignation of citizens who have had to become spectators. Listen to the awakening of those who have been abused and duped by the government show. Listen to their cry. It is a single word: *enough!*

Notes

PART ONE: THE CAST

[1]Cited by Emmanuel Berl, *Principat et liberté* (Paris, 1962).

[2]Cited by Marguerite Sarfatti, *Mussolini, L'homme et le chef* (Paris: Albin Michel, 1927), p. 57.

[3]See A. Rambaud, ''L'Art de la déformation historique dans les Commentaires de César,'' *Annales de l'Universite de Lyon* (1953).

[4]As in the title of Michel Poniatowski's book, *Conduire le changement* (Paris: Fayard, 1975).

[5]See Jean Cazeneuve, *L'Homme téléspectateur* (Paris: Denoël-Gonthier, 1974), pp. 184-194.

[6]Niccolò Machiavelli, *The Prince*, French edition, (Paris: Seghers, 1972), pp. 144-145.

[7]Hannah Arendt, *Crises of the Republic; lying in politics, civil disobedience on violence, thoughts on politics, and revolution* (New York: Harcourt Brace Jovanovich, 1972).

The Hero

[1]In his *Cahiers* (Notebooks), Montesquieu gives this definition: ''Dictator: an extreme remedy for extreme difficulties. It was a Divinity who descended from heaven to put things right.''

[2]Jean-Jacques Rousseau, *Du Contract social* (The Social Contract), book IV, chapter 6 (Paris: Seghers, 1971), pp. 226-229.

[3]Thomas Carlyle, *Heroes and the Cult of Heroes* (1840).

[4]Charles de Gaulle, *Le Fil de l'epée* (The Sword's Edge) (Paris: 10/18, 1932), pp. 24, 26. We might also recall Napoleon's answer to the remonstrances of the legislators on January 1, 1814: ''You speak of the throne. But what is the throne? A few pieces of wood covered with velvet. Everything depends on who is sitting on it. The throne is a man, it is I, with my will, my character, and my renown.''

[5]Stanley Hoffmann, *Decline or Renewal? France since the 1930s* (New York: Viking Press, 1974); see chapter IV.

[6]De Gaulle, *Le Fil de l'epée*, p. 183.

[7]De Gaulle, *Le Fil de l'epée*, p. 38.

[8]De Gaulle, *Le Fil de l'epée*, p. 74.

[9]De Gaulle, *Le Fil de l'epée*, p. 55.

[10]De Gaulle, *Le Fil de l'epée*, p. 78.

[11]De Gaulle, *Le Fil de l'epée*, p. 79-80.

[12]De Gaulle, *Le Fil de l'epée*, pp. 80-81.

[13]De Gaulle, *Le Fil de l'epée*, pp. 86-87.

[14]De Gaulle, *Le Fil de l'epée*, p. 89.

[15]De Gaulle, *Le Fil de l'epée*, pp. 78-79.

[16]*Le Monde* (October 28, 1965).

[17]*Le Monde* (November 4, 1965).

[18]*Le Monde* (November 6, 1965).

[19]*Le Monde* (December 16, 1965).

[20]*Le Monde* (December 17, 1965).

[21]*Le Monde* (December 15, 1965). On the election, see also Roger-Gérard Schwartzenberg, *La Campagne présidentielle de 1965* (Paris: P.U.F., 1967).

[22]Branko Lazitch, *Le Rapport Khrouchtchev et son histoire* (Paris: Seuil, 1976), p. 133.

[23]Translated from the French, this advertisement appeared in *France-Soir* (April 16, 1975).

[24]Muammar el-Qaddafi, *Le Livre Vert* (The Green Book), French edition (Paris: Cujas, 1976).

[25]*Le Figaro* (January 10, 1969).

[26]*Le Monde* (April 13-14, 1975).

[27]He briefly changed his name to Salah Eddine Ahmed Bokassa after meeting Colonel Qaddafi and converting to Islam.

[28]*Le Monde* (December 22, 1976).

[29]Official communiqué signed by Prime Minister Ange Patassé, and broadcast on December 8, 1976, by Central African Radio. *Le Monde* (December 10, 1976).

[30]Jean Lacouture, *De Gaulle* (Paris: Seuil, 1965), p. 27.

[31]Charles de Gaulle, *Mémoires de guerre*, volume III ("Le Salut") (Paris: Livre de Poche, 1959), p. 334.

[32]Francisco Javier Conde, *Representación política y regimen español* (Madrid, 1945).

[33]See Mohamed Ben Hamdene, "La Personnalisation du pouvoir au Maghreb," thesis in political science at the University of Paris II (1976).

[34]Interview in *Playboy*, French edition (September, 1976).

[35]Roy Medvedev, *Le Stalinisme* (Paris: Seuil, 1972), pp. 194-199.

[36]Victor Serge, *Seize fusillés*, p. 23.

[37]Jean-Jacques Maris, *Staline* (Paris: Seuil, 1967), p. 186.

[38]*Novy Mir,* 5 (1962), p. 152.

[39]Medvedev, pp. 412-416.

[40]Zozulia, Lakhouti, and Tchatchikov, *Vers et chants sur Staline* (Poems and Songs about Stalin), pp. 52-53.

[41]*Pravda* (November 27, 1936).

[42]Rakhimov, in *Pravda* (August 28, 1936).

[43]*Literatournaia Gazeta* (December 30, 1936).

[44]Paul Éluard, "Joseph Stalin," in *Cahiers du communisme* (January, 1950).

[45]Cited by Stuart Schram, *Mao Tse-tung* (Paris: Armand Colin, 1963), pp. 382-384. Original source: *Zui Weida De Yougi* (Peking).

[46]Nikita Khrushchev, *Souvenirs* (Memoirs), French edition (Paris: Laffont, 1971).

[47]Mao Tse-tung, *Le Grand Livre Rouge* (Little Red Book), French edition (Paris: Flammarion, 1975), p. 44.

[48]*Le Monde* (October 24-25, 1976).

[49]*Le Monde* (May 21, 1975).

[50]*Le Monde* (March 2, 1976); *L'Humanité* (March 1, 1976).

[51]*Le Monde* (March 2, 1976). Rachidov, Kounaiev, Rassoulov, Voos, and Griskiavicius are, respectively, first secretaries of Uzbekstan, Kazakstan, Tajikstan, Latvia, and Lithuania.

[52]*L'Aurore* (May 10, 1976); *Le Monde* (May 11, 1976).

[53]Le Monde (March 2, 1976).

[54]*L'Aurore* (May 10, 1976); *Le Monde* (May 11, 1976).

[55]*Le Monde* (October 16, 1976).

[56]*Le Monde* (December 21, 1976).

[57]*Daily Telegraph* (January 16, 1951).

[58]Jane Rouch, *Ghana* (Lausanne: Editions Rencontre, 1964), p. 71.

[59]Radio program by Jean-François Chauvel on station TF1. See also *Le Monde* (August 9, 1975).

[60]Pascal Delobel, *Paris-Match* (August 9, 1975).

[61]Claude-Richard M'Bissa, "La Personnalisation du pouvoir au Ghana: le phénomène Nkrumah," thesis for doctorate in political science at the University of Paris II (1975).

[62]Mpongo Bokako Bautolinga, "La Personnalisation du pouvoir à travers Mobutu Sese Seko," thesis for doctorate in political science at the University of Paris II (1975).

[63]*Le Figaro* (March 20, 1975).

[64]Louis Vallon, *L'Anti-de Gaulle* (Paris: Seuil, 1969).

Just Folks

[1] Cyrus L. Sulzberger, *The Age of Mediocrity* (New York: Macmillan, 1973).

[2] Jacques Fauvet, *La IVe République* (Paris: Fayard, 1959), p. 200.

[3] Françoise Giroud, France-Dimanche (March 23-29, 1952).

[4] On the Pinay legend, see Jean Couramiaud, *Antoine Pinany, cet honnête homme* (1953); A. Derome, *La Dernière carte: qui est Pinay?* (Editions Médicis, 1952); André Stibio, *Antoine Pinay* (Editions du Journal du Parlement, 1956).

[5] See Stéphane Rials, *Les Idees politiques du Président Georges Pompidou,* preface by Roger-Gérard Schwartzenberg (Paris: P.U.F., 1977).

[6] *Newsweek* (April 19, 1976).

[7] *Time* (October 4, 1976).

[8] Jean-Marie Naggiar, "Le Profil des chanceliers allemands depuis 1949," thesis for doctorate in political science at University of Paris II (1975), p. 107.

[9] *Le Monde* (September 14, 1976).

[10] *Le Figaro* (September 28, 1976).

[11] *Time* (August 19, 1974).

[12] *Newsweek* (August 19, 1974).

[13] *Newsweek* (August 19, 1974).

[14] *Newsweek* (July 21, 1975).

[15] Ford's State of the Union Message (January, 1976).

[16] *Time* (January 26, 1976).

[17] *Time* (January 5, 1976).

[18] *Le Monde* (March 11, 1976).

[19] *Time* (August 2, 1976).

[20] *Le Monde* (July 17, 1976).

[21] *Le Monde* (May 14, 1976).

[22] *Time* (August 2, 1976).

[23] *Le Monde* (March 11, 1976).

The Charm Leader

[1] Jean Duvignaud, *La Planète des jeunes* (Paris: Stock, 1975).

[2] P. Cahn, *La Relation fraternelle chez l'enfant* (Paris: P.U.F., 1962), p. 166.

[3] Maurice Edelman, *Disraeli Rising* (London: Collins, 1974).

[4] Interview with Jacques Chancel, TF2 (May 22, 1975).

[5]Emilien Carassus, *Le Mythe du Dandy* (Paris: A. Colin, 1975).

[6]Chancel interview.

[7]Murray Burton Levin, *Kennedy Campaigning* (Boston: Beacon Press, 1966).

[8]Theodore White, *The Making of the President, 1960* (New York: Atheneum, 1961).

[9]White, p. 378.

[10]*Time* (July 8, 1974); *Newsweek* (July 22, 1974).

[11]Marvin and Bernard Kalb, *Kissinger* (Boston: Little, Brown & Co., 1974).

[12]Naggiar, p. 120.

[13]*Time* (December 29, 1975); *Newsweek* (January 5, 1976).

[14]*Time* (December 29, 1975).

[15]*Time* (December 29, 1975).

[16]*Le Monde* (November 27, 1974); see also *The Observer, The Economist, The Financial Times, The International Herald-Tribune, Time, The Times*.

[17]*Time* (September 23, 1974).

[18]A. de Segonzac, *France-Soir* (October 26, 1970).

[19]André Laurens, *D'une France à l'autre* (Paris: Gallimard, 1974), p. 105.

[20]*Le Monde* (May 19, 1976).

[21]*Le Figaro* (February 28, 1975).

[22]*Le Monde* (January 5-6, 1975).

[23]Interview with Philippe Bouvard on radio station RTL (May 21, 1975); see *Le Monde* (May 22, 1975).

[24]*Le Monde* (December 20, 1974).

[25]*Le Monde* (December 17, 1976).

[26]See Geneviève Galey, *Le Point* (August 9, 1976).

[27]*Le Monde* (May 22, 1975).

Our Father

[1]Radio station Europe 1 (January 30, 1977).

[2]Roger Garaudy, *L'Humanité* (October 16, 1952); cited in *Est-Ouest,* no. 168, p. 49.

[3]*Pravda* (March 7, 1953).

[4]*Le Monde* (November 21, 1975).

[5]*France-Soir* (February 12, 1976).

[6]Jean Plymyene, *Pétain* (Paris: Seuil, 1964), pp. 101-102.

[7]Olga Blanc-Uchan, "L'Image du père dans la vie politique française de 1870 à nos jours," thesis for political science degree at the University of Paris II (1976), pp. 21-28.

[8]*Sondages* (1968), p. 87.

[9]Maurice Schumann, *Le Figaro* (April 3, 1974).

[10]*Le Monde* (November 15, 1975).

[11]Broadcast on August 25, 1976.

[12]Giscard d'Estaing, January 5, 1977. Barre describes himself as "a square man in a round body."

[13]At a discussion sponsored by *L'Expansion* and TF1 (January 6, 1977).

[14]Jean Cau, "Super-Chirac, or the Political Animal," *Paris-Match* (November 9, 1976).

[15]Catherine Clessis, Bernard Prévost, and Patrick Wajsman, *Jacques Chirac ou la république des "cadets"* (Paris: Presses de la Cité, 1972).

[16]On December 5, 1976; see *Le Monde* (December 9, 1976).

[17]Harold Lasswell, *Power and Personality* (New York: W. W. Norton, 1948).

[18]Philippe Braud, *Le Comportement électoral en France* (Paris: P.U.F., 1973), pp. 151-164.

[19]Sigmund Freud, *Moses and Monotheism,* French edition (Paris: Gallimard, 1967), pp. 148-149.

[20]Gérard Mendel, *La Crise de générations* (Paris: Payot, 1969), pp. 221-222.

[21]Gérard Mendel, *La Révolte contre le père* (Paris: Payot, 1972).

[22]Mendel, *La Révolte contre le père.*

[23]Jacques Chaban-Delmas, *L'Ardeur* (Paris: Stock, 1975), p. 104.

[24]See Margaret Mead, *The Generation Gap* (New York, 1970).

[25]Alvin Toffler, *Future Shock* (New York, 1970).

The Political Nonwoman

[1]Mendel, *La Révolte contre le père;* see also J. Bowlby, "The Nature of the Child's Tie to His Mother," *International Journal of Psychoanalysis* (1958), pp. 355-372.

[2]Golda Meir, *Ma Vie* (My Life), French edition (Paris: Laffont, 1975), p. 402.

[3]Mendel, *La Révolte contre le père,* pp. 220-222.

[4]Mendel, *La Révolte contre le père,* pp. 132-135, 230-233.

[5]*Le Monde* (September 3, 1976; October 31, 1976).

[6]*Le Monde* (January 23-24, 1977).

[7]*International Herald-Tribune* (August 26, 1975).

[8]*International Herald-Tribune* (August 26, 1975).

[9]Interview on TF1 (January 22, 1976).

[10]*Newsweek* (July 7, 1975); *Time* (July 7, 1975).

[11]*France-Soir* (June 14, 1975).

[12]*Le Monde* (March 25, 1976).

[13]*Le Monde* (February 6, 1975).

[14]*Time* (February 24, 1975).

[15]*France-Soir* (December 7, 1974).

[16]See Olivier Todd's article in *Le Nouvel Observateur* (December 30, 1974) and Pierre Desgraupes' article in *Le Point* (December 22, 1975).

[17]*Jours de France* (February 26, 1977).

The Private Life of a Public Man

[1]*Le Monde* (November 21, 1965).

[2]Special issue of *Le Courrier des Démocrates*.

[3]TV interview with Michel Droit (December 15, 1965).

[4]In Marseille (April 27, 1974).

[5]Theodore Sorensen, *Kennedy* (New York: Harper and Row, 1965).

[6]Speech to the American Society of Newspaper Editors.

[7]Pierre Salinger, *With Kennedy* (Garden City: Doubleday and Company, 1966), pp. 57-58.

[8]Salinger, p. 50.

[9]White, pp. 389-390.

[10]*France-Soir* (February 12, 1976).

[11]*Le Monde* (October 10, 1974).

[12]Salinger, pp. 381-382.

[13]*Le Figaro* (August 19, 1976); *L'Aurore* (August 19, 1976).

[14]Radio station RTL (May 23, 1969).

[15]*Paris-Match* (June 1, 1974).

[16]Sorensen, p. 308.

[17]*Newsweek* (February 23, 1976).

[18]*Time* (February 16, 1976); *Newsweek* (February 16, 1976).

[19]*Time* (July 19, 1976).

[20]*Time* (August 25, 1975).

[21]Myra MacPherson, *The Power Lovers: An Intimate Look at Politicians and Their Marriages* (New York: Putnam's, 1975).

[22]*France-Soir* (November 5, 1976).

[23]*Time* (January 23, 1977).

[24]Ellen Proxmire, *One Foot in Washington* (1974).

[25]*Time* (February 16, 1976).

[26]*Newsweek* (February 16, 1976). The Trudeaus separated in May 1977 after Margaret, as a photographer, followed Mick Jagger of the Rolling Stones to New York.

[27]*Time* (October 17, 1974).

[28]*Time* (January 13, 1975).

[29]White, pp. 326-327.

[30]Salinger, p. 392.

[31]*Newsweek* (July 22, 1974).

[32]*Newsweek* (December 23, 1974).

[33]Bob Armstrong, Carter's Texas campaign manager, cited in *Time* (October 11, 1976).

[34]*Time* (July 19, 1976).

[35]Salinger, p. 393.

PART TWO: THE SHOW

The Art of Politics

[1]Directed by Michael Ritchie, the film denounced American campaign methods. Quotes from *Lui* (September 1976).

[2]Bertolt Brecht, *La Resistible ascension d'Arturo Ui,* French edition (Paris: L'Arche, 1960), pp. 51-56.

[3]Jean Lacouture, *Cinq hommes et la France* (Paris: Seuil, 1961), p. 115.

[4]Jean-Louis Barrault, "Le Métier," *Esprit* (May 1965).

[5]Roland Barthes, *Essais critiques* (Paris: Seuil, 1964), p. 277.

[6]See Richard Demarcy, *Elements d'une sociologie du spectacle* (Paris: 10/18, 1973), p. 89.

[7]De Gaulle, *Le Fil de l'epée,* pp. 79-80.

[8]De Gaulle, *Le Fil de l'epée,* pp. 55, 78.

[9]De Gaulle, *Le Fil de l'epée,* p. 125.

[10]Odette Aslan, *L'Acteur au XXe siècle* (Paris: Seghers, 1974), pp. 125, 128-129.

[11]Denis Diderot, *Paradoxe sur le comedien* (Paris: Garnier-Flammarion, 1967), p. 133.

[12]Diderot, p. 190.

[13]Charles Dullin, "L'Emotion humaine," in *L'Art cinematographique* (Paris, 1976), p. 61.

[14]Bertolt Brecht, *L'Achat du cuivre,* French edition (Paris: L'Arche, 1970), p. 83.

Government as Cinema

[1] See John Schlesinger's film, *The Day of the Locust,* based on the novel by Nathanael West.

[2] Joseph Kessel, *Hollywood, ville mirage* (Paris: Gallimard, 1937), pp. 7, 9, 57, 50-52.

[3] See Irving Schulman, *Valentino, l'amant du monde,* French edition (Paris: Editions René Chateau, 1976).

[4] Maurice Bessy, *Hollywood d'hier et d'aujourd'hui* (Paris: Editions Prisma).

[5] Roland Barthes, *Mythologies* (Paris: Seuil, 1957), pp. 70-71.

[6] Pierre Leprohon, *Le Monde du cinéma* (Paris: Hermes, 1967), p. 70.

[7] Leprohon, p. 69.

[8] De Gaulle, *Le Fil de l'epée,* p. 55.

[9] De Gaulle, *Le Fil de l'epée,* p. 78.

[10] De Gaulle, *Le Fil de l'epée,* p. 79.

[11] De Gaulle, *Le Fil de l'epée,* p. 80.

[12] Edgar Morin, *Les Stars* (Paris: Seuil, 1974), p. 25.

[13] Leprohon, p. 147.

[14] See Guy Abitan, *Une Legende américaine: Hollywood d'aujourd'hui, de Brando à Redford* (Paris: La Table Ronde, 1976).

[15] Frank Westmore, *The Westmores of Hollywood* (Philadelphia: Lippincott, 1976).

[16] Kessel, pp. 48-50.

[17] Garson Kanin, *Hollywood, The Crazy Years* (1975), p. 176.

[18] *Playboy,* French edition (April 1975).

[19] Jacques Berne, "La Campagne de Valéry Giscard d'Estaing pour les elections présidentielles de 1974," thesis for doctorate in political science at the University of Paris II (1975), p. 128.

[20] Sylvie Colliard, "La Campagne présidentielle de François Mitterand en 1974," thesis for doctorate in political science at the University of Paris II (1976), p. 54.

[21] Cited by Richard L. Neuberger, "Madison Avenue in Politics," *Esquire* (August 1957).

[22] *Time* (June 17, 1966).

[23] *Time* (February 2, 1976).

[24] *L'Express* (July 2, 1973).

[25] *Time* (April 28, 1975).

[26] Salinger, pp. 134-137.

[27] Statement made in May 1975 and cited in *Le Nouvel Observateur* (December 2, 1975).

[28]See also Altman's *Buffalo Bill and the Indians,* which portrays Cody capitalizing on his image as a Wild West hero by becoming a pioneer of American show business.

Mediapolitics

[1]Jacques Ellul, *Histoire de la propagande* (Paris: P.U.F., 1967), p. 90.

[2]Jean Lacouture, *Quatre hommes et leurs peuples* (Paris: Seuil, 1969), pp. 119-121.

[3]Jean-Jacques Servan Schreiber, *Le Pouvoir d'informer* (Paris: Laffont, 1972), p. 167.

[4]Olof Palme, *Le Rendez-vous suèdois,* French edition (Paris: Stock, 1976), p. 12.

[5]Jean-Claude Lamy, *Pierre Lazareff à la une* (Paris: Stock, 1975).

[6]Jean Ferniot, *La Presse et la personnalisation du pouvoir* (Paris: P.U.F., 1964), p. 349.

[7]Ferniot, pp. 347-349.

[8]Robert de Jouvenel, *La République des camarades* (Paris: Grasset, 1914), p. 225.

[9]André Tardieu, *La Profession parlementaire* (Paris, 1937), pp. 110, 115-116.

[10]Salinger, pp. 46-47.

[11]Salinger, p. 54.

[12]White, p. 329.

[13]White, p. 423.

[14]Salinger, p. 157.

[15]Sorensen, p. 272.

[16]A reference, of course, to Cecil B. DeMille. See *Time* (July 12, 1976).

[17]Salinger, p. 184.

[18]Claude-Jean Bertrand, *Les Mass media aux Etats-Unis* (Paris: P.U.F., 1974), p. 100.

[19]Salinger, p. 181.

[20]Salinger, p. 184.

[21]Sorensen, p. 268.

[22]Salinger, p. 74.

[23]Charles de Gaulle, *Memoirs d'espoir,* volume I, ("Le Renouveau") (Paris: Livre de Poche), pp. 365-366.

[24]Pierre Viansson-Ponte, *Les Gaullistes* (Paris: Seuil, 1963), pp. 46-47.

[25]Cited by Francis Balle, *Institutions et publics des moyens d'information* (Paris: Montchrestien, 1973), p. 121.

[26]Marshall McLuhan in *L'Express* (February 5, 1972).

[27]Harold Mendelsohn and Irving Crespi, *Polls, Television and the New Politics* (Scranton: Chandler Publishing Company, 1972), p. 260.

[28]E. J. Wrage and B. Baskerville, *Contemporary Forum* (New York: Harper and Row, 1962), p. 137.

[29]Cited by Hadley Cantril, *Public Opinion: 1935-1946* (Princeton: Princeton University Press, 1951), p. 759.

[30]Pierre Mendès France, *Dire la verité, causeries du samedi* (Paris: Juillard, 1955), pp. 3-5.

Man in the Public Eye

[1]Marcel Bleustein-Blanchet, *La Rage de convaincre* (Paris: Laffont, 1970).

[2]De Gaulle, *Memoirs d'espoir,* volume I, pp. 363-364.

[3]Cited by Dan Nimmo, *The Political Persuaders* (Englewood Cliffs: Prentice-Hall, 1970), p. 149.

[4]M. Bonnefoy, *Nixon President* (Paris: Solar, 1968), p. 86.

[5]Jacques Chaban-Delmas, *L'Ardeur,* p. 390.

[6]Cited by Salinger, p. 64.

[7]Douglass Cater, *Power in Washington* (New York: Random House, 1964).

[8]White, p. 366.

[9]Sidney Kraus, *The Great Debates* (Bloomington: Indiana University Press, 1962), p. 200.

[10]Braud, p. 85.

[11]Robert Fabre, *Quelques Baies de Genièvre* (Paris: J. C. Lattès-J. P. Ramsay, 1976), p. 218.

[12]Enrico Fulchigoni, *Civilisation de l'image,* French edition (Paris: Payot, 1969).

[13]*Time* (September 27, 1976).

[14]*Time* (September 27, 1976).

[15]Gallup poll published in *Newsweek* (October 4, 1976).

[16]*Le Monde* (October 9, 1976).

[17]*Time* (October 4, 1976).

[18]François Mitterand, *La Paille et le grain* (Paris: Flammarion, 1976), pp. 49, 271.

[19]Joe McGinniss, *The Selling of the President, 1968* (New York: Trident Press, 1969), p. 213.

[20]White, p. 155.

[21]McGinniss, p. 90.

[22]Joseph Napolitan, *The Election Game and How to Win It* (New York: Doubleday, 1972), p. 49.

[23]*Le Figaro* (April 20, 1976).

[24]Napolitan, p. 162; see also James M. Perry, *The New Politics: The Expanding Technology of Political Communication* (London, 1968), p. 48.

[25]McGinniss, p. 144.

[26]*Newsweek* (April 12, 1976).

[27]*Newsweek* (April 12, 1976).

[28]Marshall McLuhan, *The Gutenburg Galaxy,* French edition (Paris, 1967); *Understanding the Media,* French edition (Paris, 1968); *The Medium is the Message,* French edition (Paris, 1969).

[29]Machiavelli, *The Prince,* French edition, p. 145.

[30]Cited by McGinniss, p. 197.

[31]McGinniss, p. 45.

[32]McGinniss, p. 36.

[33]Napolitan, pp. 85-86.

[34]Cited by McGinniss, p. 190.

[35]Sorensen, p. 158.

[36]Cited by Sorensen, p. 274.

[37]J. G. Blumler and D. MacQuail, *Television and Politics: Its Use and Influence* (London: Faber and Faber, 1968).

[38]Emeric Deutsch, Denis Lindon, and Pierre Weill, *Les Familles politiques aujourd' hui en France* (Paris: Editions de Minuit, 1966).

[39]Cited by McGinniss, p. 162.

[40]*France-Soir* (September 24, 1976).

[41]L. A. Dexter and D. M. White, *People, Society and Mass Communications.*

The Political Show Business Industry

[1]See Serge Tchakhotine, *Le Viol des foules par la propagande politique* (Paris: Gallimard, 1939, 1952).

[2]Jean-Claude Boulet in his preface to Gary Yanker, *Prop Art* (Paris: Editions Planète, 1972).

[3]Ernest Dichter, *The Strategy of Desire* (Garden City: Doubleday and Company, 1960), p. 37.

[4]Cited by Vance Packard, *The Hidden Persuaders* (New York: McKay, 1957), pp. 7-8.

[5]Dichter.

[6]Packard, p. 6.

[7]Dichter, p. 152.

[8]Dichter, p. 118.

[9]Stanley Kelley, Jr., *Professional Public Relations and Political Power* (Baltimore: Johns Hopkins Press, 1966), p. 15.

[10]Ralph D. Casey, "Republican Propaganda in the 1936 Campaign," in *The Public Opinion Quarterly,* I (April 2, 1937), pp. 31-32.

[11]Cited by David Lee Rosenbloom, *The Election Men: Professional Campaign Managers and American Democracy* (New York: Quadrangle Books, 1973), p. 11.

[12]*L'Express* (March 28, 1966).

[13]See Kelley, p. 202; Perry, pp. 7-40.

[14]See Rodney C. Minott, *The Sinking of the Lollipop* (San Francisco: Diablo Press, 1968).

[15]On marketing see Armand Dayan, *Le Marketing* (Paris: P.U.F., 1976); Denis Lindon, Marketing politique et social (Paris: Dalloz, 1976); Michel Noir, "Le Marketing politique, l'exemple américain," thesis for doctorate in political science at the University of Paris II (1976).

[16]Louis Harris, "Polls and Politics in the United States," in Robert Agranoff, ed., *The New Style in Election Campaigns* (Boston: Holbrook Press, 1972), p. 206.

[17]Napolitan, p. 121.

[18]Joseph T. Klapper, *Bandwagon: A Review of the Literature* (Office of Social Research, CBS, June 17, 1964), p. 55.

[19]Mendelsohn and Crespi, p. 25.

[20]Mendelsohn and Crespi, p. 164.

[21]P. Lazarsfeld, B. Berelson, and H. Gaudet, *The People's Choice* (New York: Duell, Sloan and Pearce, 1944).

[22]B. Berelson, P. Lazarsfeld, and W. McPhee, *Voting* (Chicago: University of Chicago Press, 1954).

[23]Harris, p. 210.

[24]On "pseudo-events" see Daniel Boorstin, *The Image: or What Happened to the American Dream* (New York: Atheneum, 1962).

[25]Perry, pp. 139-140.

[26]Napolitan, p. 109.

[27]Perry, p. 167.

[28]Salinger, p. 89.

[29]According to Kennedy himself, as quoted by White, p. 82, who adds that Sorensen had become, as it were, one of the lobes in Kennedy's brain.

[30]Sorensen, pp. 53-54.

[31]*Time* (August 30, 1976).

[32]William Wingfield, "The Man Who Discovered Nixon," *UUA Now*, 60 (December, 1968), pp. 24-25.

[33]Napolitan, p. 150.

[34]Napolitan, p. 150.

[35]Napolitan, p. 4. Napolitan's office advised Jean d'Ornano, a conservative, in the Paris municipal elections of March 1977, in cooperation with Michel Bongrand.

[36]*Time* (August 30, 1976).

[37]Kurt and Gladys Lang, "The Mass Media and Voting," in E. Burdick and A. Brodbeck, eds., *American Voting Behavior* (New York: Glencoe Free Press, 1959), p. 218.

[38]Nimmo, pp. 2-4.

[39]See Berelson *et al.*, pp. 132-137.

[40]See Lazarsfeld *et al.*, p. 151.

[41]See Elihu Katz and David Failkes, "On the Use of the Mass Media as Escape," The Public Opinion Quarterly, XXVI (Fall 1962), pp. 377-389.

PART THREE: THE PUBLIC

Why Star System Politics?

[1]Hannah Arendt, *The Origins of Totalitarianism* (New York: Harcourt, Brace, 1951).

[2]Ludwig Feuerbach, *L'Essence du Christianisme* (1841).

[3]Wilhelm Reich, *The Mass Psychology of Fascism*, trans. Theodore P. Wolfe (New York: Orgone Institute Press, 1946).

[4]Feuerbach, pp. 403-404.

[5]James Burnham, *Les Machiaveliens, Defenseurs de la liberté* (Paris: Calman-Levey, 1949); Vilfredo Pareto, *Traite de sociologie general* (1917-1919); Gaetano Mosca, *Elementi di scienza politica* (1896); Roberto Michels, *Les Partis politiques, Essai sur les tendances oligarchiques des democraties* (Paris, 1914).

[6]Sigmund Freud, *Moise et le Monotheism* (Moses and Monotheism), French edition (Paris: Gallimard, 1967), p. 148.

[7]Reich, p. 208.

[8]Gabriel Almond and G. Bingham Powell, *Comparative Politics: A Developmental Approach* (Boston: Little, Brown, 1966).

[9]Jean Ziegler, *Le pouvoir africain* (Paris: Seuil, 1971).

[10]*Le Monde* (April 11, 1975).

[11]In December 1976, Marshal Bokassa went one better and proclaimed himself Emperor.

[12]Joseph Barsalou, *La Mal-aimée: Histoire de la IVe République* (Paris: Plon, 1964). That same year, referring to the Fourth Republic, de Gaulle declared: "Nothing is more urgent than to get rid of this shadow-play government."

[13]Clemenceau, for instance, defied his own party colleagues on May 14, 1907: "I've had enough! I will not be smothered by murmurs. Speak up! My rostrum is open to any Radicals brave enough to use it." Jean de Malafosse, *Histoire des institutions et des régimes politiques de la Révolution à la IVe République* (Paris: Montchrestien, 1975), pp. 198-199.

[14]Maurice Duverger, *Les Partis politiques* (Paris: A Colin, 1961), p. 210.

[15]Otto Kirchheimer, "The Transformation of Western European Party Systems" in J. LaPalombra and M. Weiner, eds., *Political Parties and Political Development* (Princeton, 1966).

[16]Mattei Dogan, "Le Personnel politique et la personnalité charismatique," in *Revue Française de Sociologie,* 3:6 (1965), p. 310.

[17]Michel Habib-Deloncle, report on the first UNR convention at Bordeaux (November 1959), on "The Role of the UNR in the Fifth Republic," cited by Jean Charlot, *Le Gaullisme* (Paris: A. Colin, 1970), p. 106.

The Goals of Star System Politics

[1]Guy Rocher, *Introduction à la sociologie générale* (Paris: Seuil, 1968), vol. II, p. 165.

[2]Robert King Merton, *Eléments de théorie et de mèthode sociologique* (Paris: Plon, 1965), p. 118.

[3]Merton, p. 126.

[4]Jean Lacouture, *Quatre hommes et leurs peuples* (Paris: Seuil, 1969), p. 53.

[5]*Newsweek* (December 8, 1975).

[6]See Paul-Henri Siriex, *Félix Houphouet-Boigny: L'Homme de la paix* (Paris: Seghers, 1975).

[7]Lucian Pye, "The Concept of Political Development," in *Annals of the American Academy of Political and Social Science,* 358 (March 1965), pp. 1-13.

[8]LaPalombra and Weiner, pp. 402-404.

[9]David Easton and Jack Dennis, *Children in the Political System* (New York, 1969).

[10]David Easton, *A Systems Analysis of Political Life* (New York, 1965).

[11]Edgar Morin, *Les Stars* (Paris: Seuil, 1972), p. 125.

[12]Bertrand de Jouvenel, *Du Pouvoir* (Geneva, 1945), pp. 541-557.

[13]Victor Hugo, *Les Rayons et les ombres,* I (1839).

[14]W. E. Mülhmann, *Messianismes révolutionnaires du tiers monde* (Paris, 1968).

[15]*Paris-Match* (August 9, 1975).

[16]Jean-Claude Vajou, *JJSS par JJSS* (Paris: La Table Ronde, 1971), pp. 58-60.

[17]White, p. 416.

[18]*Time* (May 31, 1976).

[19]Marvin and Bernard Kalb, p. 19.

[20]Agranoff, p. 261.

[21]*France-Dimanche* (May 19, 1975) ran this headline: "Giscard without his usual fire." It gave a more domestic image of him: "Yes, here is Valéry bringing breakfast himself to his wife in bed . . . . He is a thoughtful husband who still is as attentive to Anne-Aymone as a young bridegroom."

[22]Violette Morin, *Communications* (Paris: Seuil, 1967).

[23]Sigmund Freud and William C. Bullitt, *Portrait psychologique de Thomas Woodrow Wilson,* French edition (Paris: Albin Michel, 1967), p. 89.

[24]Reich, pp. 183-184.

[25]Gilles Deleuze and Félix Guattari, *L'Anti-Oedipe* (Paris: Editions de Minuit, 1973).

[26]Arendt, p. 148.

[27]Jean Paulhan, preface to Pauline Réage, *Histoire d'O* (Paris: Pauvert, 1954).

[28]In the collective work *Eléments pour une analyse au fascisme* (Paris: 10/18, 1976), Maria-Antoinetta Macciocchi underscores "the immense frustration which is at the bottom of fascism."

[29]Cited by Jean-Marie Domenach, p. 35, who adds: "When the people mass together they take on a more sentimental, feminine character."

[30]Jean Plumyene, *Pétain* (Paris: Seuil, 1964), p. 101.

[31]Plumyene, p. 104.

[32]Gerard Miller, *Les Pousse-au-jour du Maréchal Pétain* (Paris: Seuil, 1975).

[33]Daniel Boorstin, L'Image (Paris: Julliard, 1963), p. 90.

[34]Gaston Bouthoul, *Sociologie de la politique* (Paris: P.U.F., 1967), pp. 28-29.

[35]Machiavelli, *The Prince,* French edition (Paris: Seghers, 1971), p. 166.

[36]According to the rating done by *France-Soir* (January 29, 1977), 23 percent of the viewers watched Giscard answer women's questions, 18 percent watched a TV film entitled "Jacob et Josephe," and 59 percent watched a film with François Rosay and Louis Jouvet. *France-Soir*'s headline: "Jouvet beats Giscard."

[37]Thorstein Veblen, *Theory of the Leisure Class* (1899).

[38]See Milovan Djilas, *La Nouvelle classe dirigeante* (1957); Marc Paillet, *Marx contre Marx: La Societé technobureaucratique* (Paris, 1971); Claude Lefort, *Eléments d'une critique de la bureaucratie* (Paris, 1972); Charles Bettelheim, *Les Luttes de classes en URSS* (Paris, 1974).

[39]See the controversy between Ralph Miliband and Nicos Poulantzas in *Politique Aujourd'hui* (March 1970).

Star System Government: Government of Illusion

[1]At a discussion organized by the magazine *Stratégies,* held January 27, 1977, in Paris; reported in *Le Monde* (January 29, 1977).

[2]*Le Monde* (March 11, 1976).

[3]*Le Monde* (May 27, 1976).

[4]*Time* (May 31, 1976).

[5]Pierre Mendès France and Michel Debré, *Le Grand Debat* (Paris: Editions Gonthier, 1966), p. 189.

[6]Press conference on December 16, 1965; reported in *Le Monde* (December 18, 1965).

[7]See Roger-Gérard Schwartzenberg, *La Guerre de succession: les élections présidentielles de 1969* (Paris: P.U.F., 1969), p. 169.

[8]Valéry Giscard d'Estaing, *Démocratie Française* (Paris: Fayard, 1976).

[9]Napolitan, pp. 85-86.

[10]Karl Deutsch, *The Nerves of Government: Models of Political Communication and Control* (New York, 1966).

[11]T. C. Smith, *Life and Letters of James A. Garfield* (New Haven, 1922), p. 1044.

[12]Nixon preferred TV talks to the nation to press conferences. During the first four years of his presidency he held the same number of press conferences, 28, as Franklin Roosevelt held in his first three months.

[13]Mary McGrory, "A Talk with John Dean," *New York Post* (June 18, 1973).

[14]Cited by Herbert Poter, interview in the *New York Times* (August 5, 1973).

[15]Lou Cannob, "The Siege Psychology and How It Grew, *Washington Post* (July 29, 1973).

[16]Arthur M. Schlesinger, Jr., *The Imperial Presidency* (Boston: Houghton, Mifflin, 1973).

[17]Hannah Arendt, *Crisis of The Republic,* p. 152.

[18]Jeb Stuart Magruder, interview in the *New York Times* (June 15, 1973).

[19]Bob Woodward and Carl Bernstein, *The Final Days* (New York: Simon and Schuster, 1976).

[20]Mao Tse-tung, editorial in *Renmin Ribao* (April 5, 1956), cited by Stuart Scram, p. 385.

[21]Roy Medvedev, p. 550.

[22]Zhores Medvedev, *The Greatness and Fall of Lyssenko* (Paris, 1971). In Mao's China many scientists and doctors also made excessive references to the thought of Chairman Mao.

[23]Branko Lazitch, *Le Rapport Khrouchtchev et son histoire,* French edition (Paris: Seuil, 1976), pp. 111-112.

[24]Lazitch, p. 119.

[25]Lazitch, p. 125.

[26]Tombalbaye was assassinated in April 1975.

[27]*Le Monde* (April 16, 1975).

[28]*France-Soir* (June 13, 1975).

[29]*Time* (July 19, 1976). Also in July, Amin's pride received a severe blow when Israeli commandos freed hostages aboard a hijacked airliner at Entebbe airport.

[30]*Le Monde* (December 21, 1976).

[31]*Le Monde* (January 27, 1977).

[32]Message to the nation on January 1, 1971.

[33]See *Le Monde* (October 15-16, 1976).

[34]*Le Monde* (August 5, 1976).

[35]Dany Cohen, "Assassinat politique et personnalisation du pouvoir," thesis for doctorate in political science at the University of Paris II (1976).

[36]See Sigmund Freud, *Introduction to Narcissism* (1915). Vice-President Walter Mondale was a good critic of state narcissism. When he withdrew from the presidential primary race he said: "To think I am the only man in America who is worthy of being president takes a sort of arrogance that I don't like. If my children had that idea, I would give them a spanking." *Le Monde* (July 17, 1976).

[37]*Le Monde* (March 19, 1976).

[38]Feuerbach, preface *Passim*.

[39]Boorstin, *The Image*.

[40]Boorstin, *The Image*.

[41]Bertolt Brecht, *Ecrits sur la politique et la societé,* French edition, p. 57.

[42]See Pierre Gonidec, *Les Systèmes politiques africains,* II (Paris: L.G.D.J., 1974), p. 18.

[43]See *Le Monde* (April 10, 1976).

[44]*Congressional Quarterly* (September 12, 1968).

[45]Figure given by Henry Kimelman, finance director of the campaign, reported in the *International Herald-Tribune* (November 8, 1972).

[46]Perry, p. 48.

[47]Claude Julien, *Les Suicide des démocraties* (Paris: Grasset, 1972), p. 153.

[48]Perry, p. 48. The figure was $3 million according to Agranoff, p. 34.

[49]Julien, p. 151.

[50]Agranoff, p. 31; Perry, p. 136.

[51]In 1966 Napolitan spent $120,000 on such productions for Shapp.

[52]*Time* (November 1, 1976); *Newsweek* (November 8, 1976).

[53]For legislative campaigns in West Germany in 1976, excluding expenditures by local organizations, costs were 46 million marks for the CDU-CSU, 40 million marks for the SPD, and 10 million marks for the FDP; reported by *Le Monde* (October 3-4, 1976).

[54]François Mitterand, *Ma Part de verité* (Paris: Fayard, 1969), pp. 51-52. See also Roger-Gérard Schwartzenberg, *La Campagne présidentielle de 1965* (Paris: P.U.F., 1967), p. 73.

[55]*L'Humanité* (May 13, 1969).

[56]Roger-Gerard Schwartzenberg, *La Guerre de Succession*, pp. 254-259.

[57]Jacques Berne, "La Campagne de M. Valéry Giscard d'Estaing pour les élections présidentielles de 1974," thesis at the University of Paris II (1975), p. 113.

[58]Colliard, p. 120.

[59]Mitterand, *La Paille et la grain*, p. 275.

[60]Cited by Nimmo, p. 63.

[61]White, p. 131.

[62]*New York Times Magazine* (November 22, 1970).

[63]*Congressional Quarterly,* special number (1968), p. 59.

[64]Julien, p. 151.

[65]Ralph Nader, *Citizens Look at Congress* (New York: Goorrman, 1972), p. 24.

[66]Nader, pp. 45-49; *Newsweek* (February 7, 1972); *Time* (February 2, 1972).

The Last Performance

[1]On these organizational, systematic, and functional approaches and the cybernetic techniques, see Roger-Gérard Schwartzenberg, *Sociologie politique*, pp. 99-172.

[2]Alain, *Eléments d'une doctrine radicale* (Paris: Gallimard, 1925).

[3]Jean-Jacques Rousseau, *Du Contrat social* (The Social Contract), book IV, chapter 1 (1792).

[4]See Roger-Gérard Schwartzenberg, "Le Droit de savoir," in *Le Monde* (May 7, 1975) and "Le Secret du roi," in *Le Monde* (March 3, 1976).

[5]See *Liberté, Liberté* (Paris: Gallimard, 1976), pp. 59ff, especially the preface by François Mitterand.

[6]See *Le Pouvoir communal,* the municipal manifesto of the Radical Left Movement (1976).

[7]See Roger-Gérard Schwartzenberg, "Rendre le suffrage universel," in *Le Monde* (April 5, 1974).

Photographic Credits

10   Wide World Photos

38   United Press International, Inc.

51   United Press International, Inc.

52   Wide World Photos

67   United Press International, Inc.

68   United Press International, Inc.

76   United Press International, Inc.

86   Photoworld, Division of F.P.G.

104 Photoworld, Division of F.P.G.

115 United Press International, Inc.

116 United Press International, Inc.

133 Wide World Photos

134 Photoworld, Division of F.P.G.

150 United Press International, Inc.

179 United Press International, Inc.

180 Wide World Photos

204 Wide World Photos

224 United Press International, Inc.

245 Photo from European

246 United Press International, Inc.

274 Freelance Photographers' Guild